£15.00

GW00777034

SUFFOLK RECORDS SOCIETY
SUFFOLK CHARTERS

General editor   *R. Allen Brown*

I

LEISTON ABBEY CARTULARY
AND BUTLEY PRIORY CHARTERS

SUFFOLK RECORDS SOCIETY
SUFFOLK CHARTERS

General Editor
Professor R. Allen Brown

External Advisors

Professor G. W. S. Barrow

Dr Pierre Chaplais

Dr Marjorie Chibnall

Miss Kathleen Major

LEISTON ABBEY CARTULARY
AND
BUTLEY PRIORY CHARTERS

Edited by Richard Mortimer

Published by the Boydell Press
for the Suffolk Records Society

© R. Mortimer 1979

Published for the Suffolk Records Society by The Boydell Press
PO Box 24 Ipswich IP1 1JJ

First published 1979

ISBN 0 85115 106 X ·

British Library Cataloguing in Publication Data

Leiston Abbey
   Leiston Abbey cartulary and
   Butley Priory charters. – (Suffolk charters).
   1. Leiston Abbey 2. Church lands – England – Leiston
   3. Cartularies 4. Butley Priory 5. Charters
   I. Title II. Butley Priory III. Mortimer, Richard IV. Series
   333.3'22'0942646   HD610.L/

ISBN 0-85115-106-X

Photoset by Galleon Photosetting and
printed in Great Britain by Redwood Burn Ltd, Trowbridge and Esher

Contents

General Editor's Foreword

This volume, edited by Dr Richard Mortimer, is the first of an intended special series in which the Suffolk Records Society, through an editorial sub-committee set up for the purpose, proposes to print the whole of the abundant pre-Reformation charter material relating to the county. The basis of the series will be the cartularies, of which some eleven survive from medieval religious houses in Suffolk without counting various secular registers, and without counting the great corpus of material from the abbey of Bury St. Edmunds. It is, of course, this last which is of particular importance, both national and international. The method of proceeding will be to tackle first the foothills, so to speak, of the lesser houses, and issue their cartularies and charters, while the ascent of the Everest of Bury is prepared to follow. Volumes will be issued annually. Volume ii, for 1980, edited by Dr C. Harper-Bill, will comprise the cartulary of Blythburgh Priory. Two subsequent volumes for Stoke-by-Clare are in hand, as are two further volumes respectively for Eye and Sibton.

The cartularies and/or collections of original charters will be printed in full, including documents relating to lands outside Suffolk. Where original charters survive, they will be given preference to the cartulary texts when both are extant. In such a case, or in the case of original charters of which there is no entry in the relevant cartulary, the originals will either be inserted in their appropriate places in the cartulary text, or gathered together in an appendix, as may seem appropriate. Where original charters survive for a house which has no extant cartulary, they will be printed in separate volumes or, in certain cases, incorporated in some other volume to which they relate (as with the Butley charters in this present Leiston volume). The few secular cartularies will form separate volumes.

All documents will be printed *in extenso* (and, so far as is practicable, whether they have been printed before or not) up to a date of *c*.1250. Beyond that date a full English abstract will generally be deemed sufficient. The charters of each house will usually be printed in the order in which they appear in the cartulary, and so numbered. Documents in Latin (or French or Anglo-Saxon) will be printed with a brief English abstract at the head, and all documents which require it will have a short note at the foot dealing with such essentials as date, the particulars of the document and seal in the case of originals, and the whereabouts of previous editions. Each volume (or series of volumes in the of, e.g., the larger cartularies) will have an introduction and a full index of persons, places and subjects. Punctuation and capitalization will be modernized and abbreviations extended.

The Society most gratefully acknowledges a generous grant from the British Academy to cover the cost of the publication of this first volume. Thereafter it is hoped that the series of *Suffolk Charters* will stand upon its own merits through sales and subscriptions. Particulars of favourable subscription rates should be obtained from The Boydell Press, PO Box 24, Ipswich, Suffolk, IP1 1JJ – to whom, and Richard Barber especially, our grateful thanks are also due for their generous and painstaking care in seeing this volume through the press.

Thelnetham, Suffolk   *R. Allen Brown*
26 December, 1978

TO MY PARENTS

Preface

My thanks are due to the Dean and Chapter of Ely, the British Library, the Bodleian Library and the Master and Fellows of Corpus Christi College, Cambridge for permission to publish the documents which follow. Crown copyright material in the Public Record Office appears by permission of the Controller of HM Stationery Office.

The appearance of this volume would have been greatly retarded had it not been for generosity from many quarters, and my gratitude is due to two institutions in particular: to Bedford College, for the award of a Research Studentship, and to the Institute of Historical Research for a Special Research Fellowship which helped very much in the later stages. I have also accumulated great debts to a number of people: to Dr M. M. Chibnall and Professor C. J. Holdsworth, who read this work in its earlier incarnation as a thesis, to its great benefit; to Professor T. J. Brown in matters palaeographical, and Professor C. H. Lawrence in matters ecclesiastical; to Mr T. A. Heslop, who came to my assistance in the matter of seals, writing the individual descriptions as well as the general note in the Introduction; to Mr M. W. Aylward, Mr S. Chopra and Mr P. N. Lewis for assistance of all kinds; to Mrs V. Brown and Dr C. Harper-Bill, whose work on other Suffolk cartularies, forthcoming in this series, has been of the greatest help; and to the dedicatees, who have lent indispensable support and encouragement as well as much assistance with the index. To two scholars in particular my debt is too great to repay: Professor R. M. T. Hill solved my problems with astonishing ease, and a patience and generosity which only those fortunate enough to be her pupils can fully appreciate. Professor R. A. Brown suggested this as a research topic, supervised it as a thesis, and as General Editor of the series has overseen its publication. My debt to him is self-evident: it is as much his book as mine, except that I alone am responsible for the errors.

Hethersett, Norfolk   *R. Mortimer*
December, 1978

ABBREVIATIONS

BL	British Library MS
Bk Fees	*Liber Feodorum: The Book of Fees commonly called Testa de Nevill*, ed. H. C. Maxwell-Lyte, 3 vols, London 1920–31.
Bk Seals	*Sir Christopher Hatton's Book of Seals*, ed. L. C. Loyd and D. M. Stenton, Oxford 1950.
CChR	*Calendar of Charter Rolls*, 6 vols, London 1903 etc.
CCR	*Calendar of Close Rolls* (full text to 1272), 67 vols, London 1902 etc.
C Misc Inquis	*Calendar of Miscellaneous Inquisitions*, 7 vols, London 1916 etc.
C Inq PM	*Calendar of Inquisitions Post Mortem*, 16 vols, London 1904 etc.
C Lib R	*Calendar of Liberate Rolls*, 6 vols, London 1917 etc.
C Pap Reg	*Calendar of Entries in the Papal Registers relating to Great Britain . . .*, 14 vols, London 1893 etc.
CPR	*Calendar of Patent Rolls*, 60 vols, London 1901 etc.
CRR	*Curia Regis Rolls*, 16 vols, London 1923 etc.
DB	*Domesday Book, seu liber censualis . . .*, ed. A. Farley, 2 vols, Record Comm., 1783.
Exc e R Fin	*Excerpta e Rotulis Finium*, ed. C. Roberts, 2 vols, Record Comm., London 1835–6.
EYC	*Early Yorkshire Charters*, ed. W. Farrer and Sir C. T. Clay, Yorkshire Record Soc., 1914 etc.
Fasti	John Le Neve, *Fasti ecclesiae anglicanae 1066–1300*, ed. D. E. Greenway, London 1968–71.
IESRO	Ipswich and East Suffolk Record Office.
Monasticon	Sir W. Dugdale, *Monasticon Anglicanum*, ed. J. Caley, H. Ellis and B. Bandinel, 6 vols, London 1817–30.
NRS	Norfolk Record Society.
NS	New Series.
PBKJJ	*Pleas before the King or his Justices 1198–1212*, ed. D. M. Stenton, Selden Society, 4 vols, 1948–9, 1966–7.
PL	Migne, *Patrologia Latina*.
PR	*Pipe Roll* (i.e. printed in Pipe Roll Society).
PRO	Public Record Office.
PR Soc	Pipe Roll Society.
PSIA	*Proceedings of the Suffolk Institute of Archaeology.*
Red Bk Exchq	*The Red Book of the Exchequer*, ed. Hubert Hall, RS, London 1896.
R Chart	*Rotuli Chartarum*, ed. T. D. Hardy, Record Comm., London 1837.
R Lib	*Rotuli de Liberate ac de misis et praestitis*, ed. T. D. Hardy, Record Comm., London 1833.
R Litt Claus	*Rotuli Litterarum Clausarum*, ed. T. D. Hardy, 2 vols, Record Comm., London 1833.
R Litt Pat	*Rotuli Litterarum Patentium*, ed. T. D. Hardy, Record Comm., London 1835.

R Obl et Fin	*Rotuli de Oblatis et Finibus*, ed. T. D. Hardy, Record Comm., London 1835.
RS	Rolls Series.
Salter Essays	*Oxford Essays in Medieval History presented to H. E. Salter*, Oxford 1934.
Taxatio	*Taxatio Ecclesiastica Angliae et Walliae auctoritate P. Nicholai IV*, Record Comm., London 1802.
VCH	*Victoria County History.*
VE	*Valor Ecclesiasticus*, ed. J. Caley and J. Hunter, Record Comm., London 1810–34.

BIBLIOGRAPHY

Works listed in the bibliography are cited in the notes by the author's name and, where two or more works are listed, by abbreviated title.

Bedingfeld, A. L.   *A Cartulary of Creake Abbey*, NRS xxxv, 1966.

Brown, R. A.   'Early Charters of Sibton Abbey' *in* P. M. Barnes and C. F. Slade, *A Medieval Miscellany for D. M. Stenton*, PR Soc NS xxxvi, 1962.

Cheney, C. R.   *English Bishops' Chanceries, 1100–1250*, Manchester 1950.

Cheney, C. R. and M. G.   *The Letters of Pope Innocent III (1198–1216)*, Oxford 1967.

Clapham, A. W.   'The Architecture of the English Premonstratensians', *Archaeologia* lxxiii, 1922–3.

Colvin, H. M.   *The White Canons in England*, Oxford 1951.

Copinger, W. A.   *The Manors of Suffolk*, London 1905–11.

Dodwell, B.   *Feet of Fines for the County of Norfolk (1198–1202)*, PR Soc. NS xxvii, 1950 (*Fines i*).

Dodwell, B.   *Feet of Fines for the County of Norfolk (1202–1215) and of Suffolk (1199–1214)*, PR Soc. NS xxxii, 1958 (*Fines ii*).

Dodwell, B.   *Charters of Norwich Cathedral Priory*, PR Soc. NS xl, 1974.

Evelyn-White, H. G.   'An unpublished 14th-century rent roll from Butley Priory', *The East Anglian, or Notes and Queries*, 2nd ser. xi, 1905–6.

Eyton, R. W.   *Court, household and itinerary of Henry II*, London 1878.

Farrer, W.   *Honors and knights' fees*, London and Manchester 1923–5.

Gasquet, F. A.   *Collectanea Anglo-Premonstratensia I–III*, Camden Soc. 3rd ser. vi, x, xii, 1904–6.

Giraldus Cambrensis   *Opera*, ed. J. S. Brewer et al., RS 21, 1861–91.

Holtzmann, W.   *Papsturkunden in England*, Berlin and Göttingen 1930–52.

Jaffé–Wattenbach: Jaffé, Philipp, ed. W. Wattenbach   *Regesta pontificum romanorum . . . ad . . . MCXCVIII*, Leipzig 1885–8.

Knowles, D., Brooke, C. N. L. and London, V. *The heads of religious houses: England and Wales, 940–1216*, Cambridge 1972.

Landon, L. C. *Cartae Antiquae, Rolls 1–10*, PR Soc. NS xvii, 1939.

Landon, L. C. *The Itinerary of Richard I*, PR Soc. NS xiii, 1935.

Lefèvre, P. L. *Les statuts de Prémontré*, Louvain 1946.

Liebermann, F. *Ungedruckte anglo-normannische Geschichtsquellen*, Strasburg 1879.

Mortimer, R. 'Religious and secular motives for some English monastic foundations', *Studies in Church History* xv, 1978.

Myres, J. N. L. *Archaeological Journal* xc, 1933, 242–81.

Palgrave, Sir F. *Rotuli Curiae Regis*, Record Commission, London 1835.

Raban, S. 'Mortmain in Medieval England', *Past and Present* no. 62, Feb. 1974.

Rye, W. *A Calendar of the Feet of Fines for Suffolk*, Ipswich 1900.

Rye, W. *A Short Calendar of the Feet of Fines for Norfolk*, Norwich 1885–6.

Sayers, J. *Papal judges delegate in the province of Canterbury, 1198–1254*, Oxford 1971.

Stenton, F. M. *Transcripts of Charters relating to the Gilbertine Houses of Sixle, Ormsby* (etc.), Lincoln Record Soc., xviii, 1922.

Suckling, A. *The history and antiquities of the county of Suffolk*, London 1846–8.

West, J. R. *Register of the Abbey of St Benet of Holme*, Norfolk Record Soc., ii–iii, 1932.

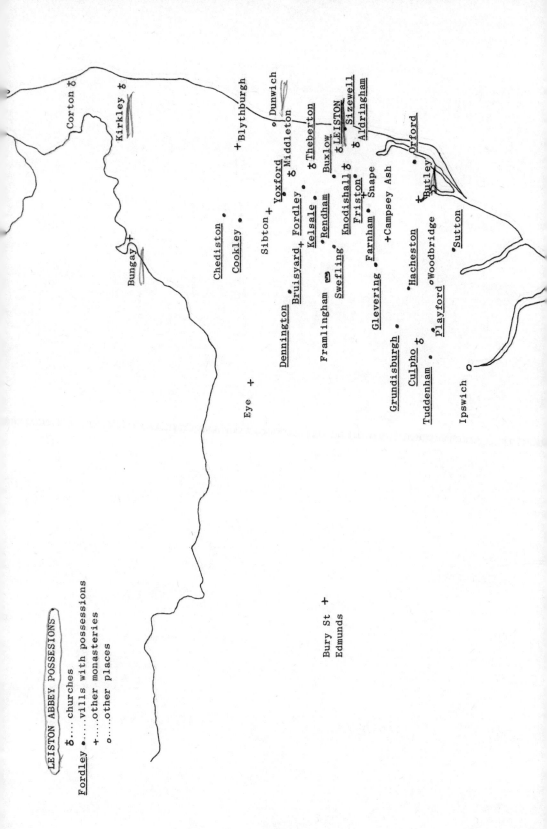

LEISTON ABBEY POSSESIONS

Fordley &....churches
&.....vills with possessions
+.....other monasteries
o.....other places

Corton &
Kirkley &
Blythburgh +
Dunwich o
Middleton &
Theberton &
Buxlow &
LEISTON &
Sizewell •
Aldringham &
Orford •
Bungay +
Chediston •
Cookley •
Sibton +
Yoxford +
Bruisyard + Fordley +
Kelsale •
Rendham •
Knodishall &
Friston +
Snape •
Campsey Ash +
Butley +
Sutton •
Dennington
Framlingham
Swefling
Farnham
Glevering •
Hacheston •
Woodbridge o
Playford •
Grundisburgh •
Culpho &
Tuddenham •
Eye +
Ipswich o
Bury St
Edmunds +

Biker, Lincs ⱦ

Bylaugh ⱦ

Upton ⱦ   West Somerton ⱦ

Norwich o

ⱦ Worlingham
ⱦ Ringsfield?
ⱦ Redisham

ⱦ South Cove?
+ Blythburgh

o Dunwich

+ Leiston

ⱦ Iken?

o Redgrave

Bungay +

+ Mendham
ⱦ Weybread
ⱦ Wingfield

Instead •

+ Sibton

• Dennington

Framlingham
Knodishall ⱦ ⱦ Benhall
Glemham { Nth ⱦ   ⱦ Parham
          Sth ⱦ • + Snape
Campsey Ash +   Stratford ⱦ
St Andrew
Wantisden
BUTLEY ⱦ   o Capel
ⱦ Redgrave
+ Ramsholt
ⱦ Bawdsey

Winfarthing? ⱦ
ⱦ Gissing

ⱦ Kilverstone

Eye +

ⱦ Rishangles?

Aspall ⱦ
Debenham ⱦ
ⱦ Ashfield
Winston •

Bredfield ⱦ

Woodbridge •

Kesgrave o

Ipswich o

Harleston ⱦ
ⱦ Finborough

Shelley ⱦ

Thetford o

Bury St Edmunds +

London, St Stephen
Coleman Street ⱦ

ⱦ Dedham

INTRODUCTION

Butley priory was a house of Augustinian canons; Leiston abbey was a foundation for Premonstratensian canons, an order originating at, and long dependent upon, Prémontré in northern France. Both were the foundations of Rannulf de Glanville, a Suffolk man, born at Stratford St Andrew in the honour of Eye,[1] and successively sheriff of Yorkshire and chief justiciar of England. Butley was founded in the early 1170s and Leiston in the early 1180s. From Leiston abbey there survives a cartulary, an early thirteenth century register of deeds with some miscellaneous later additions, but very few original documents. This volume is largely an edition of the Leiston cartulary along with such originals as have come to light. Butley priory was a wealthy house, and has left a considerable number of scattered documents of various kinds, many of which are already in print. Its later history, in many respects similar to that of Leiston, has already been thoroughly dealt with in two articles by J. N. L. Myres, while for the sixteenth century there is a remarkable chronicle.[2] A number of miscellaneous additions to a fragmentary late fourteenth-century rent roll[3] include a brief history of the descent of the advowson, and some extracts almost certainly from the lost 'Calendare Evidentiarum' of the priory[4] giving a list of benefactors and their gifts. It is not intended to reprint any of this material here, but instead to print the surviving charters, nearly all hitherto unpublished, which relate to the foundation and the Suffolk possessions of the priory, and illustrate its close connections with Leiston. The Introduction covers aspects of the history of both houses and their documents, but is chiefly concerned with Leiston as the better documented and less investigated of the two.

1. Foundation and Later History

The traditional date for the foundation of Butley priory is 1171. This is given among the miscellaneous additions to the rent roll mentioned above, originating from the house, and is confirmed in the chronicle of Colchester.[5] The founder, Rannulf de Glanville, was then only a minor royal servant, having just been deposed as sheriff of Yorkshire, and the site chosen was on land which had come to him as the marriage-portion of his wife, Bertha de Valeines.[6] The foundation charter was given before 1174, but survives only in a sixteenth century copy (120). The first prior, Gilbert, had previously been precentor of Blythburgh, and resigned as prior in 1192, four years after the dedication of the church on 24th September 1188.[7] Gerald of Wales says that the foundation was for 36 canons, and was especially directed towards

[1] See R. Mortimer, 'The Family of Rannulf de Glanville', forthcoming.
[2] *Archaeological Journal* xc, 1933, 177–228; *Salter Essays*, 190–206; A. G. Dickens, *The Register or Chronicle of Butley Priory, Suffolk, 1510–1535*, Winchester 1951.
[3] Evelyn-White.
[4] G. R. C. Davis, *Medieval Cartularies of Great Britain*, London 1958, no.139.
[5] Liebermann, 163.
[6] Evelyn-White, 30.
[7] Liebermann, 164–5.

1

hospitality and charity;[8] he implies that both Glanville's religious houses were forbidden to buy lands and rents, and to amass money to increase their possessions, but while we know that similar conditions were written into the foundation charter of Leiston (27), there is no such clause in Butley's charter. How the site was colonised we do not know; it seems unlikely that all the canons could have come from Blythburgh, which was a relatively unimportant cell of the priory of St Osyth in Essex, and more natural to turn to St Osyth.

In contrast to this speculation, the foundation of Leiston abbey is relatively well documented.[9] The founder first asked the advice of the abbot of Welbeck; they discussed the appointment of an abbot for the new foundation, and agreed on Robert, abbot of Durford, whom Rannulf knew and liked.[10] As the candidate was already an abbot, pressure had to be brought to bear, and the abbot of Welbeck went to Prémontré armed with letters from the king and other great men to obtain his translation,[11] which was duly granted. About now Rannulf must have given Leiston manor to found the abbey on, and the church of the neighbouring vill of Knodishall. Abbot Robert began by 'borrowing' canons from Welbeck: among them Ralph, to be prior and novice-master, and afterwards abbot of West Dereham, W. de Lincoln the *provisor exteriorum*, and a certain 'G.', afterwards abbot of Beauchief, who went to lay out the site, which process took two months and more. He also borrowed some canons from Durford, and some books which he afterwards returned.[12] The reason given for borrowing from two houses rather than from just one was that Glanville, who wished his house to be the greatest of its order in England, wanted no *corporalem exactionem* (probably meaning a money payment) to be made from it by any senior foundation. Before 1185 pope Lucius III issued a solemn privilege confirming to the infant monastery the manor of Leiston, 'as is testified by the charter of Rannulf the donor' (1). The charter thus referred to is not 27, which dates from 1186 or later: it is thus possible that Rannulf gave the canons an initial charter which has not survived.[13] Next, Leiston and Butley exchanged churches: Leiston abbey resigned Knodishall (the only evidence that they ever possessed it) and received in exchange the churches of Leiston and Aldringham (6, 31).

In the spring of 1185 Rannulf obtained royal confirmation of his foundation. This charter, 24, mentions the exchange of churches with Butley, describing the abbey church as *constructa* and the *abbatia* (conventual buildings?) as *construenda*. The manor, which was given to Rannulf 'for his good service', is confirmed to the canons. A year or so after this, in January 1186, the bishop of Norwich at an appropriate ceremony received the surrender of Leiston and Aldringham churches from Gilbert, prior of Butley, as well as the demesne tithes of Leiston (36). He then granted the vacant churches to Leiston abbey. No mention is made of Knodishall church. Only

[8] Giraldus Cambrensis, iv.245.
[9] Colvin, 118–25, 345–8; Mortimer.
[10] Colvin, 345–6.
[11] Colvin, 346.
[12] Colvin, 346–7.
[13] The phrase *sicut carta testatur* occurs quite frequently, e.g. Holtzmann, i. no.231, ii. no.220, but is missing from some otherwise very similar privileges of the same pope (*ibid.* i. no.209, and West, no.69).

now did Rannulf formally grant the manor and churches to the canons (27). About a year later the bishop issued a formal confirmation of churches and manor (34), and the documents of the foundation process are complete.

The foundation of a monastery is a process, not an event – this is obviously the case, if only because buildings take time to construct. There is no evidence to tell us when the canons began to sleep in their dormitory and sing the divine office in their church, or where they lived and used their borrowed books until they could do so. A group of masons witnessed a deed in 1219 (76) but there is no indication of what they were building, or repairing. Thus when a marginal note in the Colchester chronicle by the year 1183 says 'eodem anno facta est abbacia de Laistun',[14] it could well refer to the beginning of the process.

Each house stands at the head of a new chapter of expansion in its own order. The number of houses founded by Rannulf de Glanville's relatives has been discussed elsewhere.[15] Butley was an early contribution to a flurry of Augustinian foundations in Norfolk and Suffolk, being roughly contemporary with Ixworth and Walsingham, and followed by Holy Trinity, Ipswich, Dodnash and Woodbridge before 1200. Nor were Leiston and Butley the only religious foundations of Rannulf de Glanville: he also endowed a hospital for 13 lepers at West Somerton, Norfolk, the guardian of which was to be the prior of Butley; the hospital was put to dubious uses later on in its history, and by the later fourteenth century had ceased to be a hospital at all.[16]

It is noticeable, but surely not remarkable, that Leiston abbey was founded according to the Premonstratenoian rules. No house should be started, say the Statutes of Prémontré, without books – a psalter, a hymnal, a book of collects, an antiphoner, a gradual, a copy of the Rule, and a missal,[17] and presumably it was these that abbot Robert borrowed from his old house in Sussex 'which he afterwards returned'[18] (perhaps when the canons had made their own copies). In the next clause of the Statutes we read that the canons, or at least the abbot, may not move to the new site unless an oratory, dormitory, refectory, guest house and gate lodge have already been built. We know that the site was laid out by a canon *secundum formam ordinis*;[19] the buildings would thus have been of the simple, austere early Premonstratensian type.[20]

When Robert ceased to be abbot cannot be fixed with certainty. He is mentioned in 47, witnessed by Hubert Walter as archbishop, and thus was still in office in December 1193, and probably later; he also occurs in 51, which cannot be much earlier than the late 1190s. His successor Philip first occurs with certainty by 1205 (130). He is mentioned in 35, which dates almost certainly from before the winter of 1205/6, but after 1200. The balance of probability is thus that Philip replaced Robert within a few years of 1200, and certainly between 1193 and 1209.

[14] Liebermann, 164.
[15] Mortimer, 81.
[16] *VCH Norfolk*, ii.450; BL Harley Roll N20.
[17] Lefèvre, 92.
[18] Colvin, 346.
[19] Colvin, 347.
[20] Clapham, 117–46.

At no time is the history of Leiston abbey lavishly documented. Best illustrated are the foundation period, and the late fifteenth century thanks to the visitation records. The most obscure period of all is the thirteenth century, when even the succession of the abbots is sketchy. Abbot Hugh occurs in 1228 or 1229, and Abbot 'P.' is mentioned in 1243 (22). An abbot Gilbert of Leiston is entered in the Beauchief obituary in a thirteenth century hand which also enters abbot Philip.[21] Suckling mentions an abbot Matthew ascribed to 1250, but gives no reference.[22] For the later thirteenth century we have two names, Nicholas and Gregory. Nicholas occurs as the recipient of a weekly market in 1278,[23] and again in the cartulary as engaged in litigation in and after 1293 (112). Gregory's date depends on the dating of 116; if, as Suckling suggests,[24] this dates from 1285–6, we should have two abbots called Nicholas. In fact reasons are given below, in the note to the charter, for preferring 1260–75 as its terminal dates, and Suckling's suggestion is unsupported by evidence or argument. We can thus fit abbot Gregory before abbot Nicholas, of whom there need only be one.

Apart from the abbots we have the names of four canons of Leiston in 1219 (76). A brother Henry is found representing the abbey in secular courts in 1219 and 1221, who is most likely to be identified with the brother Henry 'the cellarer' performing the same task in 1225.[25] As we have seen, the monastery at first had a *provisor exteriorum*: this office is provided for in the Statutes[26] and is broadly equivalent to the cellarer in Benedictine houses, having charge of the *curia* with its ploughs and animals and presenting his accounts four times yearly. The 'cellarer' so called, in a Premonstratensian house was a sort of kitchener, in charge of the preparation and distribution of food, and overseer of the bakers, cooks and gardeners. Brother Henry is more likely to have been the former, whether he called himself 'provisor' or 'cellarer'. We have no indication how many canons made up a full complement at Leiston at this period: Gerald of Wales says the house was founded for 26, but in the late fifteenth century the number was usually about 15 including novices.[27]

The site of the first Leiston abbey is repeatedly referred to as an island (3, 14, 36, 43, 44, 48), and once as a marsh (54). Precisely where this was I have not been able to discover: either in a belt of low-lying land by the sea now washed away, or somewhere in the vicinity of Minsmere. As Mr Colvin points out, 'the chapel of St Mary in the old monastery' still existed in the sixteenth century.[28] A small rectangular building, now very overgrown, survives on a low eminence overlooking the marshes of Minsmere and the sea: it can hardly be the remains of the first monastery, as it is far too small

---

[21] BL Cotton Caligula A viii, ff.5v–6r. A very similar hand enters Rannulf de Glanville (fo 21v) and abbot Robert of Leiston (fo 19v).
[22] Suckling ii.442; Matthew occurs in the 'Malet' cartulary of Eye priory, fo 49v, in a charter of the 1230s or 1240s, which may be the charter to which Suckling refers. I owe this reference to Mrs Vivien Brown.
[23] *CCR*, v.321.
[24] Suckling, ii, 442–3.
[25] *CRR*, viii.2; x.27; xii.788.
[26] Lefèvre, 52–5.
[27] Giraldus Cambrensis iv.245; Gasquet, 49–55.
[28] Colvin, 125.

for even a Premonstratensian conventual church, and quite the wrong shape; it could, possibly, be a chapel, even the chapel of St Mary, but there is no sign of any other remains in the vicinity to represent 'the old monastery'.

The site of Butley priory was excavated in the 1930s,[29] revealing an aisleless twelfth century church virtually rebuilt in the thirteenth, with choir aisles extended in the fourteenth century. The monastic buildings were mostly thirteenth century. As well as a quantity of embossed tiles and fragments of stained glass, a number of human remains were found, apparently of extremely large individuals.

The descent of the patronage of the two monasteries has been traced by J. N. L. Myres[30] and H. M. Colvin[31]. It went with Rannulf de Glanville's daughter Matilda to the d'Auberville family along with the manor of Benhall. Matilda's grandson William made an attempt to assert unspecified rights as patron of Butley, but was resisted at the gates by the convent; finally an agreement was reached whereby no guardian should be appointed during vacancies, suggesting that this was the point at issue.[32] The patronage went with Benhall manor to William's daughter Joanna who married Nicholas de Crioil or Cryel, by whom it was sold to Guy Ferre (115). The patrons from the middle of the fourteenth century were the successive earls of Suffolk.[33] Both houses had their freedom of election confirmed by pope Celestine III in the 1190s[34]: there is no further evidence to illuminate the patron's role at Leiston and Butley.

Royal interest in the two houses during the first century of their existence seems confined to visits by Henry III in 1235 and 1248,[35] and isolated acts of charity – a chasuble for Butley from Henry II,[36] and a pyx for Leiston from Henry III.[37] But late in the reign of Edward I we have evidence of the use of both houses as homes for retired royal servants. The first of whom we have record are Roger le Usher at Butley and Hugh Warde at Leiston, both in 1303.[38] The royal foot was firmly in the door, and they both had a stream of successors despite the objections of the hosts. The last known pensioner at Leiston occurs in 1367[39]: in 1388 Richard II conceded freedom from this type of demand (119).

Both houses were members of large organisations. Leiston from its foundation belonged to an international order, though indications of what this meant are very infrequent. It seems likely that the charter of the Count of Guines (12) granting freedom from toll in his territories, near Calais, *in eundo et redeundo*, is, as Mr Colvin suggests, connected with the annual visit of the abbot to the general chapter at Prémontré. There is only one reference to an abbot actually performing this obligation: in 1316 abbot Simon and five of his colleagues were allowed to attend the general chapter as long as no 'census' or

[29] J. N. L. Myres, *Archaeological Journal* xc 242–81.
[30] *Salter Essays*, 191–3.
[31] Colvin, 34, 292.
[32] *Salter Essays*, 192; Evelyn-White, 30.
[33] *Salter Essays*, 192.
[34] **1** below: *Salter Essays*, 192.
[35] *Salter Essays*, 193; *CChR 1247–51*, 36–8; *CPR 1247–58*, 11.
[36] *PR 32 Henry II*, 49.
[37] *C Lib R 1251–60*, 278.
[38] *Salter Essays*, 193; *CCR 1302–7*, 88.
[39] *CCR 1364–8*, 398.

'apportum' was taken out of the country.[40] There is certainly no evidence to suggest that the founder's wish for Leiston to be independent of the order was ever fulfilled. Butley's connections were not international; triennial chapters for the English Augustinian houses were instituted in 1215, and seem to have been held quite regularly at least from the 1220s.[41] In the 1350s it is possible that Butley was making a bid to join the Arroasian canons, money being collected to prosecute Butley, but otherwise relations with the general chapter seem to have been good.[42]

The Curia Regis Rolls show both houses engaged in that constant stream of litigation over lands and rights which seems to have been inseparable from the ownership of property. Relations between Leiston abbey and the men of Dunwich especially do not seem to have been good, though two of the deeds in the cartulary record small gifts by burgesses (**14, 60**). Bad relations began almost immediately (see **11**), with what seems to have been an attack on the abbey for which the townsmen were punished. There was more violence a century later (see **111, 113**), one possible reason for dispute being suggested by **112**, concerning the right to take toll from ships landing in what was then the harbour of Minsmere, between Leiston and Dunwich. The two monasteries were themselves engaged in a dispute in 1235, over the tithes of Leiston's estate at Westhouse in Butley's parish of Knodishall (**90**): the dispute was settled by papal judges-delegate incorporating the outlines of an earlier agreement.

The early fourteenth century abbots of Leiston are only slightly better known than their predecessors. Abbot John is found in 1302 and 1308,[43] Alan in 1310, and Simon in 1316.[44] Another John was abbot in November 1344,[45] and there follows an abbot John in 1367 (**117**); in the 1390s we find presumably another John,[46] though the dates of the individual abbots cannot be recovered. Despite the infrequency of named abbots, the later fourteenth century is well documented. Before then, we have only licences in mortmain showing the increase of the estate, confirmations of charters, and references to the employment of the abbot as a collector of subsidies (one a pardon for deeds of oppression as collector, given on payment of a £50 fine.[47] The prior of Butley was similarly employed, and equally oppressive.[48])

The ruins visible today do not represent the original monastery. That Leiston changed its site has long been known, though it was doubted by William St John Hope on the grounds of the 'archaic' appearance of the capitals at the crossing of the present ruins: not very good evidence in view of the documents to be cited, and in itself disputable, though Clapham thought

---

[40] *CCR 1313–18*, 427. Money was paid despite the royal order: Colvin, 217.

[41] See H. E. Salter, *Chapters of the Augustinian Canons*, Canterbury and York Society xxix, 1921–2.

[42] *Salter Essays*, 200–4.

[43] *CPR 1307–13*, 88; *C Misc Inq*, i. no. 2414.

[44] *CCR 1313–18*, 427. An abbot William occurs in Bodley Suffolk Charter no.221, which I cannot date to within a century: it is, in Mr Colvin's understatement, 'mutilated'.

[45] *CCR 1343–6*, 478.

[46] *C Pap Reg* v.233 (1399).

[47] *CPR 1338–40*, 503; *CPR 1340–3*, 154; *CPR 1343–5*, 559.

[48] *CPR 1334–8*, 39; *CPR 1343–5*, 6.

the capitals were brought from the old monastery and re-set.[49] Suckling, writing in the 1840s, knew that Leiston abbey moved, and suggested that the canons found the old site 'bleak and inconvenient'.[50] This is an understatement, as we shall see.

Leiston was an unfortunate house in the late fourteenth century. The first indication that all was not well comes in November 1362, when Adam de Cockfield and others are given licence to alienate to the canons the advowson of Corton.[51] The reason given is that the abbey's buildings are threatened with ruin by the recent inundations, and cannot be repaired because the foundations have been weakened; therefore the abbey must be rebuilt. The move was thus decided upon before 1362, as steps are being taken to provide the required increase in income. Three years later the canons obtained licence from pope Urban V to transfer from 'the swampy site near the sea' to the town of Leiston one and a half miles away, as long as the church of the old monastery should continue to be served by a priest. In addition, a relaxation of one year and 40 days of enjoined penance was granted for ten years to penitents giving alms for the reconstruction.[52] Each of these processes must have taken time: **117** is the *submissio* of John, abbot of Leiston, concerning the first fruits of Corton church, dated July 1367. Corton was evidently not sufficiently profitable (it was worth just over £7 10s annually in the 1530s), and in 1372 Margaret, countess of Norfolk, obtained licence to alienate the church of Theberton to the canons in exchange for 40s rent and the provision of two canons as chaplains to celebrate daily there.[53] **118** is the bishop of Norwich's confirmation of the appropriation, dated May 1380. In 1382 the countess obtained licence to grant to the abbot and convent the 40s rent, and to release them from finding one of the chaplains. In return the canons granted her the advowson of Kirkley.[54]

By 1380 the abbey had clearly moved to its second site, but a further disaster had overtaken it: in June of that year the collectors of the subsidy were ordered to stay their demands on the abbey until Michaelmas and to release any goods sequestrated out of compassion for the abbey's poverty.[55] The following October the canons were relieved from payment: the monastery was burdened with debt, its possessions were barren (possibly damaged by flooding like the old monastery), the church had been rebuilt at great cost inland, and then, to crown it all, everything except the church had been destroyed by fire.[56] This makes it possible that the church we see today, with its numerous bricks embedded in the flint, and its flushwork, dates from the 1360s or 1370s, though of course it could have been added to, or even rebuilt, in the fifteenth century or later.

69 below is a letter from the king, addressed probably to the pope,[57]

[49] W. St John Hope, *PSIA*, vii, 1891, 227–8; Clapham, 137–41.
[50] Suckling, ii.444.
[51] *CPR 1361–4*, 264–5.   [52] *C Pap Reg*, iv.50.
[53] *CPR 1370–4*, 226.
[54] *CPR 1381–5*, 177.
[55] *CCR 1377–81*, 464.
[56] *CCR 1377–81*, 486.
[57] Though Mr Colvin suggests the bishop of Norwich (Colvin, 425), perhaps the bishop would not need to be informed of Leiston's circumstances and patronage, and the pope is a more likely candidate for the title 'très saint père'.

requesting the papal licence to transfer which was granted in 1365.[58]

This collection contains no document later than the 1360s, so the later history of the two monasteries is strictly irrelevant to our purposes. A good deal can be discovered about the state of Butley priory during the last fifty years of its life, thanks to the records of diocesan visitations[59] and the chronicle mentioned above. The prior, Augustine Rivers, seems to have had a reputation as an autocrat, and there were grumbles about the state of repair of the buildings and choir books, the food, and the lack of harmony between the brothers. For Leiston too there are reports of visitations conducted by the authorities of the Premonstratensian order,[60] but here the house receives unstinted praise for the efficiency of the prior and the general spirit of devotion, just a few small points of observance being worthy of correction. In both sets of visitation reports we have the names of the canons, and from Leiston there is also a list from 1411.[61] The majority of surnames are those of villages in the vicinity, though some are as far afield as Bury St Edmunds and Norwich. The evidence is not easy to interpret, but it seems likely that recruits for the monasteries were drawn in the main from the locality.

The documents we have are concerned almost entirely with properties and rights: there is very little to remind us that these foundations were not, in intention, concerned with this world at all. Only one manuscript book survives from the library of each house. From Leiston there is a copy of a commentary on the concordance to the Gospels by Zacharias Chrysopolitanus, a Premonstratensian writer of the later twelfth century.[62] The volume itself seems to date from the early thirteenth century, but is in none of the hands at work in the cartulary. From Butley there is a fourteenth century volume now in Sydney containing the statutes of the realm and other legal material.[63] The motives of the founder are quite visible to us, those of the other benefactors rather less so; but the religious life as lived at Butley and Leiston is scarcely illuminated at all before the very end of the Middle Ages.

2. Donors

We shall deal with the donors alphabetically, but begin with the founder's relatives.

The family tree of Rannulf de Glanville, founder of both houses, has been discussed elsewhere.[1] The *Roger de Glanville* who granted Middleton church to Leiston (**39**) was almost certainly Rannulf's uncle, and the *William de Glanville* who granted half a mark annually (**19**) could have been Rannulf's

---

[58] *C Pap Reg*, iv.50.
[59] A. Jessopp, *Visitations of the Diocese of Norwich 1492–1532*, Camden Society NS xliii, 1888.
[60] Gasquet, 49–55.
[61] *Cal Pap Reg*, vi.330.
[62] Corpus Christi College, Cambridge, MS 27; F. Petit, *La Spiritualité des Prémontrés aux XIIe et XIIIe siècles*, Paris 1947, 99–100. The commentary is apparently a 'catena' of patristic quotations possibly used as a preparation for preaching.
[63] K. V. Sinclair, 'Another MS belonging to Butley Priory', *Notes and Queries* ccvii, 1962, 408–10.

[1] See R. Mortimer, 'The Family of Rannulf de Glanville', forthcoming.

brother, or alternatively a more remote relative from the senior branch of the family. We have a list of donors to Butley copied into the fourteenth century rent roll mentioned above,[2] from which it seems that Rannulf's sister *Gutha* or *Gytha* granted the church of Weybread, and, if the identification is correct, Rannulf's brother or nephew *Osbert* the church of Harleston; a *William de Glanville* granted the church of Bredfield. Rannulf's daughter *Matilda* married *William d'Auberville*, and this couple granted a quarter of the church of Dickleburgh in Norfolk. Rannulf's wife Bertha was a member of the Valeines family of Parham; she was in all probability a relative of *William de Valeines*, donor of Culpho church to Leiston (**43**). This William, the son of Alan de Valeines (probably the sheriff of Kent who died in 1194[3]), is found in possession of half a knight's fee of the honour of Lancaster in Culpho in 1169[4] which is continually accounted for until, presumably, his death in 1208.[5] He had two coheiresses, Isabel who married *Osbert 'de Wachesham'* (Wattisham), and Matilda the wife of *William de Verdun*: both men are duly found in possession of a quarter-fee at Culpho,[6] and both confirm the gift of Culpho church (**44, 96**). William de Verdun, the son of Guy, is found from 1209 onwards as far as the printed records take us,[7] and John, William's son, in 1245 and 1255.[8] Osbert of Wattisham, who added 3s rent in Bruisyard to the possessions of Leiston (**45**), was the tenant of a knight's fee and 30 acres in serjeanty[9] at Wattisham, and an estate at Marlingford, Norfolk;[10] he succeeded between 1194 and 1197,[11] and was himself succeeded by his son Giles in March 1235.[12] Rannulf de Glanville was related through his wife to the *Walter* family, whose most famous member *Hubert*, bishop of Salisbury and then archbishop of Canterbury, contributed a number of documents to this collection, and another member, *Peter*, was among the donors to Butley of the church of Bylaugh, Norfolk. Hubert's father *Hervey* gave some land to Butley (**146**). Agnes, the daughter of Rannulf's brother William, married *Robert de Crek*;[13] they were ultimately responsible for Robert de Glanville's inheritance, and Crek confirmed the gift of Middleton church (**41**) as well as adding a small gift of his own (**58**).

One more problematical relative remains to be considered: *Jocelin de Hispania* makes a number of grants in Glevering (**56, 93, 94**), and claims to be doing so for the soul of Rannulf his 'uncle'. The Hispanias or d'Espaines were an old Essex family[14] into which the Glanvilles could have married at

[2] Evelyn-White, 46.
[3] See p.8 n.1 above.
[4] *PR 15 Henry II*, 133.
[5] *Pipe Rolls*, passim; *PR 10 John*, 46.
[6] *Bk Fees*, 223–4.
[7] *PR 11 John*, 42; Dodwell, *Fines* ii.no.528; *PR 14 Henry III*, 350; *CRR* xiii. nos 41, 198; *CRR* xiv. no.1320.
[8] *CPR 1247–58*, 454; *Exc e R Fin*, i.446.
[9] *Red Bk Exchq*, ii.527; *Bk Fees*, 1151.
[10] *PR 28 Henry II*, 72; *PR 3 Richard I*, 36.
[11] Palgrave, i.239.
[12] *Exc e R Fin*, i.276.
[13] Farrer, iii.428–31.
[14] D. C. Douglas, *Feudal Documents from the Abbey of Bury St Edmunds*, British Academy Records of the Social and Economic History of England and Wales, viii, 1932, no.169; *EYC*, v.230–3.

any time. From a fine of 1205[15] the following family tree can be reconstructed:

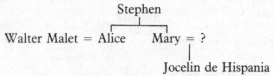

Stephen

Walter Malet = Alice   Mary = ?

Jocelin de Hispania

The name of Jocelin's father is not given but was presumably Hispania, the Stephen is most unlikely to be a Glanville since no appropriate candidate can be found – Stephen de Glanville of Bacton was succeeded by his brother William on his death, not by any sons-in-law.[16] If Jocelin's mother was not a Glanville, and we must suppose his father to have been a Hispania, he could not have been Rannulf's nephew strictly speaking; there is no evidence as to how Jocelin was related to Rannulf, and we have only his statement that he was.

The Bernesheg Family (**95, 99, 100, 101**). William son of Hervey of Bernesheg granted to the abbey a total of seven acres with a messuage, transferring all his rights in his parents' holdings. This land was in 'Aldulueston', shown to have been in Culpho by the rubric to **99**, and was held of his brother Robert for 6*d* annually, with ½*d* scutage payable when necessary to Hugh Ruffus. The gift is confirmed by the brother and by Ruffus. The acre given in **100** was not confirmed by the brother, though it was held of Ruffus and confirmed by him. The abbey steps into William's shoes, taking over a tenurial arrangement reminiscent of 'parage', though the scutage is paid direct to the lord and not to the eldest brother. The mention of rights in the parents' land (**100**) suggests the possibility of partible inheritance, often regarded as characteristic of sokemen. That William's personal legal status was not high is suggested by the phrasing of the lord's charter as a grant of William personally.

Hugh Ruffus, or le Rus, succeeded to the lands of his father Ernald between 1209 and 1212,[17] and having been deprived of them by King John was restored between 1215 and 1222.[18] He was dead by 1231.[19]

Saer de Biskele is responsible for more Leiston charters than any other donor. He grants two men with their holdings and families (**53** and **57**), some land in Leiston and the tenements which the abbey's men held of him (**54**), two small woods and a family in Theberton (**55**), and the small estate of 'Caldham' (**67** and **92**); he also sells six acres in an unspecified village (**66**). In addition there are confirmations by his lords: **74** from Herbert d'Alencun, **84** from Martin de Beaufo and **85** from Martin's wife Egidia.

From litigation which can be traced from Hilary term 1203 to Saer's victory in Easter term 1205,[20] the following family tree can be reconstructed:

[15] Dodwell, *Fines* ii. no.444.
[16] See p.8 n.1 above.
[17] *PBKJJ*, iv. no.4200; *Bk Fees*, i.223.
[18] *R Litt Claus*, i.215b, 332b, 493b.
[19] *CRR*, xiv. no.1661.
[20] *CRR*, ii.180, 309; iii.48, 85–6, 99, 277–8.

```
              Osbert
                |
Geoffrey (1) = Alpasia = (2) Ernald fitz Peter
              |_____|
Ada = Saer de        Matilda = Robert Belet
      Biskele
```

Saer was apparently a minor when his father died, and Ernald had the custody. His first occurrence is in 1194[21] and he was dead in 1224.[22] Barely a year after his death litigation began over his wife's dower: from the pleading Saer's estate can be seen to have been concentrated at Bixley, near Norwich, whence the family took its name, and at Theberton and Cove in Suffolk.[23] He died indebted to the Jews; financial difficulties are also suggested by **103**, concerning land in pledge to William son of Theobald.

Some of Saer's gifts were of land which was his mother's (**53, 54**). His tenurial situation is hard to disentangle, as the confirmations do not always correspond to the gifts (see **84n**). Herbert d'Alencun, his lord for certain lands in Theberton, was a prominent local justice, and sheriff of Norfolk and Suffolk, 1227–32.[24] The terms of **84** and **85** make it likely that the fee of which other tenements in Theberton were held was of the inheritance or marriage-portion of Martin de Beaufo's wife Egidia. They were married by 1194;[25] Martin's last recorded appearance was in 1225.[26] Egidia was the mother of Hugh de Rickinghall, a donor to Leiston and Butley.[27]

Birchard Burdun, who granted Leiston a man, his family and tenement in Middleton (**70**), is perhaps the Burchard de 'Gnateshale' (= Knodishall?) who appears in 1202.[28] He was sued in 1219 by his daughter-in-law Alexandria, who claimed her dowry from him now that Reginald her husband was dead, but the jury declared that despite an altercation at the church door no dowry had ever been mentioned.[29] Apart from these occurrences he is completely obscure.

Richard de Caen (de Cadomo) granted to Butley an acre of his fee at Instead, between Weybread and Wingfield, which William Cubald was holding, over which he had sued the canons. In addition he granted half an acre in Instead by a bridge called 'Anhand': if the amount cannot be made up on one side of the bridge, he will complete it on the other – which seems to imply that Richard did not know how much meadow he held there (**148**). The de Caen family appear as Malet tenants in Domesday Book, and had interests in Rutland, Cambridgeshire and Huntingdonshire as well as Suffolk. Richard first occurs in 1184 and last in 1203.[30] In all probability he was dead by 1216,

[21] Palgrave, i.34.
[22] *R Litt Claus*, i.611b.
[23] *CRR*, xii. nos 788, 829, 1561, 2124, 2596, 2598–9. 'Bischeleia' = Bixley, cf. Dodwell, Charters no.29.
[24] *List of Sheriffs of England and Wales*, London 1896, 86.
[25] Palgrave, i.19.
[26] *CRR*, xii. no.198.
[27] *CRR*, xi. no.2633.
[28] Dodwell, *Fines* ii, no.328.
[29] *CRR*, ix.60.
[30] *PR 30 Henry II*, 12; *PR 5 John*, 239.

when Walter de Caen junior gave Richard his brother, both of whom occur in the witness list, as a hostage.[31] There seems to be no other reference to the plea between Richard and the canons.

Gerard de Campo in **149** and **150** confirms to Butley some land held in Wingfield by his brother Henry, presumably dead. Of some of this the canons were already lords, buying out Gerard's claims for the large sum of 30*s*. The lord of the rest was Warin de Saham, also lord of one fee of the honour of Richmond in Cambridgeshire,[32] where he was coroner in 1220 and probably still in 1234–5.[33] Warin's earliest appearance is in 1211.[34] Gerard de Campo himself is obscure, and most of the witnesses equally so. The charters are not precisely datable.

Roger de Cheney or 'Kedney' granted Leiston some land in an unspecified village (**59**), and agreed to rent land belonging to Middleton church in **13**. Perhaps he was related to the distinguished family of Chesney, or 'de Caisneto': if so, his connection with the Leiston area could stem from William de Kesneto, alias William of Norwich, who held Blythburgh for the service of one knight by gift of Henry II.[35] In 1211 Margaret of this family held Blythburgh;[36] a Roger is found confirming to Blythburgh Priory the gifts of his mother Emma in Cove, and confirming and granting land in Darsham.[37]

Ralph de Cookley. **87** is a grant to Leiston by Ralph de Cookley of 10*d* annual rent from John of Derneford, who of course need not be related to the family of that name found elsewhere in the Leiston deeds. From it we can deduce:

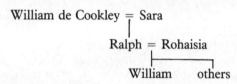

Ralph is active by 1213, and subsequently occurs on juries with various men prominent in the Leiston cartulary.[38] A date well into the thirteenth century is suggested for this charter by the sophisticated legal terminology deployed in it.

Hemfrid de Criketot. Relative obscurity does not prevent a family from being complex, and the Criketots are to be found in at least four East Anglian cartularies. Hemfrid is variously spelt Hamfrid, Ennfrid, Heynfrey, Homfrid and Amfrid; Criketot is presumably one of the three Criquetots in the vicinity of Le Havre.[39]

Hemfrid granted Leiston 20 acres of land in Fordley (**46**), and his rights over a man and his family (**104**). He also sold the 'homage' of a woman and

[31] *R Litt Claus*, i.216.
[32] *R Litt Claus*, i.446.
[33] *CRR*, ix.274; *CRR*, xv. no.1356.
[34] *CRR*, vi.138.
[35] *Bk Fees*, i.133.
[36] *PR 13 John*, 4.
[37] BL Add. 40725 ff 23^r, 28^v.
[38] Dodwell, *Fines* ii, no.557; *CRR*, viii.21; *CRR*, xii.53.
[39] L. C. Loyd, *The Origins of Some Anglo-Norman Families*, ed. C. T. Clay and D. C. Douglas, Harleian Society ciii, Leeds 1951, 36.

her children (51), and occurs frequently as a witness. He was a tenant of the honour of Boulogne for one fee at 'Westdone', perhaps Coney Weston or Market Weston (but also spelt 'Uuesdune', so perhaps Euston), which he is found holding from 1201 to 1221.[40] He was disseised of his fee in 1205 for not coming to cross the Channel in the royal service, and had to pay 100s to get it back; in 1210 he went to Ireland with King John, who was obliged to lend him money.[41] He occurs on a number of juries, and could not always be relied upon to attend.[42] 46 introduces us to Mary his wife and William his heir; Mary must have died before her husband, as Catherine his widow is found suing her stepson for dower.[43] Hemfrid himself had been left a minor, his mother marrying Osbert de Glanville, the justiciar's brother: he had come of age by 1199,[44] and was dead by September 1221.[45] His heir William married Agnes, eventual coheiress of the Blund barony[46]:

William de Criketot(1) = ? = Osbert de Glanville
|
William Blund (d. 1228)   Mary(1) = Hemfrid = (2)Catherine
                                     | (d. 1221)
William   Rose = Robert de   Agnes = William
(d. 1264)   Valeines

The Criketot lands at Middleton were held of William 'de Blancmuster' or 'de Blanmoster'.[47] This is Whitchurch, Shropshire, and the family is the Fitz Alans of Oswestry and Whitchurch. It consequently comes as no surprise to find Criketots inhabiting the Marches.[48]

The Culpho Family. John, son of Roger the Seneschal of Culpho, granted to Leiston some land and rent in Culpho in 83; his sister Margaret added some land in Grundisburgh in 105, which may well be some of the land given to her by her father in 82; and in two further charters (106 and 107) John confirms 105, and others of his sister's gifts. These charters have to be dated from their surely truncated witness-lists, as there is virtually no information about this family other than what can be gleaned from these documents. John's lord is William de Verdun, who witnesses 106, and with his brother-in-law Osbert de Wachesham, 105 and 107. This implies that the family were originally tenants of Alan and William de Valeines, and perhaps even seneschals of the Valeines fee. This would provide a connection with Leiston, which they may not have had were ours the John who was seneschal of the earl of Clare in 1193.[49]

The Dearneford Family. In 17 Robert de Dearneford grants to Henry de Bosco 3s 2d rent in Rendham and Swefling, of which 12d is to go to Leiston abbey, 12d to Blythburgh priory and 2d to 'the hospital of Dunwich' –

[40] *PR 3 John*, 141; *Bk Fees*, 241, 1435.
[41] *R Obl et Fin*, 301; *PR 7 John*, 236; *PR 8 John*, 30, *R Lib* 182, 197.
[42] *CRR*, ii.153, 200; v.244.
[43] *CRR*, x.238, 269.
[44] Palgrave, ii.10–11.
[45] *Exc e R Fin*, i.71–2.
[46] I. J. Sanders, *English Baronies*, Oxford 1960, 4.
[47] *C Inq PM*, i.no.704.
[48] *PR 22 Henry II*, 45; *R Lib*, 225.
[49] *PR 5 Richard I*, 27.

leaving 12*d* for Henry himself. In the next charter Henry de Bosco grants to Leiston whatever rights he had over the men from whom the rent is drawn (i.e. the 12*d*). The cartulary contains two additional title deeds (**15** and **16**) which show how Robert bought his elder brother Bartholomew out of the land belonging to another brother, Roger, and had the transaction confirmed by the lord, Theobald de Valeines. The arrangement within the Dearneford family must date from the 1180s (see **15**), but the gift to Leiston could be later. Again, very little is known about this family; the mere phrase 'holding by knight service' is no guarantee of knightly status at the level of a fraction contributing 9*d* in the pound scutage – they need not have been higher in the social scale than the Bernesheg family. They were tenants of Theobald de Valeines, which provides one possible connection with Leiston: but Robert's patronage went to Blythburgh and a Dunwich hospital as well. A Robert de Derneford held one fee in Derneford of Gilbert Pecche in 1242–3: though sharing the name, he need not be a relative. Later in the thirteenth century Gilbert son of Hamo Pecche confirmed the gifts of various 'Dernefords' to Sibton.[50] 'Derneford' was in Cookley.[51]

Dunwich. We have two grants from men of Dunwich, one (**14**) of land in Leiston, the other (**60**) of half an acre in Middleton. William son of Peter, donor of **14**, and a witness of Master Richer's grant in Dunwich (**61**), may be the man of that name who was fined in 1193;[52] John son of Robert was perhaps under-sheriff of Norfolk and Suffolk for Theobald de Valeines in 1200, as well as joint collector of the aid of 1235–6.[53] There is a fairly continuous flow of references between those dates,[54] but we have no way of knowing how many Johns had fathers called Robert, and there could have been many.

Gilbert de Hawkedon granted 6*d* annual rent in Instead to Butley at the request of his lord Theobald Walter (**147**), a request that the charter implies was rather pressing. Theobald Walter died before Michaelmas 1205.[55] Gilbert himself is obscure.

John de Hopton granted Leiston four acres in Hopton in **71**. The Hopton concerned was the one in Yoxford which has now vanished, bordering on Kelsale and Middleton,[56] rather than either of the other Suffolk Hoptons, which are both at a considerable distance from Leiston. A Roger of Hopton essoins himself from a Suffolk jury in 1210,[57] and he may be John's grandfather referred to in the charter.

Robert Hovel. Copinger traces three Robert Hovels, lords of Wyverstone, in the thirteenth century. The donor of **137** is Robert II (d. 1286), since he mentions Eleanor his wife, and the charter is referred to in **141**, dated 1271.[58] *Robert Maloisel*, who in effect sold certain lands and rights in Weybread to

[50] *Bk Fees*, 913; BL Arundel 221 fo 29[r].
[51] BL Arundel 221 fo 59[r].
[52] *PR 5 Richard I*, 25.
[53] *PR 2 John*, 130; *Bk Fees*, 490.
[54] eg *PR 16 John*, 167; *R Litt Claus*, i.338b; ii.210.
[55] *PR 7 John*, 178.
[56] R. T. L. Parr, 'Two Townships in Blything Hundred', *Proceedings of the Suffolk Institute of Archaeology* xxv part 3, 1952, 297–304.
[57] *CRR*, vi.2.
[58] Copinger, iii.345–6.

Butley, was on a Suffolk jury in 1200,[59] and if he is to be identified with a namesake in Herefordshire, he was dead by 1214.[60] His son and heir Alexander granted further lands in Weybread (**135**).

The *Parcarius* or Parker family of Dennington were donors to both Leiston and Butley. Gerard granted the site of the mill of 'Holyoak' to Leiston (**49**), and to Butley two of his men (**124**) and 11½ acres in Dennington (**125**) along with his body for burial. **125** is confirmed by Gerard's nephew and heir Richard (**126**) and by his lord Godfrey de Wavere (**127**).

```
                          Benedict
                             |
          ┌──────────────────┴──────────────┐
  Margery, Ida = Gerard         Henry = Isabella
                              (d. 1230)|
                                   Richard
```

This family tree is by no means complete. In 1205, Godfrey de Wavere sued Henry Parcarius for one ninth of a knight's fee, being the dower of his wife Basilia, formerly widow of Walter Parcarius.[61] This Walter cannot be fitted in, but it looks as if the family was related by marriage to their lord. Isabella sued Godfrey le Parker for her dower in 1230,[62] which implies that Henry was then dead. Unfortunately Gerard's dates are unknown.

The Peasenhall Family. In **63** and **64**, Rannulf de 'Onhus' (Onehouse) and Norman de Peasenhall grant to the abbey their mill of Langwade, except for an annual pension of two marks which is Rannulf's wife Petronilla's marriage portion. The relationship between them is:

```
            Ralph
              |
       Norman (d. 1217)           Robert
       ┌──────┴──────┐              |
    Ralph      Petronilla = Rannulf de Onehouse
                             |
                          William
```

They would appear to have been joint owners of the mill before two marks from it were given (presumably from Norman's share) as Petronilla's marriage portion. They then agreed to give the mill to the abbey except for the two marks.

In a late twelfth century charter from Sibton[63] Norman confirms amongst other things land which Rannulf de Glanville gave Sibton from his father Ralph's fee, from which we can surmise either that Norman was Rannulf's tenant, or that Rannulf obtained the wardship of Norman as a minor. Furthermore, Robert de Valeines was Norman's *avunculus*; this is probably Robert the father of Theobald de Valeines, and brother-in-law of Rannulf de Glanville, which makes Norman a distant relative by marriage of the justiciar. Norman himself is found active in the years around 1200, once in a

[59] Palgrave, ii.197.
[60] *CRR*, vii.104.
[61] *CRR*, iii.249.
[62] *CRR*, xiv. no.141.
[63] Brown, no.9.

final concord over property in Newcastle;[64] and in October 1217 his son Ralph recovered his lands on going over to the young Henry III, presumably implying that Norman was dead by then.[65] Ralph son of Robert 'de Onhus' occurs in 1199, and he and his son William witness Rannulf de Peasenhall's charter to Sibton.[66]

Master Richer. In **61** Master Richer, son of Alexander, grants all the tenement in Dunwich which he held of William 'de Falesham' and in **62** William confirms the gift, reinforced by **72**, William's son William's confirmation. Of the donor nothing else is known: he was presumably a cleric, and obviously had property in Dunwich. We know there were two William de Faleshams, and the name occurs in the public records from 1180 to 1224;[67] it is impossible to distinguish between father and son. 'Falesham' is presumably Felsham.

Hugh de Rickinghall was a donor to Leiston, granting a marsh with meadow and pasture in Playford (**79**); and a man with his family and tenement in the same vill (**80**). Both these grants were confirmed together by Hugh's lord, Alan de Witherdale (**108**). Hugh de Rickinghall was a moderate local landholder: he held of Osbert de Wachesham in Cropfield and 'Horswold', amounting to one quarter of a fee, and he and Ralph de Nereford held ¾ fee in Cropfield of the Raimes barony then given to Roger Bigod.[68] He held at Rickinghall too, as Eye Priory is found disputing the tithes of his estate there.[69] We can see that he held land in Playford, and it seems at Theberton as well.[70] He is involved in final concords over property in Wetheringsett, Gisleham and Witnesham, and Debenham in Suffolk, and 'Greinsevill' in Norfolk.[71] His earliest appearance seems to be in 1194,[72] and he is still litigating in 1231.[73]

William, son of William fitz Roscelin granted 10s rent in Sutton to Leiston in **73**. Two complicated lawsuits permit us to reconstruct the following tree[74]:

```
Roger      William fitz Roscelin = Alice = Gilbert Blund     William II
                                |                             d. c 1169
           Lecia de Edgefield = William
                              |  (d. by 1230)
                    John    Andrew    Margaret = ?
                                                 |
                                               Alice
```

The marriage of Alice to William took place in Henry II's reign, and the arrangements were confirmed by John as Count of Mortain (charters of both were produced in the pleading), hence it could be that ours is the William

[64] PR Soc, 1st ser. xx, no.1; Dodwell, *Fines* ii, no.482; Palgrave, ii.268.
[65] *R Litt Claus*, i.337b.
[66] Palgrave, i.397; *Bk Seals*, no.290.
[67] Brown, no.9, to *CRR*, xi. no.2109; in between, eg Palgrave, ii. 268; *CRR*, ii.153, 200; iii.196, 284; vi.2, 297, 359; viii.21.
[68] Dodwell, *Fines* ii, no.124; *Bk Fees* i.136, 233.
[69] Sayers, 197.
[70] *CRR*, xiv. no.470.
[71] Dodwell, *Fines* ii, nos 310, 487; also Rye, *Norfolk* s.v.
[72] Palgrave, i.1.
[73] *CCR 1227–31*, 539.
[74] *CCR* iv.107–9; xiv. no.253.

who first appears in 1198,[75] and proceeds to a laborious career as juror and justice,[76] as guardian of Yarmouth fair,[77] and under-sheriff in 1211 and 1212.[78] He was out of favour for a time in John's reign, having to offer 60 marks and a good hawk to get his land back,[79] and in March 1216 he had to deliver his son and granddaughter as hostages at Orford castle.[80] It is clear from the litigation mentioned above that he was dead by 1230, when a suit began over his wife's dower. During his life William fitz Roscelin sued a wide variety of people, from the prior of Norwich to John Hunipot of Wingfield,[81] but the family was not without generous impulses, also occurring among the benefactors of Sibton, Blythburgh, and Langley abbey in Norfolk.[82]

Baldwin de Ufford gave the canons of Butley the tithes of a mill at Woodbridge which they let out to Woodbridge ,priory in **153**. Baldwin himself is very obscure.

Oliver de Vaux granted Leiston some land (**50**) which is proved to be in Chediston by **88**. The de Vaux family had been settled at Chediston and in its vicinity since Domesday, so this Oliver is likely to have been in possession of some at least of his eleventh century ancestors' lands. The de Vaux family is either extremely large, or not a single family at all: some are Arundel tenants in Sussex and East Anglia, and there were Devonshire de Vaux by 1140.[83] The Suffolk de Vaux have been charted,[84] showing two Olivers:

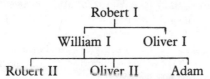

Robert II died before 1202, so the balance of probability is that ours is Oliver II. By a final concord of 1202, Oliver agrees with Adam that he will hold two carucates in Chediston with reversion to Adam's heirs after Oliver's death.[85] This, of course, may not be the only land Oliver held in Chediston. A fairly lengthy biography of an uncertain and possibly conflated Oliver can be built up from the public records, but its usefulness to us is doubtful as it does not help separate the two.

William son of Alan granted Leiston abbey Theberton church (**75**), quit-claimed a number of men (**42** and **102**), granted two acres in an unnamed vill (**52**) and some tenements in Theberton with the proviso that if they could not

[75] Dodwell, *Fines* ii, no.100.
[76] Eg *CPR 1216–25*, 259, 344, 393–4, 559; *CPR 1225–32*, 151, 305, 352; *R Litt Claus*, i.552, 633; ii.72, 159.
[77] *CPR*, i.469.
[78] *PR 13 John*, 14; *PR 14 John*, 170.
[79] *PR 9 John*, 164; *PR 10 John*, 12, 13.
[80] *R Obl et Fin*, 589; *R Litt Claus*, i.257b (bis).
[81] Eg *CRR*, i.276; Dodwell, *Fines* ii, no.455.
[82] BL Add. 5948 fo 48r.
[83] Farrer, iii, index s.v.; H. R. Watkin, in *Transactions of the Devonshire Association*, 1, 1918, 75–9.
[84] Brown, 72 n.l, 73 n.l.
[85] Dodwell, *Fines* i, no.321.

be warranted they would be replaced from his demesne at Creeting (**86**). Abbot Philip is mentioned in **102**, so we are dealing with an early thirteenth century tenant in Theberton and Creeting: therefore very probably the William son of Alan 'of Hacheston' who granted two acres of his demesne in Theberton to Blythburgh priory.[86] A final concord of July 1200, between William son of Alan and Roger Bigod, in which William agreed to hold for life of the earl half a fee in Theberton with reversion to the Bigods after his death,[87] can be connected with litigation in Trinity term 1223[88]: in this, the abbot of Leiston was summoned to answer why he held an acre and 2s rent of the half fee, since William had only a life interest in it; William son of Alan came and said that some of the tenants were enfeoffed before the fine, but that he would give the others, including the abbot, land elsewhere. The proviso clause in **86** thus suggests a date after the fine, and the remaining charters could be the replacements after the court case. The mention of demesne in Creeting allows us to identify him with the William son of Alan who granted rent from a mill in Creeting to Bromholm priory.[89] Creeting, near Stowmarket, included Glanville holdings in Domesday, and this, together with his donations to the two Glanville foundations, makes it likely that he was also a Glanville tenant. Thus we have a Bigod and probably Glanville tenant at Creeting, Hacheston and Theberton, who flourished c 1189–1223. We can hesitantly attribute to him a modest career as a juror,[90] and a position as one of eight bailiffs of Yarmouth in 1208.[91]

William son of Theobald. **48** is an early exchange between abbot Robert and Theobald son of William, virtually certainly the father of the William son of Theobald who appears in **47** as the tenant of a 'militia' in the soke of Leiston. The latter is also responsible for a gift (**65**) and an exchange (**78**), as well as **103**. It is clear that he is a knightly landholder in the Leiston area, a tenant and small benefactor of the abbey. He is very likely the William vouched to warrant land in Knodishall by his brother Thomas son of Theobald in 1229, and possibly he is the William Thebaud who was a tenant of Saer de Biskele in Theberton in 1225.[92] He is not likely to have been the only man in Suffolk with his name, which makes it hazardous to attribute entries in the legal or financial records to him. It seems reasonable to suppose that his family held the other manor in Leiston, Wade Hall: some Bodleian Suffolk charters of the thirteenth century show William and his relatives granting land in the Leiston area,[93] and the occurrence of the name Theobald among the holders in the fourteenth century adds a little more support.[94]

William de Winderville granted three and a half acres in Tuddenham for a term of six years in a charter datable to 1220 (**81**). Nothing further is known about him, except that a man of that name concorded over land in Mellis in 1198.[95]

[86] BL Add. 40725 fo 59v.
[87] Dodwell, *Charters*, no.298.
[88] *CRR*, xi. no.56.
[89] Cambridge University Library MS Mm II 20 fo 52v.
[90] *CRR*, i.188; ii.153; iv.222; v.225.
[91] *CRR*, v.168.
[92] *CRR*, xiii. no.1454; xii. no.2124.
[93] Nos 1179, 1199.
[94] Copinger, iii.115–6.
[95] PR Soc. 1st ser., xxiv, no.161.

3. Possessions

We shall begin with the two houses' churches, and go on to discuss their temporal possessions.

The churches of Leiston and Aldringham were given to Leiston abbey by its founder. The early rearrangement has been mentioned above (p.2). Leiston is described in Domesday as having three churches with a hundred acres of free land[1]: Aldringham must surely be one of them, and the third may be Thorpe or Knodishall. When the bishop sanctioned the transfer of Leiston and Aldringham churches (**36**), the latter is described as a 'chapel', but when confirmed to the abbey a year or so later (**34**) it is a 'church'. In **22**, Aldringham is again a 'chapel', and in **31** it is one of the 'two churches of Leiston'. The two are found in the abbey's possession throughout its history down to the dissolution. Sizewell was another chapel of Leiston: it is mentioned in **22** as *de novo constructa*, whether because it is a new foundation, or simply a rebuilding, or even whether it has had to be moved as a result of coastal erosion, is unclear.

In **39** Roger de Glanville, Rannulf's uncle, grants to Leiston the church of the neighbouring vill of Middleton, which is 'of his fee'. The grant is confirmed in **41** by his eventual heir, Robert de Crek, and by the superior lord, Roger Bigod, in **40**. Both Robert and the earl regard the church as an appurtenance of their lay fee. The gift is confirmed by John of Oxford, bishop of Norwich, in **37**: the church is *in usus proprios*, except for the rights of Roger 'clericus', surely the parson, as long as he shall live.

The church of Culpho, near Ipswich, was granted to Leiston by William de Valeines (**43**), and confirmed by his eventual heirs Osbert de Wachesham (**44**) and William de Verdun (**96**). It is confirmed to Leiston by Honorius III in **5**, and by William Raleigh in **22**, but no earlier episcopal confirmation survives.

Theberton is a more complicated case. William son of Alan's charter of gift, **75**, dates from 1189–93, but St Peter's Theberton is not mentioned by Honorius III in **5**, nor by the bishop in **22**. There is no specific confirmation anywhere, and no mention that Leiston possessed Theberton church in the *Taxatio Ecclesiastica*. The earl of Norfolk presented to Theberton church in 1305.[2] In 1302 licence was given for the alienation to Leiston abbey of Theberton church by Margaret, countess of Norfolk, in exchange for 40*s* rent, and finding two canons as chaplains to say service daily in the church.[3] Ten years later she remitted the 40*s* rent and the obligation to provide one of the chaplains, receiving in exchange the advowson of Kirkley.[4] From this it would seem that the earlier gift did not take effect, or if it did, that the canons were subsequently deprived of the church. It could be that William son of Alan gave the church against the terms of his final concord with Roger Bigod in 1200 (see above, p. 18), and as a result of this the canons were deprived. At all events they had to wait until the 1370s before finally obtaining the church,

[1] Domesday, i.311b.
[2] Norfolk and Norwich Record Office, Norwich Episcopal Register i, (John Salmon) fo 19ᵛ.
[3] *CPR 1370–4*, 226.
[4] *CPR 1381–5*, 177; *CPR 1345–8*, 427.

which was appropriated to them by the bishop in 1380 (**118**).

Kirkley church was obtained in 1347, when licence in mortmain was given to William Scarlet, parson of Chillesford, John Gerard, chaplain (who two years before had helped Leiston to acquire the manor of Wade Hall), and Robert de Cliff to alienate the church to Leiston abbey.[4] The canons thus had it for less than thirty-five years.

The church of Corton was acquired in 1362 with the aid of two local parsons and a layman, in the same way as Kirkley had been.[5] In 1367 the church was appropriated (**117**), and in 1383 it received royal ratification despite technical irregularities in its acquisition.[6]

The income of a parish church derived partly from oblations at the altar, and partly from the glebe land – 100 acres for the three Domesday churches of Leiston, as we have seen. **13** below is a lease of such land, showing that however Middleton church was served in the early thirteenth century, Leiston had control of the glebe, and **130** and **131** demonstrate Butley's close interest in the land of Weybread church.

But to judge from the surviving quantity of litigation, the most valuable source of income was from tithes. Tithes were due to parish churches from the inhabitants of the parish; however, the tendency was to free religious corporations from this burden, the Premonstratensians having a papal privilege to this effect as early as 1139.[7] Leiston's first papal document, **1**, frees the monastery from payment of tithes on newly cultivated ground and on animal foodstuffs, a formula developed under Innocent II. The Fourth Lateran Council, in 1215, restricted monastic freedom from payment to these 'noval' lands, thus implying that tithe still had to be paid from newly acquired, already tithe-paying land. It is à propos of this clarification of the position that we should see **20** and **21**, which emphasise that all monastic freedom has not been revoked by the council.

The tithes of the demesne of Leiston were given to the monks of Eye by their founder, Robert Malet;[8] it would seem that when Glanville was granted the manor, Butley priory acquired an interest in them, to be superseded by Leiston in the 1180s: the agreement reached (**31**) was that Leiston should pay Butley a 10*s* pension for the demesne tithes, and Butley would then 'acquit' the canons of Leiston to the monks of Eye. This involved paying Eye the 10*s*: the monks are being paid the money in the thirteenth century, at the Michaelmas synod at Ipswich,[9] and were still receiving it in the sixteenth century.[10] The canons of Leiston were themselves the holders of the demesne.

In 1235 Butley brought a case against Leiston, complaining that the latter was detaining the tithes of Leiston's house called 'le Westhus' which were due to Butley's church of Knodishall, as well as the offerings of secular servants living in 'the said grange' (**90**). Butley renounced the tithes, but

[4] *CPR 1381–5*, 177; *CPR 1345–8*, 427.
[5] *CPR 1361–4*, 264.
[6] *CPR 1381–5*, 268.
[7] G. Constable, *Monastic Tithes from their Origins to the Twelfth Century*, Cambridge 1964, 242.
[8] Eye Cartulary, 'Malet', fo 17[v].
[9] *Taxatio*, 118b.

retained the right to the offerings of their own parishioners, and of those living there who were neither their own nor Leiston's parishioners. Butley also renounced parochial rights over those parts of the demesnes of 'le Westhus' and of Leiston from which tithes were not being paid to Knodishall church at the relaxation of the interdict, and over certain other stated pieces of demesne; Leiston agreed to pay tithes from other stated pieces of land. The agreement made between abbot Philip and prior William was to stand. This *puralea* is incorporated in **89**: it is a list of those within the parish of Knodishall who shall pay tithes to Leiston, and although made at the time of the relaxation of the general interdict, as it says, it is sealed by the litigants of 1235; the interlined names are thus probably those of the tenants of 1235, those of the body of the text belonging to the original document. The date of the original document is uncertain: William, prior of Butley was dead by January 1213; negotiations to end the interdict continued for eighteen months at least, before it was officially lifted in July 1214. We should allow the agreement to have been made by prior William, perhaps shortly before his death, and assume the reference to the interdict to be the attempt of a later generation to provide an approximate date: the original document detailing the agreement would very likely contain the prior's name, but would not necessarily carry a date.

It is thus clear that Butley was taking tithe from Knodishall church in the thirteenth century, and also had an interest in oblations at the altar. In the 1360s they had been receiving the greater tithe from their parish of Debenham from time out of mind (**123**), as had Ely from Winston.

The most valuable of Leiston abbey's churches by far was Leiston itself. In the *Taxatio* it is assessed at £34 and more annually, with Aldringham and Middleton at about £8 each, and Culpho just over £5. The spiritualities together were worth over £56, rather more than a third of the assessed income of the house – the temporalities came to over £91. The church of Knodishall, resigned to Butley, was worth £6 13s 4d, while Kirkley, which they subsequently acquired, was valued at only £4 13s 4d.[11] The *Valor Ecclesiasticus* shows a dramatic decrease in the value of Leiston church. Aldringham and Middleton are much the same as 250 years earlier, at just over £7; Leiston is still worth more than they are, at nearly £15. Corton church has been added to the roll, at roughly the same value as Aldringham; Theberton is under a secular rector with no sign of a pension.[12] Culpho is described as appropriated to Leiston, but is served by a rector.[13] The proportion of the house's income contributed by spiritualities has gone down to barely one fifth – £37, as against nearly £145 from temporalities.

Right from its foundation, Butley priory was exceptionally well endowed with churches. The founder gave the churches of Butley, Capel, Bawdsey, Benhall, Farnham, Wantisden and part of South Glemham (see **120**) in Suffolk, Upton in Norfolk[14] and very likely also Finborough and Gedgrave in Suffolk.[15] He also founded a hospital on the manor, and endowed with the

---

[10] *VE*, iii.438.
[11] *Taxatio*, 116–18.
[12] *VE*, iii.439.
[13] *VE*, iii.427.
[14] *Monasticon*, vi(i).380 no.3.
[15] Evelyn-White, 45.

church, of West Somerton near Yarmouth, giving the general oversight to Butley.[16] Knodishall, resigned by Leiston in **6**, occurs among Butley's spiritualities in the late thirteenth century; in the sixteenth it has a secular rector.[17] By the time of the *Taxatio Ecclesiastica* in the late 1270s there had been added the churches of Debenham, Weybread,[18] Little Worlingham (see **154**), Redisham, Harleston, North Glemham, Kesgrave, Aspall, Ashfield, Shelley and Bredfield in Suffolk,[19] Gissing in Norfolk,[20] St Stephen Coleman Street in the city of London,[21] and probably also Biker in Lincolnshire.[22] By the time of the *Valor Ecclesiasticus* in the sixteenth century Butley also possessed Bylaugh and Kilverstone in Norfolk, Dedham in Essex and Ramsholt in Suffolk, but Bylaugh at least may have been given centuries earlier.[23] Other churches described as Butley's in a fourteenth century list, but not mentioned as such in the *Taxatio* or the *Valor*, are Ringsfield, Rishangles, Eyken and South Cove in Suffolk, and Winfarthing in Norfolk.[24] Butley thus certainly possessed at least twenty-nine churches, and may at some stage have had claims on another five.

With an endowment on this scale it is not surprising to find that the house's income from spiritualities (£138) is greater than that from temporalities (£100) in the *Taxatio*, though by the time of the *Valor* the temporalities (£210) are double the spiritualities (£108). The two most valuable churches in both the thirteenth and sixteenth centuries were Debenham and Upton, and as with Leiston the actual income assessed has diminished – at Debenham from £30 to £12 6s.

The question of how these parish churches were served is difficult to answer. The early statutes of Prémontré forbade accepting a church *nisi possit esse abbatia*,[25] but Leiston, like the other English houses of its order, was from the start given churches which could not be the abbey. Leiston and Butley shared with the whole canonical order the right to hold churches 'in their own hand' and 'for their own use', and to serve them with their own canons if they wished.[26] A fourteenth century note mentions a bull of pope Lucius III specifically allowing Butley to do this,[27] and the privilege is ascribed to Leiston by the bishop of Norwich in **22**. When a church was granted to them, the rights of the sitting incumbent would be safeguarded (**36**), but thereafter the canons, now the patrons, could appoint an outside vicar or one of their own number as they thought fit, as long as he was decently maintained (**22, 36**). There is very little evidence to show what actually happened. Butley could hardly depute canons to all its numerous

[16] BL Harley Roll N 20.
[17] *Taxatio*, 118b; *VE*, iii.439.
[18] Before 1205 – see no.130.
[19] *Taxatio*, 115b, 117, 117b, 118, 119, 123.
[20] Bodleian Library, Suffolk Charter 191, a late 13th-century *inspeximus* of an appropriation by 'bishop John' – therefore before 1214.
[21] *Taxatio*, 19.
[22] *Taxatio*, 74; Biker in *VE*, iii.418.
[23] *VE*, iii.418–22; Evelyn-White, 46.
[24] Evelyn-White, 46.
[25] Colvin, 8.
[26] Colvin, 277.
[27] Evelyn-White, 60.

churches, some of them distant: Upton in Norfolk was served by a vicar in the 1240s (**154**). **118** shows Theberton church served by a brother Robert of Darsham, clearly a canon of Leiston, who is referred to as *rector*, paying a pension to the abbey. He is to be replaced by a temporary secular priest. The next information comes from the 1482 visitation, when one canon is *custos* of Middleton church, and another of Thorpe,[28] and in 1499 Thomas Went, formerly the precentor, was instituted to Theberton.[29]

The charters from Butley must represent a very small proportion of that house's title deeds. The Leiston cartulary is much more complete, though still not containing all the charters even of the first generation of donors, and as far as Leiston's estate is concerned it can be supplemented by a number of unpublished documents, notably the wreck rolls.[30] These are the records of the sessions of the 'hithe ward moot' held on St Nicholas's day (6th December). A jury from Thorpe and Sizewell made presentations of the objects washed ashore, which had to be viewed by the cellarer or his bailiff, who then estimated their value. The abbot and the finder had a right to half the value each, though how this was administered is unclear. There also survives a cellarer's account for the year 1305[31] – whatever the statutes may say, Leiston was by this time conforming to the normal practice as regards the duties of its cellarer. On the dorse of the roll is an interesting English-Latin glossary of agricultural terms. There is also an undated, but probably early fourteenth century, extent of the manor of Leiston, recording the names of dozens of small tenants of the abbey along with their holdings.[32]

Leiston manor formed the nucleus of the property: on it the abbey was itself situated. It was the gift of the founder, and was confirmed by popes and kings (**1, 3, 23, 24, 27**). The manor consisted of demesne, tenant land, and various jurisdictional rights and dues.

Demesne land was in existence in Domesday Book, and if the figure for ploughs is any guide to its extent, was twice as large as the tenant land: under Edric of Laxfield there were eleven ploughs on the demesne, and the tenants had six; *modo*, the demesne had seven ploughs and the tenants three and a half. The wood had diminished – then, pannage for five hundred pigs, *modo*, two hundred. This, together with the over-all diminution in the number of ploughs, compares interestingly with a rise in value from £16 to £28 for the whole manor.[33] The tithes of the demesne were given to Eye priory by Robert Malet – Leiston manor was part of the honour of Eye. While the demesne must have continued to exist, it is not illustrated by the charters: they are not concerned with it, though **68** mentions a *dominica aula*. Possibly the absence of leases of land implies that the canons were farming it directly, with

[28] Gasquet, iii.48. Presumably Thorpe near Aldringham.
[29] C. Harper-Bill, *The Register of Cardinal Morton*, Canterbury and York Society, forthcoming, no.1330.
[30] For a charter not in the cartulary, see *Monasticon* vi(ii).880 (Gilbert Pecche). For the wreck rolls, see B. Schofield, in J. Conway Davies (ed.), *Studies Presented to Sir Hilary Jenkinson*, 1957, 361–71. Rolls for 1378–97 (10 membr.), 1398–1407 (5 membr.), 1495–1518 (missing).
[31] IESRO, HD 371/4.
[32] IESRO, HD 371/5.
[33] Domesday, i.311–311b.

'conversi' or hired labour. It is clear from the cellarer's roll that they were doing so later, and the Leiston entry in the *Taxatio Ecclesiastica* seems to imply direct exploitation.[34] For the very end, the *Valor Ecclesiasticus* provides evidence that the demesne lands of Leiston Hall were let out for £14 annually, the largest single source of income of the many under the heading 'Leiston cum membris';[35] other large sums (£10 and £6) are due from pieces of demesne let to others. A large number of 'closes' are named, all of them let. Some parcels of land, however, are described as retained in the abbot's hand to pasture the monastery's livestock and to 'sustain their husbandry'. It would seem on the whole that most of the demesne was leased by the 1530s, in line with the process on much greater estates than Leiston's. It could be that the home farm of Leiston, when directly exploited, provided enough produce for the canons and their dependants to live off, but only an edition of the cellarer's account could provide such information.

On the main estate Domesday enumerates 25 villeins, 27 bordars and 7 serfs (up from 3 in 1066). In addition, Gilbert held 140 acres under Robert Malet, formerly held by Edric as a manor, with a small complement of 4 bordars, 2 villeins and 2 ploughs; Fulchred held of Malet an estate consisting of 3 demesne ploughs and 8 freemen with 1½ carucates; and an anonymous freeman held 40 acres as a manor, valued in the main estate; to which were attached a further 47 freemen with 7 carucates and 6½ ploughs between them.[36] Two centuries or so later there were at least two estates in Leiston: the abbey's manor, and Wade Hall, belonging to a family represented at the time of our charters by Theobald and William his son (see above, p 18). **114** shows the size and value of Wade Hall in the fourteenth century – the abbey's own estate must surely have been larger. We must assume that the abbey's manor had its quota of dependants who are not mentioned in the charters; however, other lords had men in Leiston, whom they could, and did, grant. We have the names of eight men of the abbey who also held of Saer de Biskele, who are granted by him with their holdings in **54** – evidently the tenurial situation was not simple. In an interesting charter (**47**) William son of Theobald granted, amongst other things, Walter the reeve and his sons. Other men also had demesne land in Leiston which they could grant – both the charters just referred to include gifts of land – and we have a grant of rights over land in Leiston from a man who appears to be a burgess of Dunwich (**14**).

The jurisdictional rights of Leiston were obviously rather extensive – it was in fact a soke. The soke of Leiston is found acting as a judicial unit in the time of king John, owing ten marks *pro falso clamore*.[37] A cryptic entry on the Curia Regis Rolls suggests that the abbot's jurisdiction in some matter was being contested in 1219,[38] and certainly in the Hundred Rolls accusations of appropriating jurisdiction are easy to find: the abbot has taken away the suit of Aldringham which was once in the body of the hundred; he is holding a market at Sizewell and taking tolls, to the damage of the royal vill of Dunwich. He has usurped the assize of bread and beer over his tenants at

[34] *Taxatio*, 126.
[35] *VE*, iii.437.
[36] Domesday, i.311–311b.
[37] *PR 7 John*, 253; paid off, *PR 13 John*, 18.
[38] *CRR*, viii.2.

Culpho, but has been deprived of that in Buxlow.[39] The manor of Leiston has had right of wreck, gallows, warren and the assize of bread and beer 'for a long time past'.[40] Wreck we know about from the surviving rolls; the warren crops up again when in 1348 a number of local men were accused of entering the abbot's free warren and taking rabbits, hares, partridges and pheasants, felling his trees and trampling his grass;[41] in the *Valor*, the warren is let for the large sum of £10.[42] The soke could be regarded as a unit for the purposes of extortion by Robert Garveys, the crooked head constable of Blything hundred in 1388.[43] Despite the centuries of history behind it, the abbot was accused in 1399 of claiming a soke called 'Leyston sokene' where he had none, and of preventing the king's sheriffs and bailiffs from executing writs, receiving plaints, and delivering goods unjustly siezed within it, insisting on holding such pleas in his court.[44] Possibly he was claiming some rights he did not have; the printed enrolments do not give the outcome of the case. A complicated transaction on the dorse of the Close Roll for 1450[45] shows us, amongst other things, men holding 'by the rod' in the courts of Leiston, and being freed, by agreement, of suit to the court leet. In the *Valor*, the perquisites of the court at Leiston amount to £3 6s 8d.[46]

47 is the only charter which illustrates the soke. William son of Theobald was the holder of a *militia* within the soke of Leiston, and thus the abbot's man; as we have seen, this was probably the manor subsequently called Wade Hall. He resigns the rights which he or his ancestors have acquired in the soke, and the gifts his father made to the abbey; he confirms that two of his men shall help the abbot with the 'common aid of the vill'. For this, the abbot confirms to William the lands, rents, men and tenements which his father held within the soke, plus land in Theberton and some men at Fordley returned to him as part of his 'militia' within the soke. Thus the soke had a tenurial as well as an administrative and legal aspect, affecting by no means only the lower reaches of society; it also included lands and rights in vills neighbouring Leiston.

Abbot Nicholas was granted a weekly market in 1278 (see above, p 4). By 1391 this had ceased to be of any value and had not been held for some years: the manor, being on the coast, had become impoverished because of 'the enemy', and 'other misfortunes'; also 'the people of the neighbourhood will not buy on Fridays as readily as on other days', so the abbot surrendered the earlier letters patent for cancellation and obtained new ones granting a weekly market on Tuesdays.[47] Leiston also had a yearly fair, which in 1315 was changed from July to 29th November and the following three days.[48]

Assised rents in Theberton, Aldringham, Knodishall and Buxlow are

---

[39] *Rotuli Hundredorum temp. Hen. II et Edw. I*, Record Commission, London 1812–18, ii.186, 200, 189, 147.
[40] *Rotuli Hundredorum* (cf. n.39) ii.148.
[41] *CPR 1348–50*, 157–8.
[42] *VE*, iii.437.
[43] *C Misc Inquis*, iii.263.
[44] *C Misc Inquis*, vi.374.
[45] *CCR 1447–54*, 287–9.
[46] *VE*, iii.437.
[47] *CChR*, v.321–2.
[48] *CChR*, iii.289.

included under Leiston manor in the *Valor Ecclesiasticus*. The cartulary contains several gifts in Theberton, of lands and woods (**48, 55**), of men and rent (**84, 86**), and of the small estate of 'Caldham' (**92**). Theberton was second only to Leiston in value in the *Taxatio*, and the abbey's holdings there continued to increase in the fourteenth century.[49] For Aldringham we have only one charter, **30**, an agreement to lease just over four acres of meadow. Probably the gift of Leiston manor carried with it lands and rights in Aldringham. Knodishall is a comparatively well documented vill. The estate of Westhouse was called a 'grange' in **90**, and presumably was being farmed directly, possibly even with lay-brothers, who have however left no trace in the documents. In 1451 it is again called a grange.[50] **89** is a unique document allowing us to see the descent of certain peasant holdings in Knodishall (see below, p. 29).

Further afield, the abbey possessed substantially less. In the *Valor* the most valuable estate outside the Leiston area was at Glevering, presumably that given by Jocelin de Hispania (**56, 93, 94**). In the same district near Ipswich, at Grundisburgh, Tuddenham, Playford and Culpho they received small grants (**77, 79, 80, 83, 97, 105–7**) which cannot be precisely traced: at Culpho in the sixteenth century there was an estate called 'Abbot's Hall', which still survives, and the *Valor* enters rents from all those villages.[51] There were smaller gifts in Chediston (**50**), Cookley (**87**), Rendham and Swefling (**17, 18**), Bruisyard (**45**), a messuage in Orford (**77**), and mills in Dennington and Farnham (**63, 64**).

From 1279 a licence in mortmain was necessary in order to alienate lay fee to a religious house, and how this worked in Butley's case has been elucidated by Dr Myres.[52] At Leiston the first specific licence occurs in 1290,[53] and the three churches added during the fourteenth century were all acquired under specific licences.[54] In 1311 the escheator was ordered to enquire whether the abbot had acquired lands contrary to the Statute of Mortmain, the result being a fairly long list of such acquisitions: the abbot was pardoned for a fine of five marks.[55] From 1344 Leiston, like Butley, purchased licences in advance, setting off subsequent acquisitions against the value allowed in the licence: thus Wade Hall, obtained in 1345, was held to represent ten marks (£6 13s 4d) of a licence granted the previous year to acquire lands worth £20 annually.[56] The inquisition *ad quod damnum* held before Wade Hall was alienated reported that the total value of the land concerned was £2 15s 3d (**114B**) – in fact nothing like ten marks, an example of the way this method could work to the royal advantage. Monasteries were in the habit of appointing trustworthy nominees who would acquire land on the monastery's behalf before licence was obtained; this had the advantage that land could be acquired when the opportunity arose without having to negotiate a licence.[57]

[49] *CPR 1307–13*, 482.
[50] *CCR 1447–54*, 288.
[51] *VE*, iii.437.
[52] *Salter Essays*, 195–6; Raban.
[53] *CPR 1281–92*, 392.
[54] *CPR 1345–8*, 427; *CPR 1361–4*, 264; *CPR 1370–4*, 266.
[55] *Calendar of Chancery Warrants*, i.348; *CPR 1307–12*, 482.
[56] *CPR 1343–5*, 349, 529.
[57] Raban, 10–13.

Such nominees were often secular clergy (eg **145**). A chain of people could gather land, each enfeoffing the next in line, and ultimately enfeoffing the church: such a chain lies behind the acquisition of Wade Hall (**114**).

The initiative in these transactions seems to come from the monasteries themselves, and one may question how far earlier acquisitions represented pious gifts rather than concealed purchases. Several of the deeds below are quite clearly purchases (**132**, **134**), and others could be without the phraseology making it obvious. It was contrary to the terms of the foundation charter for Leiston abbey to amass money to buy lands and rent, and the attempt to erase the tell-tale clause from the cartulary and its subsequent restoration speaks of a crisis of conscience. The re-writing, in emphatic gold ink, seems to date from the fourteenth century: the clause was mentioned in an inquisition in 1399, but without the canons being accused of breaking it.[58]

Butley priory was the second wealthiest religious house in Suffolk in the sixteenth century,[59] though a very long way behind Bury St Edmunds. Butley was worth some £318, Leiston barely half as much at £180. Though Butley held land as far away as Yorkshire, given by an associate of the founder,[60] its estates were concentrated in east Suffolk. The Taxatio Ecclesiastica shows that the most valuable lands in the 1270s were at Butley itself, worth over £16, followed by Bawdsey (£12), Harleston and Capel (£7 each), and Stratford St Andrew and Great Finborough (£6 each). Most of the original charters printed here refer to Weybread, where Butley's holdings were assessed at £1 6s 9d, and Wingfield (19s 4d).[61] These figures give some idea of the relative unimportance to Butley of the vills to which the charters refer, and indicate how much of the priory's archive must have been lost.

The Weybread deeds, the only surviving Butley series large enough to have any coherence, show the canons consolidating their holdings by purchase (**132**, **134**, possibly **136**) and exchange (**139–40**) during the thirteenth century; in the fourteenth, the canons are letting out land there (**143**, **144**). Perhaps this can be taken, without straining the evidence too far, to imply direct exploitation giving way to a policy of leasing soon after 1300, a pattern often noticed elsewhere on monastic estates. If so, this would be interesting since Butley's holdings there were relatively small, and Weybread was among the more distant vills in which they held land.

The pattern of both houses' estates is similar, being concentrated in the vicinity, and especially at Leiston the founder's gifts are the basis of the abbey's income for the rest of its existence. Butley is a more difficult case since we have less information, but here too it seems likely that the largest estates came from the founder or his daughters. Generally the vills where the canons have most are those in which they possess the parish church; in some cases the church seems to have come first and to have acted as a centre of attraction for small gifts in the vicinity, for example at Culpho, and perhaps, for Butley, at Weybread.

[58] *C Misc Inquis*, vi.no.374.
[59] Valor figures collected in D. Knowles and R. N. Hadcock, *Medieval Religious Houses, England and Wales*, London 1971.
[60] *EYC*, i.no.370n.
[61] *Taxatio*, 124b–131b. BL Add. 23948 is a late 15th-century extent of Butley's lands in Bawdsey.

Such evidence as these charters provide of the structure of local society will have to be seen along with that from the other houses of the neighbourhood before any coherent picture can emerge. Leiston's estate lay mostly in the poor, sandy heathland along the coast – how poor can be seen in **114** – as did much of Butley's, though Weybread, Wingfield and Dennington are all on much better soil inland. Despite the scrappy nature of the evidence, certain features are worth pointing out.

It is noticeable how many of these charters record gifts of men, and in most instances of their *sequela* as well. **42** is an interesting example (though not typical); it seems likely that Alexander and Thomas are bastards whose father is not mentioned: Elena is now married to Roger. As the mother is the abbey's serf, such children are the abbey's. The implication is that Roger Wuluard is William son of Alan's serf. A man's *sequela* clearly means his children, and probably his wife as well, though in **67** Bernard Helle's wife is mentioned separately. It does not seem likely, though, that all or even many of these men were serfs. The same William son of Harvey of 'Bernesheg' who is granted (in the accusative) in **95**, himself gave two charters (**99** and **100**) granting this land. **99** and **100** are the deeds of gift, **95** is the lord's confirmation. William's charters are truncated, but the usual sealing clause is begun. Here is a man who is free enough to give a charter, who probably even had a seal, yet whose lord's confirmation charter is phrased as a gift of the man himself. William holds the land of his brother Robert (who also confirms the gift in **101**) for 6*d* rent annually, and ½*d* scutage to Hugh Ruffus. **101** makes it clear that William has resigned to Leiston abbey all his rights in their parents' land. This certainly suggests the possibility of partible inheritance, which in turn implies that these are the descendants of sokemen. If this is forcing a little too much out of the evidence, at least it is clear that the relationship between the Bernesheg family and their lord was more complicated, and less servile, than **95** by itself would suggest.

One may ask what exactly the lord got out of these men. There is no mention of labour services: the answer seems to be rent, in cash. Thus in **14** the donor grants his right in some land, which amounts to some 6*d* per annum; he also promises to warrant the land itself – the rent is a due on the land. The 'pueri Suatman' of **47** pay rent. The rights of Henry de Bosco over Harvey son of Hunteman (**17** and **18**) consist of a money rent, as does the 'service' of two men in Dennington (**124**) and of one in Weybread (**134**). In all probability the soke over these men was being transferred as well, as it is in **124**. Some of them held of more than one lord, like the men of Leiston abbey who also held of Saer de Biskele (**54**). Harvey son of Hunteman, who owed rent to the Dearnefords (**17**), was also the holder of 20 'ware' acres in Rendham; he came into court in 1205 and recognised himself a villein.[62] For these he was the tenant of Walter son of William, who granted him, his *sequela* and his 'ware' acres to Agnes, wife of William de Drinkstone.

Men are commonly granted along with their 'tenement'. In **95** we can see that such a tenement consisted of a messuage and at least seven acres lying in four different places (the tenant may possibly have held more land than the charter mentions); a tenement in Weybread (**134**) consisted of a messuage, two and a half arable acres in an assarted wood, and two and a half acres of

[62] Dodwell, *Fines* ii, no.447.

meadow; for this the tenant owed 18*d* rent and 2*d* per £1 scutage. In one case, that of Knodishall, the descent of peasant tenements can be traced from c 1212 to 1235, thanks to **89**. This is not an extent of the whole vill, only of those parts of it which pay tithe to Leiston abbey. One remarkable feature is the lack of correspondence between the earlier and later tenants. Only four tenements are held by people of the same surname at both dates, though of course surnames may not be hereditary – John Cole for example may be the heir of Halden Brun. As far as the document lets us know, all the tenements are small: if the measured ones are roughly the same size as the others, the biggest is only some seven acres. A number of the named ones are tofts and crofts. The extent of Leiston manor, now at Ipswich, shows that in that vill many of the *tenurae* have family names, and that by the fourteenth century they have been partly subdivided into many extremely small pieces. Thus the 'Ode' tenement is shared between nine people, with John Ode holding the messuage and an enclosure of eight acres, and the others holding between one rod and three acres each. The whole tenement adds up to 20 acres. The 'Lotewyne' tenement is shared between eight, of which the lion's share belongs to John Lotewene with the messuage and 13 out of 21 acres. The rest is minutely subdivided with, for instance, Robert Oky holding 2 acres 2 roods and 13 perches, and Henry Coleir and Alice his sister holding a cottage and curtilage.

A good deal of the land described in these documents is held in scattered parcels (eg **50, 105, 138, 139**), and sometimes these appear to lie in larger fields (eg **123**). We also meet a number of enclosures (**54, 89, 123**). The history of enclosure is too long and complex to discuss here, and receives very little detailed illustration from these charters; the agricultural routine is not revealed at all.

At a rather higher social level Saer de Biskele's little estate at Theberton comprised the messuage of 'Caldham', with an orchard and small adjacent wood, some 24 acres around it, a ditched enclosure of seven acres, pieces of meadow land and a number of tenants (**67, 92**). The part of Gerard the parker's estate at Dennington that he gave to Butley consisted of five acres around his house and a small wood next to it, an acre of meadow, four and a half acres in four different places (**125**), and also rent paying tenants (**124**).

Knight service and the knight's fee are mentioned occasionally; William son of Theobald held a *militia* within the soke of Leiston (**47**), while the service of 'half a knight' is due from Jocelin de Hispania's holding at Glevering, which he describes as consisting of a messuage, lands, men and rent (**93**). From **15** it is clear that the phrase 'knight service' is not only applied to the knight himself, but also to his tenants who contributed to the scutage due from his fee, the burden being passed on down the social scale. Thus we find tenements owing 1*d* and ½*d* per £1 scutage levied (**100, 132**): scutage has become a due on the land, irrespective of the status of the tenant.

4. The Documents

A. Papal Documents   The Leiston cartulary contains eight papal documents: four of Honorius III, and one each of Lucius III, Celestine III, Innocent III and Gregory IX. One papal document survives from Butley, a judicial mandate of Innocent III; we also have a brief list of certain bulls copied onto the fourteenth century rent roll mentioned earlier, none of which have survived.

The earliest is a solemn privilege of Lucius III (1). The original would have had a dating clause, but this has been omitted by the compiler of the cartulary; it cannot therefore be dated on internal evidence more accurately than by Lucius' pontificate, September 1181–November 1185, though it surely dates from after the beginning of the foundation process, c 1183. The abbey's possessions are confirmed, consisting of the site, and the manor of Leiston with its appurtenances, an unusually brief list for such a bull, suggesting that this privilege was obtained very early in the foundation process, before Leiston had acquired any other possessions. The rest of the privilege consists of a series of common form clauses taking Leiston under papal protection, establishing that the abbey shall be served by Premonstratensian canons, and confirming justly obtained gifts in advance. He forbids the exaction of tithe from noval lands and animal foodstuffs, and gives them the privilege of accepting into their house anyone, clerical or lay, who wishes to flee the world. No professed canon may leave Leiston or be retained elsewhere without permission. The canons may celebrate mass discreetly during a general interdict. The pope also grants the canons the rights of free election, and of burying anyone who wishes to be buried there, as long as the defunct is not excommunicate, subject to agreement with the church which would otherwise bury him. Privileges such as this one were issued to houses all over Europe, with slight variations, some clauses being left out and others added.[1] Butley had a bull from Lucius III allowing the canons to be used as vicars in parish churches.[2]

3 is a solemn privilege of pope Celestine III, inspected once by archbishop Hubert (4), and once by John of Oxford, bishop of Norwich (9). The archbishop's has been taken as the basic text, and the bishop's variations of it indicated in the notes. Once again the dating clause has been omitted, and there is no internal evidence to narrow the date within the pontificate of Celestine, March 1191–January 1198. It is addressed to abbot Robert, but that provides no help. The similarities between this and Lucius' privilege are manifest – it is granted 'ad exemplar . . . Lucii Pape' – and all of Lucius' specific grants recur, though in a slightly different order. Celestine adds freedom from compulsory attendance at synods, and freedom from demands for procurations and hospitality from any ecclesiastic less than a legate *a latere*. If any patron should give them a church, the canons may retain it in their own hands when it falls vacant, paying only the synodals due to the bishop. No tenants may alienate lands held of the monastery to another church without their consent, and the canons are to have free disposition of their goods when the abbacy is vacant.

A number of these privileges had already been granted to the whole Premonstratensian order by earlier popes: thus freedom to receive anyone who wished to flee the world, and to bury anyone, are found in Innocent II's basic foundation document of May 1134.[3] The same pope, in later privileges, added the prohibition from leaving the order without the relevant abbot's

---

[1] Cf. *PL*, cci, cols. 1110–15, 1136–8.
[2] Evelyn-White, 60.
[3] *PL*, clxxix, cols. 204–6.

30

permission, and release from paying tithes[4]: Leiston partakes of the privileges of its order as far as these are concerned. Butley had two bulls of Celestine III, one allowing the retention of churches to their own use, the other specifying freedom of election.[5]

Leiston's next document, in chronological order, is 2, a letter of protection from Innocent III. The prelates of the church are ordered to punish anyone who attacks the canons, their men, or their property, or who exacts tithe from them, withholds legacies, or excommunicates them contrary to their privileges. Towns where their belongings are detained are to be placed under interdict. The letter is complete, and dated 1st June 1199. This wholly common form letter is among the commonest surviving of Innocent III issued to England – 20 have been calendared, including ours.[6] Hubert Walter's Premonstratensian foundation of West Dereham obtained one on the same day.[7] Clearly some form of co-operation between the houses was at work, and it is hard to resist the suspicion that archbishop Hubert's influence was involved. Leiston's and Dereham's are identical to Innocent III's general letter to the Premonstratensian order of May 1198.[8] Since this is such a common document it would be unsafe to assume that it has a specific bearing on the attack on Leiston abbey referred to in 11.

5 is a common form letter of protection, which has also survived unabridged. Pope Honorius takes under his protection Leiston abbey and its possessions, which now include the parish churches of Leiston, Aldringham, Middleton and Culpho. The pope is certainly Honorius III – Honorius IV reigned for only two years. The date is thus 22nd June 1224.

Notwithstanding the rubric, 20 is a decretal letter or rescript rather than a 'privilege'. Certain people, claiming that the order's privileges have been revoked in the general council, or content to pervert their meaning, have been attempting to extort tithes which are not due. The Premonstratensians do not have to pay tithes except on land acquired since the council, on which tithe should be paid to the church to which it was always due. The date is 29th December 1218. The eschatocol of this document has been omitted, but the date preserved. 21, as the rubric states, is another 'interpretation' from Honorius III to the Premonstratensian order concerning tithe of noval lands, dated 18th February 1219.

In 91 Honorius III grants the abbot and prior of Leiston freedom from being called upon to serve as judges delegate, on the grounds that the monastery's business would be neglected, heavy expenditure would be incurred, and the beneficiaries do not have the requisite skill in law. It is dated 14th March 1225. The Premonstratensians were apparently quite in demand to supply judges, West Dereham and Barlings being called on the most.[9] Leiston was called upon at some time between 1214 and 1217, along with the prior of Butley and the dean of Wangford, in a case brought by Sibton abbey; once possibly earlier (1198–1216), with the abbot of Sibton and the prior of Blythburgh in a case between Holy Trinity Ipswich and the

[4] *PL*, clxxix, cols.350–1, 386–7.
[5] Evelyn-White, 60.
[6] Cheney, *Innocent III*, no.128.
[7] Cheney, *Innocent III*, no.204.
[8] *PL*, ccxiv, col.178.
[9] Sayers, 124.

nuns of Wix; and again in 1218, involving Eye priory and the church of Sedgebrook.[10] All of these, of course, are earlier than the exemption. This evidently useful and sought-after privilege was granted in the early thirteenth century to Bury St Edmunds, West Acre and the Premonstratensians of Bayham as well as the two great Canterbury houses and Westminster abbey; the tiny neighbouring house of Snape received theirs from Celestine III.[11] The reasons mentioned in Leiston's mandate are apparently the commonest alleged in order to obtain exemption.[12]

90, the final *actum* of a dispute between Leiston and Butley over the tithes of Leiston's estate of Westhouse, enshrines as is normal practice the mandate, largely common form, by which the judges had been appointed, in this case one of Gregory IX, dated 28th July 1234 at Rieti. This is a 'wide' mandate, including the clause *quidam alii*, meaning that charges could be brought against a number of people, in this instance in the dioceses of London and Lincoln as well as Norwich.[13] **131** is a surviving original final act of papal judges delegate, also including a transcript of the papal mandate, this time one of Innocent III dated 13th July 1205. It is a specific mandate, enabling only the case mentioned to be determined.

The Leiston cartulary probably contains all the early bulls of the house, but neither the basic papal privileges to the order of the 1130s, nor any of the later ones from, for instance, Innocent IV or Gregory IX, even though **91** has been added in a later hand.[14] For Butley we have only brief notes of two later bulls, one of Innocent IV granting exemption from having to concede pensions or benefices at the request of popes or their delegates (unless this privilege is mentioned), and one of Boniface IX conferring on the prior the right to use mitre, ring, and staff.[15] Butley also possessed a bull of Honorius III, given in 1221, releasing them from service as judges delegate, presumably like Leiston's.[16]

B. Royal Charters   The Leiston cartulary contains three charters of Henry II, one of Richard I, one of John as Count of Mortain and one of John as king. For Butley there is one each of Henry II and Richard I.

The earliest of these is Henry II's grant of Leiston manor, Upton, and 52s annual rent to Rannulf de Glanville (**26**). Rannulf was given the large manor of Leiston in the spring of 1173 – from 1174 £20 annually are deducted from the farm of the honour of Eye. Then in 1176 the 52s rent is allowed off the farm of Norfolk and Suffolk.[17] This makes it virtually certain that the exchequer year 1175–6 is the date for this charter, the most likely occasion being May 1176.[18] 'Selfleta' is almost certainly Shelfley, south-west of Ipswich.[19] This gift leads to a fairly complicated series of transactions: Upton

[10] Sayers, 211–2, 150, 295. For Sedgebrook, Lincs., see Eye Cartulary, f.43.
[11] Sayers, 144–5; Snape's is PRO Papal Bulls 9 (4).
[12] Sayers, 147.
[13] Sayers, 65–8.
[14] Cf. W. Farrer, *Chartulary of Cockersand Abbey*, Chetham Society 1898–1909, i(i), 26–8, 36–9.
[15] Evelyn-White, 60; Butley's bulls are discussed by Dr Myres, *Salter Essays*, 197–9.
[16] *C Pap Reg*, i.79.
[17] *PR 19 Henry II*, 132; *PR 21 Henry II*, 126; *PR 22 Henry II*, 60, 76.
[18] Eyton, 203.
[19] Cf. *Bk Fees*, i.134; *CRR*, iii.206.

manor goes to Reiner, Rannulf's steward,[20] and Butley priory receives the churches of Upton and Leiston (with Aldringham), and the 52s rent. The entire gift to Rannulf is made for the service of half a knight, which burden is then placed upon Reiner, leaving Leiston without dues in knight service and permitting the alienation of the manor in free alms without burdening Rannulf's descendants. The witnesses are all well-known *curiales*.

Leiston's second royal charter is **24**, Henry II's confirmation of manor and churches. The attestation of Baldwin as Elect of Canterbury dates it between 16th December 1184 (his postulation by the monks of Canterbury) and 19th May 1185 (his enthronement). **121**, Henry II's charter granting certain liberties to Butley, probably dates from the same occasion. The Leiston charter is lavish with details: it was requested by Rannulf; the churches are confirmed along with the manor, and the surrender by Butley is mentioned (but not Leiston's resignation of Knodishall).

It also contains the canons' promise to their founder about the purchase of land and other matters. This clause occurs no less than five times in the cartulary, or should do: here, in Glanville's foundation charter (**27**), and in Richard I's charter, which stands once by itself, once in an *inspeximus* by archbishop Baldwin, and once in an *inspeximus* by Hubert Walter (**23**, **8** and **10**). At some time an attempt was made to blot out its existence by erasing it from the cartulary, but whoever set about this only found three of its occurrences: it remains in the original hand in the two archiepiscopal copies (less obvious places to look for it, of course), and these two agree word for word on the text. At a still later stage, probably some time in the fourteenth century, it was decided to rewrite the erased clause, in proud and emphatic gold ink: but the scribe found only two of the erasures. The rewritings are not quite word-for-word the same as in the unerased versions, though the differences are not great enough to affect the meaning. Thus we have the clause in the nearest version to Rannulf's intentions in **8** and **10**, erased in **23**, and restored in **24** and **27**. The clause has been reproduced in the edition as it occurs in the earliest surviving texts, with later variations indicated in the notes.

25, Henry II's 'charter of liberties' to Leiston, is datable between archibishop Baldwin's enthronement, May 1185, and the death of king Henry in July 1189, thus coming rather later than Butley's similar document. To help narrow it down within this period we have only three other witnesses, all bishops and eminent men likely to dance attendance on the king. According to Eyton, in February 1188 Henry was attended by our four witnesses (and numerous others) at Geddington, where he granted a charter to the nuns of Bungay at the request of Roger de Glanville and his wife Gundrada, after which he went to Bury St Edmunds;[21] this is the most promising known occasion for **25**, but is very far from being the only possible one. The king confirms all reasonable future gifts in lands, men, 'alms' and churches; to the corroborative clause is attached an extensive list of liberties, which form the real interest, not to say the real point, of the charter. To the previous liberties of sac and soc, toll, team and infangentheof, 'and other liberties and free customs belonging to the manor', mentioned in **23**, are

[20] *Monasticon*, vi(i). 380 no.3.
[21] Eyton, 285; charter in *Monasticon*, iv.338.

added, amongst others, freedom from suit of court to shire and hundred, freedom from scutage, geld, hidage, hundred-penny, and from contributions to castles, bridges and roads. The canons are to be free from secular service, servile works, and all other secular customs excepting only justice of life and limb.

It is not easy to assess how significant these privileges, or at least some of them, were: whether they were valuable, or simply an ancient invocation without which no foundation would be properly complete. Two facts need to be considered: at some stage, probably early in the life of the cartulary, someone has written 'No(ta)' in the margin opposite 'suit of shire and hundred', and again at the beginning of the clause conferring freedom from toll. This implies that someone, at least, thought these two privileges worth drawing attention to, perhaps because they were more valuable than the others. The other fact is the frequent granting of such charters under Henry II. Of other East Anglian houses, Bromholm received freedom from toll, passage, pontage, and 'all other customs', and Sibton's charters of Henry II include lengthy recitals such as ours, and a specific order to maintain freedom from toll.[22] St Benet at Holme, no newcomer to the East Anglian scene, has a Henry II 'charter of liberties'.[23] Among the Premonstratensians, Welbeck's charter witnessed by Rannulf de Glanville grants such freedoms as ours.[24] Even at Christ Church, Canterbury, which one would expect to be well abreast of such developments, Henry II's charter granting exemption from shire and hundred, and 'immunity from personal service' went 'one stage further' than what had gone before.[25] It could be that this represents a committal to writing of existing privileges, or alternatively a widespread development in monastic exemption. Without more enquiry into the frequency of these grants under Henry II and his predecessors, and more information on which specific liberties had become dead letters, any definite conclusion would be unwise.

The two charters of Richard I (23 and 122) are very similar, and are both based on Henry II's charters. 23 was obtained at the petition of Glanville: at least he was not so far under a cloud in the new reign as to make that impossible. 122 was given at Marseilles, shortly before the king began his voyage to Sicily and the Holy Land.

29, a confirmation by John, Count of Mortain, can be considered most conveniently here. A latest possible date is supplied by the third witness, Roger de Planes, John's 'justiciar', who was killed during the attack on London on 1st November 1191.[26] John was enfeoffed with the county of Mortain in July 1189, when Richard became duke of Normandy,[27] but Hubert Walter was not consecrated to Salisbury until 22nd October 1189. It is uncertain exactly when John was granted the honour of Eye, whether on his marriage in August 1189, or later; but he was certainly in possession when

[22] Cambridge University Library MS MmII 20 fo 1^v; BL Arundel 221 ff 23^r–25^v.
[23] West, no.9.
[24] BL Harley 3640 fo 121^r.
[25] R. A. L. Smith, *Canterbury Cathedral Priory*, Cambridge 1943, 83; *Monasticon*, i.105.
[26] Ralph de Diceto, *Opera historica*, RS68, 1876, ii.99; Roger of Hoveden, *Chronica*, RS51, iii.140.
[27] See Landon, Appendix E, for John in this period.

Richard left England in December; it is as lord of the honour that he gave this charter. 'Evera' is Iver, Bucks. In March 1190 John joined his brother in Normandy, and there promised not to enter England for three years.[28] Hubert Walter went to Normandy at the same time: this makes the date of the charter somewhere between October 1189 and March 1190. Count John confirms in a straightforward way the manor of Leiston, and the churches of Leiston and Aldringham, in extremely royal terms, as his father and brother confirmed them. The witnesses include Hubert's brother Theobald and Rannulf's son-in-law Ralph de Arderne.

28, King John's charter to Leiston, is dated 14th May, 3 John. John was crowned on Ascension Day, a moveable feast, and his regnal years were calculated from one Ascension Day to the next. His third year thus runs 3rd May 1201 – 22nd May 1202, giving two 14ths in one year. The date is in fact 1201, when John was preparing his expedition to France, and not May 1202, by which time he had left on it. The charter is, once again, a confirmation and virtually an exact repetition of Henry II's, obviously the one mentioned in the final phrase. Butley also had a charter from John to the same effect.[29]

C. Archiepiscopal and episcopal acta   The Leiston cartulary contains three archiepiscopal *acta*, two of Hubert Walter and one of Baldwin of Ford; and seven of John of Oxford, John de Grey and William Raleigh, bishops of Norwich. A number of these documents occur several times in the cartulary, once on their own account and then again as inspected by another authority. Where a document occurs more than once, the text is given below once only, the basic text being the one given when it appears by itself in the MS, and the variations in its other appearances are indicated in the notes. There is one exception to this procedure: archbishop Baldwin's document (8, itself an *inspeximus* of Richard I's charter) has been given once by itself and once in Hubert Walter's *inspeximus* of it (10); the reason for this will become clear below. William Raleigh's confirmation of Leiston's parish churches occurs only once, in an *inspeximus* by prior Simon of Norwich. For Butley we have a document of archbishop Hubert appointing judges delegate, and another containing their judgement; two documents of Walter Suffield, bishop of Norwich, and one of bishop Henry Despenser.

Of the archiepiscopal documents the earliest is 8, of Baldwin of Ford. Its first appearance in the cartulary is under the rubric 'Confirmatio Ric' Canth' Arch''. It cannot possibly belong to any archbishop Richard, since it is witnessed by Gilbert Glanville, bishop of Rochester 1185–1214. It is highly unlikely to be of any 'archbishop R.', since neither Reginald fitz Jocelin (Nov. – Dec. 1191) nor Reginald the sub-prior of Canterbury (1205–6) was ever consecrated. The vital clue is given by 9, Hubert Walter's *inspeximus* of 'archbishop B 's' confirmation of Richard I's charter, obviously archbishop Baldwin, word for word the same as 7. It is eminently possible that a charter of Baldwin of Ford would be witnessed by bishop Gilbert and archdeacon Herbert Poore (bishop of Salisbury from 1193), and then inspected by archbishop Hubert. The scribe has mis-read the initial B as R (very easy to do), and expanded it hopefully as 'Ric.' in the rubric. Now we know what it

[28] Landon, *Itinerary*, 26.
[29] *PR 6 John*, 244; *R Chart*, i.1176.

35

is, it can be dated. It confirms Richard I's charter of 14th October 1189, and the archbishop sailed from Marseilles early in August 1190,[30] to die at Acre in October. Gilbert, bishop of Rochester did not accompany Baldwin on the crusade but went at least as far as Rouen in March 1190.[31] This gives us outside dates of October 1189 – August 1190. The most likely occasion within this period is at Canterbury in late November or early December 1189, when the archbishop, Gilbert of Rochester, and abbot Robert of Leiston are known to have been present.[32]

4 is another *inspeximus*, by archbishop Hubert of pope Celestine's privilege. Since the witness-list has been omitted, it is not possible to date it more accurately than by Hubert's tenure of the see of Canterbury, 1193–1205. **10**, as already mentioned, is also an *inspeximus* by archbishop Hubert, of Baldwin's *inspeximus* of Richard I's charter, but here even the survival of part of the witness-list does not help the dating, since the first two witnesses outlived Hubert, and the others' dates are obscure.

All three are examples of the developed *inspeximus* form, in which the inspected document is recited, which finally established itself at Canterbury during the pontificate of archbishop Baldwin.[33] The wording soon becomes more elaborate: Hubert's chancery is prepared to use far more words to enhance the solemnity of the document than Baldwin's was. Of the witnesses, the Master Silvester of **8** may be the clerk of Roger, bishop of Worcester, found witnessing in 1177[34]: Baldwin had been bishop of Worcester before his elevation to Canterbury. A Master Ralph of St Martin is associated with bishop Gilbert in the administration of Canterbury diocese during Baldwin's absence.[35] Richard, the chancellor of archbishop Hubert is highly obscure despite his frequent attestations and the large number of the products of his office. Ralph 'Testranum' (the reading is far from certain) may be Ralph the treasurer of Salisbury, whom Hubert kept by him after 1193, and who witnesses many archiepiscopal *acta*.[36]

130 is the termination of a dispute between Butley and Mendham priories concerning certain lands belonging to Weybread church (Mendham is in the next parish). The form is basically that of sentences of judges delegate on receipt of a mandate from the pope, but in this case the mandate is from archbishop Hubert. The dispute had been committed to arbitration, but Mendham refused to accept the arbitrators, whereupon Butley appealed to the archbishop's court of audience. The archbishop could either hear the case in person, or delegate it; delegations were either general commissions, or ones to hear individual cases. Here we have an early case of an appeal, showing the system of specific delegation in full working order c 1200.

Of the episcopal *acta* the earliest is **36**, of John of Oxford, relating the surrender of Leiston and Aldringham churches to Leiston abbey. There is no mention in this document of Knodishall church, which Leiston surrendered to Butley (**6**). It is a business-like document, describing the transaction in a

[30] Landon, *Itinerary*, 38.
[31] Landon, *Itinerary*, 28.
[32] Landon, *Itinerary*, 17–21. Gilbert first appears on 28th November.
[33] Though he was not the first to use it. Cheney, *Chanceries*, 95.
[34] Cheney, *Chanceries*, 10.
[35] I. Churchill, *Canterbury Administration*, London 1933, ii.1.
[36] Cheney, *Chanceries*, 15.

minimum of words, and appending a date. St Hilary's day is 13th January; thus the occasion was most likely in January 1186 by modern reckoning – it was in the later twelfth century that the Lady-Day style of reckoning 'became accepted in England'.[37] Gilbert, prior of Butley, 'willingly' resigns the churches into the bishop's hands; they and their appurtenances are then confirmed to Leiston 'at the presentation of Rannulf de Glanville'.

34 is a more elaborate, diplomatically more interesting document. In effect John of Oxford's confirmation of the young monastery's basic possessions, it is an episcopal equivalent of the privileges of popes Lucius and Celestine. After the general address it launches into a 'harangue' on the duties of a bishop to guard the property of those living a holy life. The dispositive clause, beginning *eapropter* as in a papal privilege, rehearses the property to be confirmed; the charters of Henry II and Rannulf de Glanville are both mentioned, as is the 'spontaneous resignation' of the churches by Butley. There is a clause confirming in advance possessions justly acquired (cf **1**), and an interesting closing 'sanction' on the papal model. The other Leiston document very likely to be of John of Oxford is **37**, the confirmation of Roger de Glanville's gift of Middleton church. This is a simple and business-like piece, with nothing of **34**'s elaboration.

9 presents the problem of distinguishing between documents of John of Oxford and John de Grey. It is a straightforward *inspeximus* of pope Celestine's privilege, which is almost word for word the same as archbishop Hubert's (**4**). There is no reason to attribute it to either one of the bishops rather than the other; it can only be dated 1191–1215, by the earliest date for the document inspected, and the death of John de Grey.

This leaves two documents of John de Grey: **38**, an *inspeximus* of his predecessor's confirmation of the gift of Middleton church, and **35**, his *inspeximus* of **36**. A comparison of the two shows how far common form was pervading the episcopal chancery after 1200, and how efficient and business-like it could be. The diocese of Norwich produces examples of the finished, terse *inspeximus* type of document not only within a few years of 1200 – just the time when this form is in evidence in many other dioceses – but earlier as well.[38] Of the witnesses, Master William of Lynn was a lawyer attached to the 'familia' of John of Oxford but well known to Hubert Walter. He continued to work for John de Grey until he ceases to occur in the winter of 1205–6,[39] thus providing an indication of date for **35** and **38**. The archdeacon Geoffrey of **37** could be either Geoffrey de Bocland, archdeacon of Norfolk (occurring after July 1197), or Geoffrey archdeacon of Suffolk, whose predecessor Walkelin's last known appearance is in **36**.[40] The archdeacon of Suffolk is perhaps more likely (Middleton was in his archdeaconry), but not so as to exclude the possibility of the former.

The next episcopal document is **22**, a general confirmation of Leiston's ecclesiastical documents by William Raleigh, bishop of Norwich 1239–43. It is part of an *inspeximus* by Simon, prior of Norwich cathedral, himself an

[37] R. L. Poole, 'The Beginning of the Year in the Middle Ages', in *Studies in Chronology and History*, Oxford 1934, 14.

[38] Examples in Blythburgh Cartulary, forthcoming in this series.

[39] C. R. Cheney, *Hubert Walter*, London 1967, 142–3; also *From Becket to Langton*, Manchester 1956, 198; Dodwell, *Charters*, no.144n.

[40] *Fasti*, ii.67.

unsuccessful candidate for the see from 1236 to 1239. The bishop's document, dated at the episcopal manor of South Elmham in Suffolk on 10th February 1243, a few months before Raleigh's translation to Winchester, gives the briefest imaginable précis of first the papal bulls, then the episcopal confirmations as above. His selection of salient facts from the bulls is interesting – they may serve churches in person if they wish; bishop William apparently saw an episcopal confirmation of Culpho church, which is not in the cartulary, although the deeds of gift are. It is interesting that Sizewell church, apparently a chapel of Leiston, has been constructed recently. Having seen all the other confirmations, he again confirms the abbey's possessions himself in the same terms. Prior Simon's *inspeximus* of this was executed only 17 days later, while William was still bishop of Norwich. He and the convent, having seen the bishop's *actum*, add their consent, and, as far as in them lies, their confirmation. The bishop noted that he had the assent and wish of his chapter when confirming Leiston's documents: his predecessors did not make this clear in their own confirmations.

This inspecting by the prior and chapter of episcopal documents is not uncommon in Norwich diocese in the thirteenth century, **154** being another example.[41] Here the documents inspected are of Raleigh's successor Walter Suffield, and both are short and business-like. The last episcopal document, **118**, is from the chancery of Henry Despenser, and is very different from the thirteenth century productions, being excessively verbose, even though containing interesting details. The prior and chapter now ratify and confirm instead of 'inspecting' it, and there are no witnesses.

D. Abbatial documents   We have six early documents concerning the substitution of Leiston abbey for Butley priory as possessor of Leiston and Aldringham churches and of the tithes of the demesne of Leiston. This had occurred by the time of Henry II's charter, **24**, dated above to before May 1185. **6** is the resignation of Robert, first abbot of Leiston, of all the abbey's rights in Knodishall church and all its appurtenances to Gilbert, first prior of Butley. We learn that Butley had Knodishall church in the year the canons came to Leiston. The date of the document is necessarily c 1183–1192 (fixed by the approximate beginnings of the foundation, and the resignation of prior Gilbert), and probably before 1185. **31** is Butley's counterpart, datable certainly before 1189 by the attestation of Hubert Walter unqualified as bishop of Salisbury. The similarities of phrasing are obvious: it could well be that **6** and **31** are products of the same, pre-1185, occasion, each document being a 'quid pro quo'; but the omission of **6**'s witness-list (assuming, reasonably, that it had one) prevents certainty. **7** and **32** form another pair. Both houses have changed superior, and the new heads, possibly at the time of their appointment, confirm their predecessors' quitclaims in almost identical terms. In **33** the next prior of Butley, Robert, confirms **31** and **32** in what have become the traditional terms. This was presumably done on his accession; Philip is still abbot of Leiston.

68 is a charter of Roger, prior of Eye, who has inspected the charters of Gilbert and William (presumably **31** and **32**), and also that of Robert (i.e. **33**), and who now confirms the arrangements concerning the tithes of the

[41] Eg Bedingfeld, no.138; BL Cotton Titus C 8, fo 22^r; Add. 46353, ff 74^v, 260^{r-v}.

demesne of the hall. S., abbot of Sibton, is not datable or identifiable, at least not until the Sibton cartularies have been edited. Abbot Alexander occurs in 1212, but S. could be before or after. The archdeacon of Suffolk is Robert 'de Twya', who occurs in 1205 and 1235.[42] This leaves Robert of Butley, c 1210 to 1219.

The most noticeable feature of these documents is their similarity – they are confirmations of previous charters in very nearly identical terms. The *inspeximus* form is not being used by these abbots and priors as it is by contemporary bishops, though the effect is the same.

E. Private deeds   About one third of the charters have been discussed in the previous four sections. The remaining two thirds cannot be divided into digestible units on the same plan. Here we are concerned with the formal content of the documents, and what conclusions can be drawn from that. They can be divided into types according to their basic function:

1: grants to the monasteries, of many kinds of property – lands, rents, serfs, mills, freedom from toll – mostly permanently, but sometimes for a stated period. This is by far the most numerous class.

2: grants from laymen to other laymen. These are included as title deeds, where the property concerned was subsequently given to the monastery, demonstrating the donor's right to give, and sometimes specifying the service due to the superior lord. These are substantially fewer than type 1.

3: confirmations of grants by the donors' lord. There are some well-documented transactions illustrated by all three types of document.

4: quitclaims and renunciations, seemingly arising out of complex situations where others have, or could claim, rights over property being granted, and whose position has to be taken into account when the property is to be alienated.

5: exchanges of land – only two from Leiston, both between the abbey and the same man; three from Butley.

6: leases – two from Leiston; two from Butley, both fourteenth century.

7: purchases, and agreements to rent; like the leases these contravene the terms of Leiston's foundation charter. There are only three from Leiston, and several more from Butley.

8: there is the inevitable class of miscellanea not fitting into any of the above (**11, 30, 48,** and **76**). These are not amenable to diplomatic generalisation, and are discussed in notes to the text.

Thus nearly all the deeds in this class are gifts, or intended to smooth the way for gifts. In the cartulary there are very few documents issued by the abbey itself: in other words it is the abbey's in-tray. Despite most of the abbey's possessions being held in frankalmoin what we have in these charters is an (admittedly very incomplete) sketch of local lay society. Though collected by churchmen these documents overwhelmingly illustrate the legal, tenurial and economic relationships of laymen; the canons' spiritual concerns do not obtrude at all. The cartulary records the gifts of the first generation of Leiston's patrons; as such it necessarily differs from collections of contemporary charters from older houses, such as St Benet at Holme or, in a smaller

---

[42] *Fasti*, ii.67–8.

way Blythburgh, which are concerned with the administration of an existing estate. It thus enables us to see who was patronising a new monastery in the decades around 1200. The Butley collection is too fragmentary to be regarded as representative.

The development of the private charter has attracted little attention, at least in this country, and the reason is not far to seek: the huge number of unprinted, undated deeds discourages generalisation until a great deal more work has been done on them, work which advances most conveniently in stages, on small, datable collections such as this. Fortunately the trail has been blazed by Sir Frank Stenton.[43] The fact that most of these are cartulary copies need not be a deterrent: the scribe is far more likely to sin by omission than by inventing fanciful formulae, which would contradict the whole point of compiling a cartulary. Arguments from omission are thus highly dubious (as they must always be with any set of medieval documents), but there is no basis for doubting the accuracy of what we have, especially when a coherent pattern emerges which finds confirmation from the surviving Butley originals.

Most of these charters can be dated between the 1180s and the 1220s, thus standing at the turning point between fluidity and solidification in private diplomatic. One would expect common form to be gaining ground, but still short of its deadening triumph as reflected in, for instance, the West Dereham cartulary, compiled about 1315, which contains at least 1,000 deeds hardly varying at all in the formulae used. If the diplomatic ice age is just beginning, we are still not too late to find interesting individuals.

Protocols. Most of the 21 charters which have address-clauses are addressed universally, and most often with a vague religious phrase as well, possibly thought appropriate for a donation to the church: thus the commonest is 'universis sancte matris ecclesie filiis' and its minor variant, 'omnibus Christi fidelibus'. Only six charters are addressed to the donor's men and friends (**12, 15, 47, 134, 146,** and **148**); all are from people relatively high in the social scale – and **12, 15** and **146** certainly, and **47** probably, belong to the twelfth century. The document is referred to as a 'scriptum' or a 'carta' indifferently. **50**, interestingly, is directed to the hearing rather than the vision of all Christ's faithful. 'Salutem' always occurs by itself, with none of the elaboration found in the abbatial documents. But by far the largest number of these deeds have no address-clause at all, beginning usually with 'Sciant presentes et futuri quod ego X' or some similar phrase. This group accounts for three-quarters of the charters concerned. This straightforward notification apparently has an unbroken history from earlier times, and survives the Middle Ages.[44]

Dispositive clauses. The charters with address-clauses, about a third of the total, have a notification-clause too: the most popular is 'noverit universitas vestra', followed by 'ad omnium vestram volo pervenire notitiam' and the simple 'sciatis me'. These all lead into an accusative-and-infinitive construction for the words of gift. Those which dispense with the address-clause lead straight into the words of gift, naturally in the active voice. These ordinary laymen always refer to themselves in the singular, even the earl of Norfolk (**40**). There is indeed no class-distinction in thirteenth century diplomatic:

[43] See especially Stenton, introduction, on which this section is based.
[44] Stenton, xviii.

the earl uses the same formulae as Michael son of Reginald of Orford (cf 77).

Sometimes the assent of possible objectors is specified: in 84 the donor's wife, in 12 his son; in 47 he emphasises his own willingness to quitclaim his rights. The wife of the donor of 84 gives her own charter (85) with the assent of her husband. In one case, a charter of confirmation by William de Falesham (62), given with the assent of his wife and his heir, is confirmed in another charter by the heir (72) possibly on his father's death. The practice of adding an assent-clause is apparently in decline after the early thirteenth century, being superseded by the promise to warrant against all men made by the donor for himself and his heirs.[45] One confirmation charter (96) is given at the request of the donor's wife.

The words of gift themselves are usually 'dedi, concessi et (hac) presenti carta (mea) confirmavi' (or the same in the infinitive). 'Confirmare' occurs all the time, whether the charter is a confirmation or an original grant. The omission of 'dare' is more significant, not being used in confirmation charters, such as 44, 62, 74 and 84 from the donor's heir or lord; 101 and 106 are confirmations by the donor's brother. There seems to be no instance of a confirmation charter using 'dare'.

The monasteries as recipients are nearly always defined as 'God, the church of St Mary of Leiston (Butley), and the (Premonstratensian) canons there serving God'. 'Beata' and 'Sancta' are used indifferently. This phrasing, with virtually insignificant variations, is all but universal for deeds of gift. Three charters have only 'to the abbot and convent', and two of these (42 and 57) are quitclaims; four have 'to abbot Robert (or Philip) and the convent', two being quitclaims (47 and 102), one a purchase (51) and the other (48) is described as a 'cyrograph'.

The description of the property to be granted one would expect to gain in precision as the thirteenth century advances. This can be illustrated, in a small way, from these charters: 15, 61 or 146, relatively early gifts, are vague, and in contrast to, say, 92 or 106; but these deeds are not sufficiently exactly datable to allow an elaborate chronological analysis – suffice it to say that examples of precision and vagueness can both be found. In the earlier charters land is more often defined by who holds it than by where it is; topographical directions become more common as the thirteenth century progresses, eg 125, 138, 139, 143, 145. The greatest variety obtains in descriptions of property, very naturally, and these clauses are the least patient of generalisation.

By the terms of Glanville's charter Leiston was to hold in frankalmoin tenure only, and this is by and large the case. The phrase 'free, pure and perpetual alms' occurs very frequently and is not, as Stenton points out, mere verbiage, 'free' meaning that suits so held should be heard in ecclesiastical courts, 'pure' barring the grantor and his heirs from exacting secular service, and 'perpetual' guarding against revocation.[46] This tenure does not, of course, free land from its burdens to other parties without their explicit consent. Thus Jocelin de Hispania grants land in free, pure and perpetual alms saving the forinsec service of 'half a knight' (93; cf 95, 108). Part of a holding can be so granted; in 63 Ralph de Onehouse grants a mill, but

[45] Stenton, xix.
[46] Stenton, xxvii.

41

reserves from it a pension of two marks annually which his wife has in dower – where several people have rights in a piece of property, one of the portions can be granted in free, pure and perpetual alms without prejudice to the rights of others. **106** is interesting in this connection: it is a confirmation charter, not an original gift; the canons are to hold in alms, and rent is still due to the man who confirms. A dozen or so charters have just 'pure and perpetual alms', including all the conveyances of churches (**39, 40, 43, 75**), but the rest have no other discernible common features (eg **19, 57, 98**).

In return for granting land in frankalmoin the donor received the canons' prayers: the spiritual beneficiaries are mentioned in many charters, occasionally quite elaborately, for instance in **87**, where the gift is for the health of the donor's soul and those of his wife, eldest son, other children, father, mother, predecessors and successors. *Pro salute anime mee* is the commonest expression, and predecessors and successors are usually mentioned. New spiritual beneficiaries can be added in a charter which merely confirms another's gift: not just by the earl of Norfolk (**40**), but by lesser men too – Osbert de Wachesham (**44**), and Herbert de Alencun (**74**). This clause sometimes provides valuable genealogical information. A specific pious motive is alleged for the gift in a few instances: the fabric of the church (**19, 81, 103**), or its lighting (**56**), while in **125** the donor is to be buried at Butley.

Many charters include a phrase describing the tenure by which the land is to be held, usually beginning 'habendum et tenendum' etc. As Stenton has pointed out, this is somewhat inappropriate to a gift in alms,[47] though many charters simply have 'habendum et tenendum in liberam, puram et perpetuam elemosinam . . .' The origin of these clauses is to be found in royal charters, and in some cases abbreviated versions of the elaborate royal adverbial clauses are produced: thus we have 'libere, quiete et pacifice' (**100**), 'libere et honorifice' (**59**) etc. There are four charters with 'quare volo' (**46, 60, 127, 146**), and one imitation of the common royal phrasing 'in pratis et pasturis . . .' etc (**93**). The donors who use these phrases are neither earlier than the average, nor noticeably higher in the social scale, though two of them, Saer de Biskele and Jocelin de Hispania, were exceptionally generous.

Warranty clauses are not rare by the late twelfth century. They can take slightly different forms – an overall promise, binding on heirs as well, to warrant against all men (eg **53, 66, 83**; cf **95**), though rarely specifically against Jews in this collection; or a promise to supply equivalent revenue from another source if the donor's warranty proves insufficient (**63, 86**; cf **133**). In **103** ten acres being held in pledge for a fixed period are given to the abbey until the term expires; the charter includes a promise to replace them if they are redeemed before the term is reached. The promise to warrant gradually replaces the association of others in the gift, and the clauses specifying the consent of other interested parties; there is no example with both types of clause. Some of these charters (**70, 79**) contain a promise to acquit the canons, and one (**92**) specifically against claims of service. **129** is a quitclaim following on a lawsuit, and both it and **149** are fortified by an oath.

[47] Stenton, xxviii.

Dating clauses gradually become more common during the thirteenth century, and by the fourteenth are normal. The earliest in this collection is **139** (1240).

Corroborative and sealing clauses consist mostly of infinite small variations on the theme 'ut hec (mea) donatio (concessio, confirmatio) firma sit et stabilis in perpetuum, eam (presens scriptum) sigilli mei appositione roboravi (roborare curavi).' **40, 126** and **135** are slightly more elaborate, and in **13** a similar phrase takes the place of a warranty clause. These phrases seem to be normal in deeds of gift; they are omitted slightly more frequently from other types of charter, but arguments from absence are not strong.

Virtually all the donors had seals, though a good many of them were below knightly status. In **96**, a confirmation by an heir, the donor uses his father's seal as he has not got one of his own. In **95** Hugh le Rus grants William son of Harvey and his tenement; in **99** and **100** we find the same William giving a charter, and probably even using a seal, as he starts the usual sealing clause which the scribe has not copied in full.

The problem of the witness-list is notorious. We have been warned that it is 'unwise to assume that the witnesses to a charter of the late twelfth or thirteenth century were all present at the same place at the same time'.[48] But at the very least we can assume that those on the list were believed to be alive at the time, and we can continue to use them for dating charters on the understanding that the news of their death had not yet become common knowledge when the charter was given. With most of the witnesses to private deeds all one has to go on is the approximate date of death; often some even less specific clue, such as a date by which an heir has succeeded, or a sudden absence from juries after decades of activity; most of these charters are not sufficiently closely datable for such sophistications as the presence or absence of witnesses at the ceremony to cause particular difficulty.

5. Manuscripts and Editorial Method

A. Physical description of the cartulary   Cotton MS Vespasian E 14 consists of 85 folios, plus three later flyleaves one of which bears, inaccurately, 'Registrum Cartarum prioratus de Leeston in Com' Norff'', and another 'Vespasian E 14'. These are presumably from an earlier binding made after the MS entered the Cotton collection. Six fly-leaves are associated with the present binding, stamped 31st August 1964. The 85 folios are of membrane, and are foliated in arabic numerals 1–83, the last two being blank. The average dimensions of the leaves are 18.5 cm high by 14.5 cm broad. Some incomplete or damaged folios (eg ff 1, 13, 42) have been repaired, possibly relatively recently, to bring them up to the size of the others, while quire F and possibly also quire A show signs of having been cut down – some marginal annotations have been partially sliced through (eg ff 8r, 49v, 52r).

The 85 folios are made up of nine quires, of which the collation is as follows[1]:

[48] Stenton, xxxi.

[1] Using the method described in N. R. Ker, *Catalogue of MSS Containing Anglo-Saxon*, Oxford 1957, xxiii.

A 8 + 1 leaf after 8 (ff 1–9).
B 10 + 1 leaf before 1 (ff 10–20).
C 8 (ff 21–28).
D 10 (ff 29–38).
E 10 (ff 39–48).
F 8 (ff 49–56).
G 10 (ff 57–66).
H 10 (ff 67–76).
I 10, 8 and 10 blank, wants 9 probably blank (ff 77–86).

The normal arrangement leaves flesh side opposite flesh side, and hair opposite hair, with hair outwards. Pricking is visible on the outer margins of both leaves, sometimes (eg ff 7r, 19r, 36v, 47r) in two rows of which only the outer, more widely spaced, corresponds with the ruling. The MS is written in single column throughout, the written space being on average 12.5 cm high by 8.5 cm broad, defined by vertical rulings usually prolonged to the upper and lower edges; horizontal rulings are occasionally prolonged to the outer edge.

The nucleus of the MS is written in a well-formed documentary script of a common early thirteenth century type, probably the work of one hand with assistance from a small number of contemporaries; some additions in later hands have been made at the ends of quires. Quire I is entirely an addition of the very late thirteenth or early fourteenth century. There are a number of surviving quire signatures, which correlate with the handwriting and predominant subject matter of the quires as follows:

A (1–9) (i) Papal. Fo 9 completes doc. **4**, and contains **5** in a different contemporary hand.

B (10–20) ii Episcopal confirmations. Fo 10 has two abbatial documents (**6** and **7**) in a different contemporary hand.

C (21–28) iii Private deeds. Continues **11** from quire B. **20** and **21** (ff 24v–26r), papal, different contemporary hand. **22**, episcopal, in a mid-13th century hand. Fo 28v blank.

D (29–38) viii Royal. Two contemporary hands (eg fo 31r).

E (39–48) iiii Abbatial: bishops of Norwich: then private.

F (49–56) (v) Private. Continues **52** from E (catch-words, fo 48v); **68** (55r–v) in a different contemporary hand; **69** (56v) in 14th cent. hand. Fo 56r blank.

G (57–66) vi Private, a number of contemporary hands (eg 61v–62r); **87**, **90** (abbatial) and **91** (papal) added in two later 13th cent. hands.

H (67–76) vii Private, a number of contemporary hands (eg 72r–v). The outermost sheet (67–76) may be a contemporary insertion: fo 67r has a quire signature, but fo 67v partly blank, unruled; benediction in upper margin, fo 68r. From 74r, litigation (1288 etc).

I (77–86) Litigation continues. Change of hand, fo 81v.

The rubrication, apart from one probably fourteenth century example in green ink on fo 54v, seems to be mainly the work of one hand, quite likely the scribe of much of the main nucleus, with possibly another contemporary with him rubricating ff 54r, 55r, 61v–64r, and 72r–73v in a lighter, now very faded, orange-coloured ink. The main rubricator's work stands at the head of other scribes', on eg 59r–61r; he is probably responsible for the elaborate capitulum signs which begin quires A, B, G, and H, and are common in quires D, G and H, and also for the animal heads (pigs?) which occur before **9**, **21** and **29**, and very frequently in quires G and H. There seem to be no factors common to the documents thus marked out. There are no coloured initials. Lengthy marginal notes, hard to date and often hard to decipher, accompany **2** (3v and 4r), **26** (33v), **49** (47v), and briefer ones accompany the litigation (79v–80r). There are informal-looking additions on ff 37v and 59r–60v, and 'No(ta)' appears in the margin frequently. Quires E and F have titles, often abbreviated versions of the rubrics, written vertically in the margin, presumably for ease of reference.

Date. The great majority of documents transcribed by roughly contemporary, and quite similar, hands belong to the first third of the thirteenth century. Apart from quire G there is very little later than 1225; in quire D nothing later than 1209, in B (except fo 10) nothing later than 1205. Quire G contains the greatest variety of hands, and also documents datable to 1189–90 and 1220. The items added in identifiably later hands, as described above, date from 1234–5 and 1243. **91** (1225) is added in a hand much later than the document itself. This suggests a date for the main part of the cartulary within about a decade either side of 1230; but handwriting is not very reliable as an indication of date within broad limits, and many of these deeds are not precisely datable. It is possible that some quires containing specific classes of relatively early deeds (A, B, D) were executed before c 1220; but quire G cannot have been completed down to **92** earlier than 1220, and as it includes work by the main hand, both transcribing and probably rubricating, the other quires could equally well be of the same date as G. The evidence thus permits no more precise conclusion: indeed, quite apart from obvious later insertions, the nucleus itself is a compilation which may well have been made over a period.

There is no indication of when the MS was first bound: when the quire signatures were added, D was intended to go at the end (eighth), a position it has not occupied since the Edward I litigation was put there. The quire-signatures thus pre-date 1288, but do not necessarily prove that the MS was actually bound by then. BL MS. Add. 8171, ff 61–84 contains a complete transcript of the cartulary made in the early nineteenth century, showing that none of its contents have been lost since that date.

The Butley charters are obviously a much more miscellaneous collection. A number of them have Roman numerals either on the back, which would have been visible when they were folded, or on the part of the seal tag protruding through the slits at the back. These seem to have been added in the fourteenth century, and probably represent some sort of filing system which cannot now be reconstructed. Some numbers correspond to transactions rather than to individual charters (eg **149** and **150** have the same number, as have **132** and **133**). Some charters have no number (eg **124**, **126**) though some may have been numbered on lost seal tags. Some of these charters are clearly by the same scribe: **149** and **150**, for instance. **124** and **125** seem to be by the same scribe as **127** and **132**; presumably he worked for Butley priory – perhaps he was even a canon of the house.

The cartulary is presented in MS order, with some surviving Leiston originals at the end. The Butley originals have been arranged topographically, in rough order of date within each section, preceded by charters referring to the house generally.

B. Editorial Method   The difficulty is to reconcile comprehensibility with respect for the text, to decide how far to impose standardised forms, and which forms to choose. The editor's clearest duty is to explain the method used and to apply it consistently. To take the areas of difficulty one by one:

Punctuation. One of the cartulary scribes is an enthusiastic user of the 'punctus elevatus', but is alone in this; others use an oblique dash to the same effect. As a whole, punctuation is not always used where we would (eg the end of sentences), is sometimes used where we would not (eg in the middle of phrases), and is not always used consistently (eg in witness-lists). Comprehensibility must take precedence over eccentricity on this scale, but in order to keep intervention to a minimum commas have only been added in lists. The mark . is used as a full stop, a medial stop and an abbreviation mark in the MS. Medial stops and the 'punctus elevatus' have been rendered as commas or omitted entirely, and abbreviation marks, suspension and compendium marks standardised as '. A colon or semi-colon has occasionally been added where required by the sense. The result is rather sparse punctuation, consisting largely of commas, which are nowhere to be found in the documents, but which usually represent something that is.

Spelling. It would take a more skilled palaeographer than the present editor to be confident of distinguishing *c* from *t* in these hands. Spelling has therefore been standardised in cases of doubt, usually to the form given in standard Latin dictionaries: thus, *pertinentia*, and *servitium*. Slight oddities such as *cartha, autoritas* (which occurs several times), and *relligio* have been reproduced. '*Inperpetuum*' has been made into two words in line with the more common occurrences, but *imperpetuum* given where it occurs. Obvious scribal errors such as repetition of a word have been ironed out, and are not footnoted. *Hiis testibus* followed by one name has been left as it stands, and not thought worthy of comment. The word *dominicum*, demesne, is usually abbreviated, and has been expanded as that despite the occasional occurrence of *dominium*, which is given where it occurs.

Capital Letters. The MS generally uses them indiscriminately and inconsistently, so with some exceptions they have been purged. They have been used for the beginnings of sentences, proper names and titles – eg Ministris, Ballivis, Abbas, Magister – and for Pascha and Natale. In some cases MS unanimity has been irresistible: thus we have Salutem, and capitals throughout the pope's salutation. Oddly to our way of thinking, *deus* virtually never has a capital, and it has not been given one. *Ecclesia* frequently has, but has been denied what has not been accorded to the Almighty. The same applies to *sanctus*.

Extension. Words have been extended without comment where there is no doubt; brackets are used where there is.

By far the greatest editorial problem has concerned the extension of proper names. Simple common names have been extended without comment: thus *Rog'* and *Gileb'* have become *Rogerus* and *Gilebertus*. *Ric'* could refer to Richard or Richer, and has been made 'Richard' only if such a person is known to exist. 'Rannulf' occurs in several different forms, and is usually abbreviated '*Ran*'. This has been made into *Rannulfus* throughout, except where abbreviated *Rand'*, which becomes *Randulfus*, or *Rad'*, which becomes *Radulfus*. Where spelt with *ph*, it has been given as such. Names occurring frequently, such as Saer de Biskele and Hemfrid de Criketot, have been extended to the commonest forms without comment. *Glanvill*, or *Glamvill*, or *Glanwill* has been given as it stands. Compendium marks added after names, as a concession to a Latin ending, have been given where they occur, but not added where they do not; and not added to extended forms of names. Leiston occurs as *Leestun* or *Leeston*, but most often *Leest'*: the same applies to Middleton and Sibton. These have been made into *Leeston*, *Midelton*, *Sibeton* where abbreviated in the MS; where they occur with *u*, they are left as such. Other place names are expanded without comment into the most frequently occurring form, but left as they are when an eccentric form occurs. All ecclesiastical dignitaries have their sees etc extended as adjectives. In the descriptions of originals the dimensions given are width followed by height down the left side. Endorsements are not noted in calendared documents unless of particular interest; post-medieval endorsements are not noted.

It is hoped that readers will not think the result either pedantic or misleading. No editorial techniques seem to have any merit in themselves, as all the choices are between evils.

6. Seals and Sealing   by T. A. Heslop

The small collection of seals on the Butley muniments is very well preserved considering its early date. Most of the damage the seals have sustained seems to have occurred at an early date, before a medieval campaign of repair which used vermilion wax. The impressions have hardly deteriorated since then for no unrepaired seal is badly damaged now, nor is any that was repaired in need of further attention. The date of this conservation cannot be closely limited. It is however after 1290 because Nicholas Kyriel's seal on a charter of that date (**115**) is mended with the vermilion wax. The nature of the wax, with reasonably large lumps of pigment, would suggest a date within the fourteenth century, possibly the first half. Such manifest care for seals is not common in early archives.

The earliest seals are, as one might expect, of white wax covered with a darkish varnish (ie Hervey Walter, **146**, Gilbert of Hawkedon, **147** and Mendham Priory, **130**). This was, *par excellence*, the eleventh and twelfth century method of taking an impression. Hervey Walter's and Gilbert of Hawkedon's seals are attached on tags fed through a series of parallel slits in the base of the charter.[1] This is a common enough late twelfth century method but is unnecessarily complex as it gives very little more security than passing the tag through a single pair of superimposed slits in the double layer of parchment. The latter simpler method was used almost universally on the thirteenth and fourteenth century charters in this collection. This phase is well represented by three charters of Robert Maloisel (**132–4**) and two of

---

[1] This is the method described by Hilary Jenkinson, *Guide to Seals in the Public Record Office*, London 1968, 15 and fig.3.

Gerard son of Benedict of Dennington (124–5). The concern here is no longer with lacing the tag through the charter but rather to prevent the wax falling off the tag. The two ends of the tags are separated and twisted to form a better keying to secure the wax. These five charters are early examples of this precaution which may well have been favoured by the clerk who wrote them. This system remains the most popular for fixing the later seals in this collection. In common with most seals of the early thirteenth century these five impressions are in dark green wax, though browns and buffs also occur frequently.

The design of the seals is best looked at in two sections: secular and ecclesiastical. Of the secular seals, the equestrian seal of Hervey Walter is of particular interest because it seems to reflect a change in design introduced into England around 1180. The earliest English representative of this pattern known to me is on the second seal of William de Mandeville, earl of Essex. His seal closely copies the third seal of his friend Philip d'Alsace, count of Flanders, which itself dates from 1168. The distinguishing feature is the horse whose back legs are thrust out behind and whose forelegs are off the ground in parallel curves in front of its chest.[2] Otherwise most of the medieval designs are typical with several birds and lions, a squirrel, a slender foliage scroll and a star. Of these the most impressive is Gilbert of Hawkedon's lion both because of the size of the seal, nearly 5 cm across, and the drawing of the animal.

In addition to these fairly obvious devices there is a group which presents some problems. Walter of Hesham (139), Reginald Thanur (138) and Valentine Cubald (141) have totally enigmatic images. These three seals are quite probably the work of a single maker. The lettering of the legends is very similar and the devices all have a deep but uniform relief which makes them appear strong in design if rather rustic. Since all of them could represent implements of some kind it is possible that they relate to their owner's profession. The peculiar splayed trident on Valentine Cubald's seal re-appears, along with a pair of clasped hands, on that of John Cubald (143), suggesting that it might be a family rebus of some kind. For the moment though they remain obscure.

The use of ancient engraved gems encompassed by a medieval legend is not uncommon among English seals from the middle of the twelfth century to about the mid thirteenth, though they tended to be used only by the baronial class and officials of church and state. This is splendidly demonstrated by the present collection. The non-ecclesiastical users are all men of rank, Richard de Caen (148) and Robert de Montalt (116) were both important mesne barons and Godfrey de Wavere (127), who used gems for both his seal and counterseal, was lord of Dennington. This all points to the expense and prestige of gems which were widely collected in the Middle Ages particularly for the decoration of precious metalwork, for example the shrine of the three kings at Cologne.

Of the ecclesiastical seals in this collection the counterseal of Mendham Priory (130) is also a gem as is that of William, rural dean of Dunwich (131),

---

[2] For an illustration of such a seal see C. H. Hunter Blair, 'Armorials upon English Seals from the twelfth to sixteenth centuries', in *Archaeologia* lxxxix, 1943, plate IIIc (Patrick I Earl of Dunbar and March).

though in this case the stiff awkward pose of the figure engraved upon it may indicate that this is a medieval imitation or even a deliberate forgery of an ancient intaglio.

The other ecclesiastical seals are very much what one would expect. The large seal of Mendham Priory, in common with virtually all English non-Cistercian houses dedicated to her, shows the Virgin Mary enthroned holding the Child. From its appearance the matrix would seem to date from c 1180–90. The Cistercians are represented among these charters by a typical hand and pastoral staff seal (**131**) which, though named on the legend as the seal of the Abbot of Sibton, served additionally as the conventual seal.[3] The seals of the prior of Snape and Geoffrey, archdeacon of Suffolk (**130**) show a standing figure holding a book. By about 1190 this was becoming quite standard for a prior, who occasionally also holds a staff, and for an archdeacon, who in this case, unusually, does hold a short staff.[4] The prior's seal is peculiar only in respect of its legend. There is an undue gap between SIGILLUM and PRIORI DE SNAPE. Furthermore the style of lettering changes at this point becoming smaller and less confident. The most obvious explanation is that this is a stock seal which could be bought over the counter, rather than a special commission. It would have been a few minutes work for the maker to fill in the particulars on the rim when he had found a customer. Confirmation of this interpretation will depend on the discovery of other examples of the phenomenon.

Rather isolated by virtue of its later date and its consequent complexity is the seal of Roger of Bungay, rector of Groton (**145**). Typically the owner has been relegated to a small arch at the base of the seal while saints occupy niches in the centre. The intercessory purpose of this format is here made quite clear by the legend.

---

[3] On English Cistercian seals see Charles Clay, 'The seals of the religious houses of Yorkshire', *Archaeologia*, lxxviii, 1928.
[4] On this phenomenon and on archdeacons' seals in general see W. H. St John Hope, *Proceedings of Society of Antiquaries* xv(1), 1893–5, 27–8.

Robert	first abbot; occurs 1193–[2]	William	14th century?[14]
Philip	–1205[3]	Thomas of	
Hugh	1228–9[4]	Huntingfield	1403; 1411[15]
Gilbert	13th cent.[5]	Clement Bliburgh	1437?; 1451[16]
P.	1243[6]	John	1452; 1459[17]
Matthew	1229–62, prob. 1240s[7]	Richard Dunmow	1475; 1482[18]
Gregory	1260–75[8]	Thomas Dogett	1488; 1500[19]
Nicholas	1278; 1294[9]	Thomas Waite	1504?[20]
John	1302; 1308[10]	John Green	1527?;
Alan	1310[11]		resigned 1531[21]
Simon	1316[12]	George Carlton	1531–6[22]
John	1344; 1367; 1390?; 1399[13]		

[1] Based on Colvin, 410–11.
[2] **47** below. *CChR*, i.426, cited in Knowles, Brooke & London, 196, dates from 1189 and not 1198 as stated.
[3] **130**; cf. **35**, **38**, before 1206; **30**, poss. 1204.
[4] Rye, *Suffolk*, 29.
[5] BL Cotton Caligula A viii, ff 5^v–6^r.
[6] **22** below.
[7] Essex Record Office, Eye Cartulary, fo 49^v.
[8] **116** below.
[9] *CChR*, v.321; **113** below.
[10] *CPR 1307–13*, 88; *C Misc Inquis*, i.no.2414.
[11] Gasquet, i.no.3.
[12] *CCR 1313–18*, 427.
[13] *CCR 1343–6*, 478; **117** below; Suckling, ii.442; *C Pap Reg*, v.233. It is impossible to decide how many abbot Johns there were.
[14] Bodleian Library, Suffolk Charter 221.
[15] *C Pap Reg*, v.620; vi.330.
[16] Suckling, ii.443; *CCR Henry VI*, v.287–9.
[17] *CPR*, xviii.56; Gasquet, i.135–6.
[18] Gasquet, iii.45–8.
[19] Gasquet, iii.51–4.
[20] Suckling, ii.442.
[21] Suckling, ii.442; A. G. Dickens, *The Register or Chronicle of Butley Priory*, 1951, 59.
[22] Suckling, ii.442.

PRIORS OF BUTLEY[1]

Gilbert	to 1192[2]
William de Boyton	1192–[2]
Robert	occ. Jan. 1213[3]
Adam	1219; 1235[4]
Peter	1251?[5]
Hugh	1255?[5]
Walter	1260–1; 1263[6]
Robert	1268; 1271[7]
Thomas	1277–8; 1290–3[8]
John	1292–1303[9]
Richard de Iakesle	appointed Sept. 1303[10]
Nicholas de Wictelesham	Dec. 1307
Richard de Hoxne	July 1309
William de Geytone	Feb. 1311
Alexander Stratford	Sept. 1332
Matthew Pakenham	July 1333
Alexander de Drenkeston	Sept. 1353
John Baxter	resigned Jan. 1374
William de Halesworth	Jan. 1374
William de Randeworth	Mar. 1410
William Poley	Aug. 1444
Thomas Framlingham	June 1483
Edmund Lychefeld	Aug. 1503 d. before Dec. 1504
Robert Brommer	July 1506 – suicide, 1509
Augustine Rivers	Sept. 1509
Thomas Sudborne or *Sudbury* or *Manning*	
	Feb. 1529–March 1538

[1] Based on J. N. L. Myres, in *Archaeological Journal*, xc, 1933, 242–81.
[2] Liebermann, 165.
[3] Dodwell, *Fines* ii, no.556.
[4] W. O. Massingberd, *Lincolnshire Records*, London 1896, i.119; R. E. G. Kirk, *Feet of Fines for Essex*, Colchester 1899, i. no.404.
[5] *Salter Essays*, 182.
[6] Rye, *Suffolk*, 64; Rye, *Norfolk*, 98.
[7] Rye, *Suffolk*, 66.
[8] C. W. Foster, *Final Concords of the County of Lincoln*, Lincoln Record Soc. xvii, 1920, 273; *State Trials of the reign of Edward I*, Camden Soc., 1906, 3rd ser. ix, 1906, 62–7.
[9] *Salter Essays*, 196.
[10] Henceforth established by J. N. L. Myres from Norwich Episcopal Registers and Patent Rolls, giving date of appointment unless otherwise stated. For references see *Archaeological Journal*, xc, 1933, 185–208.

LEISTON ABBEY CARTULARY
(BL Cotton Vespasian E XIV)

1. Pope Lucius III, Privilege 'Religiosam Vitam', 1181/3–1185.

fo 1r Lucius Episcopus, Servus Servorum Dei, dilectis filiis Roberto Abbati sancte Marie de Leestun', eiusque fratribus tam presentibus quam futuris regularem vitam professis, in perpetuum. Religiosam vitam eligentibus apostolicum convenit adesse presidium, ne forte cuiuslibet temeritatis incursus aut eos a proposito revocet, aut robur quod absit sacre religionis infringat. Eapropter dilecti in domino filii vestris iustis postulationibus clementer annuimus, et prefatam ecclesiam vestram in qua divino mancipati estis obsequio, sub beati Petri ac nostra protectione suscipimus, et presentis scripti privilegio communimus. In primis siquidem statuentes, ut ordo canonicus, qui secundum deum et beati Augustini regulam atque institutionem Premonstratensium fratrum in eodem loco institutus esse dinoscitur, perpetuis ibidem temporibus inviolabiliter observetur. Preterea quascumque possessiones quecumque bona eadem ecclesia vestra in presentiarum iuste et canonice possidet aut in futu/*fo 1v* rum concessione pontificum, largitione regum, vel principum, oblatione fidelium seu aliis iustis modis prestante domino poterit adipisci, firma vobis vestrisque successoribus et illibata permaneant, in quibus hec propriis duximus exprimenda vocabulis: locum ipsum in quo prefata ecclesia sita est, cum omnibus pertinentiis suis ex dono Rannulfi de Glamvilla totum manerium de Leestun', cum omnibus pertinentiis et consuetudinibus sicut eiusdem Rannulfi donatoris carta testatur. Sane novalium vestrorum que propriis manibus aut sumptibus colitis, sive de nutrimentis animalium vestrorum nullus a vobis decimas exigere, vel extorquere presumat. Liceat quoque vobis clericos vel laicos e seculo fugientes liberos et absolutos ad conversionem vestram recipere, et eos in monasterio vestro sine contradictione qualibet retinere. Prohibemus insuper ut nulli fratrum vestrorum, post factam in loco vestro professionem, fas sit absque Abbatis sui licentia de clau/*fo 2r* stro vestro discedere, discedentem vero sine communium litterarum cautione retinere. Cum autem generale interdictum terre fuerit, liceat vobis clausis ianuis, exclusis excommunicatis et interdictis, non pulsatis campanis, submissa voce divina officia celebrare. Paci quoque et tranquillitati vestre paterna sollicitudine providere volentes, auctoritate apostolica constituimus ut nullus infra ambitum locorum seu grangiarum vestrarum furtum vel rapinam committere, violentiam facere, ignem apponere, seu hominem capere vel interficere audeat. Obeunte vero te nunc eiusdem loci Abbate, vel tuorum quolibet successorum nullus ibi qualibet subreptionis astutia seu violentia preponatur, nisi quem fratres communi consensu, vel fratrum maior pars consilii sanioris, secundum dei timorem et beati Augustini regulam providerint eligendum. Sepulturam quoque ipsius loci liberam esse concedimus, ut eorum devotioni et extreme voluntati qui se illic /*fo 2v* sepeliri deliberaverint, nisi forte excommunicati vel interdicti sint, nullus obsistat, salva tamen iustitia illarum ecclesiarum a quibus mortuorum corpora assumuntur. Decernimus ergo ut nulli omnino hominum liceat prefatam ecclesiam vestram temere perturbare, aut eius possessiones auferre, vel ablatas retinere, minuere, seu quibuslibet vexationibus fatigare, sed omnia integra conserventur, eorum pro quorum gubernatione ac sustentatione concessa sunt omnimodis pro futura, salva sedis apostolice auctoritate, et diocesani Episcopi canonica iustitia. Si qua igitur in futurum ecclesiastica secularisve persona hanc nostre constitutionis

54

paginam sciens contra eam temere venire temptaverit, secundo tertiove commonita, nisi reatum suum digna satisfactione correxerit potestatis honorisque sui dignitate careat reamque se divino iudicio existere de perpetrata iniquitate cognoscat, et a sacratissimo corpore et sanguine dei, et domini redemptoris /fo 3r nostri Jesu Christi aliena fiat, atque in extremo examine divine ultioni subiaceat. Cunctis autem, eidem loco sua iura servantibus, sit pax domini nostri Jesu Christi quatinus et hic fructum bone actionis percipiant, et apud districtum iudicem premia eterne pacis inveniant. Amen.

Printed: Monasticon vi(ii).882, no. 10; Suckling ii.436–7.
Calendared: Jaffé – Wattenbach no. 15179.
See Introduction, 2, 20, 30.

2. Pope Innocent III, Letter of Protection 'Non Absque Dolore'. 1st June 1199.

Innocentius Episcopus, Servus Servorum Dei, venerabilibus fratribus Archiepiscopis, Episcopis et dilectis filiis Abbatibus, Prioribus, et ceteris ecclesiarum prelatis ad quos littere iste pervenerint, Salutem et Apostolicam Benedictionem. Non absque dolore cordis et plurima turbatione didicimus, quod ita in plurisque partibus ecclesiastica censura dissolvitur, et canonice sententie severitas enervatur, ut viri religiosi et hii maxime qui per sedis apostolice privilegia maiori donati sunt libertate passim a malefactoribus suis iniuriam sustineant et rapinas, dum /fo 3v vix invenitur qui congrua illis protectione subveniat, et pro fovenda pauperum innocentia murum se defensionis opponat. Specialiter autem dilecti filii Abbas et conventus de Leestun' Premonstratensis ordinis, tam de frequentibus iniuriis quam de ipso cotidiano defectu iustitie conquerentes, universitatem vestram per litteras petierunt apostolicas excitari, ut ita videlicet eis in tribulationibus suis contra malefactores eorum prompta debeatis magnanimitate consurgere, quod ab angustiis quas sustinent et pressuris, vestro possint presidio respirare. Ideoque universitati vestre per apostolica scripta mandamus atque precipimus quatinus illos qui in aliquem de predictis fratribus instigante diabolo manus violentas iniecerint, sive possessiones, vel res, seu domos eorum vel hominum suorum irreverenter invaserint, aut ea que predictis fratribus e testamento decedentium relinquuntur, contra iustitiam detinuerint, seu in ipsos fratres /fo 4r contra apostolice sedis indulta sententiam excommunicationis aut interdicti proferre presumpserint, vel decimas laborum seu nutrimentorum suorum spretis privilegiis apostolice sedis extorserint, si laici fuerint, publice candelis accensis excommunicationis sententia percellatis, clericos autem, canonicos, sive monachos, appellatione remota ab officio et beneficio suspendatis, neutram relaxaturi sententiam donec predictis fratribus plenarie satisfaciant, et hii precipue qui pro violenta manuum iniectione vinculo fuerint anathematis innodati, cum dyocesani Episcopi litteris ad sedem apostolicam venientes ab eodem vinculo mereantur absolvi, nisi forte monachi, vel canonici regulares per Abbates vel Priores suos post satisfactionem congruam secundum ordinis disciplinam fuerint absoluti. Villas

55

autem in quibus bona predictorum fratrum seu hominum suorum per violentiam detenta fuerint, quamdiu ibi sunt interdicti sententie supponatis. Datum Laterani kal' Junii pontificatus nostri anno secundo.

Calendared: Cheney, *Innocent III*, no. 128.
See Introduction, 31.
Marginal notes: fo 3v, Summa totius est, ne de terris (dominicis) novalibus habitis (autem) contradentur decime, sed terris (primo habitis), solvantur, de novalibus non. fo 4r, Wultu mesto . . . sobrius esto.

3. Pope Celestine III, Privilege 'Religiosam Vitam'. 1191–8.

fo 4v Celestinus[1] Episcopus, Servus Servorum Dei, dilectis filiis Roberto Abbati monasterii sancte Marie de insula de Leestun'[2] eiusque fratribus tam presentibus quam futuris regularem vitam professis, in perpetuum. Religiosam vitam eligentibus, apostolicum convenit adesse presidium, ne forte cuiuslibet temeritatis incursus aut eos a proposito revocet, aut robur, quod absit, sacre religionis infringat. Eapropter, dilecti in domino filii, vestris iustis postulationibus clementer annuimus et prefatum monasterium vestrum, in quo divino mancipati estis obsequio, ad exemplar felicis recordationis Lucii Pape predecessoris nostri sub beati Petri et nostra protectione[3] suscipimus[4] et presentis scripti privilegio communimus. In primis siquidem statuentes,[5] ut ordo canonicus qui secundum deum et beati Augustini regulam atque institutionem Premonstratensium fratrum in eodem loco institutus esse dinoscitur, perpetuis ibidem temporibus inviolabiliter observetur. Preterea quascumque possessiones, quecumque bona idem[6] monasterium vestrum in presentiarum iuste et canonice possidet aut in futurum concessione pontificum, largitione regum vel principum, oblatione fidelium, seu aliis iustis modis prestante domino poterit adipisci, firma vobis vestrisque successoribus et illibata permaneant. In quibus hec[7] propriis duximus exprimenda vocabulis, videlicet locum ipsum in quo prefatum monasterium vestrum situm est cum omnibus pertinentiis suis ex dono Rannulfi de Glamvill[8] totum manerium de Leestun' cum omnibus pertinentiis suis et consuetudinibus, ita plene et libere sicut eiusdem Rannulfi donatoris carta exinde confecta testatur. Statuimus preterea et presentis privilegii pagina prohibemus, ut de laboribus quos propriis manibus aut sumptibus colitis, tam in terris antiquitus cultis quam in novalibus, sive de nutrimentis animalium vestrorum nullus a vobis decimas exigere vel extorquere presumat. Prohibemus etiam ut nullus vos vel fratres vestros ad concilia, synodos,[9] aut aliquos forenses conventus ire compellat, nec ad domos vestras accedat causa ordines celebrandi, crisma[10] faciendi, causas

[1] B, Cellestinus
[3] B adds et
[5] B, obstatuentes
[7] A, hoc
[9] B, sinodos

[2] B, Leyston, throughout
[4] A suscepimus, B suscipimus
[6] B, ibidem, and erased in A
[8] B, Glanvilla
[10] B, crissma

56

tractandi, aut aliquos publicos conventus[11] convocandi. Paci quoque et tranquillitati vestre providere volentes, districtius prohibemus ne quis vos ad secularia iudicia provocet, sed si quis sibi putaverit aliquid in vos de iure competere, sub ecclesiastico iudice experiendi habeat facultatem. In causis autem propriis, sive civilem sive criminalem contineant questionem liceat vobis fratrum vestrorum, quos ad hoc idoneos esse constiterit, testimoniis uti,[12] ne ex defectu testium ius vestrum valeat deperire. Quod si quis in aliquem de familia vestra, donec in famulatu vestro[13] permanserit propter detentionem decimarum vel aliquid aliud a sede apostolica ordini vestro concessum excommunicationis vel interdicti sententiam promulgaverit, liceat vobis eos absolvere, et in metu mortis ecclesiastica sacramenta cum sepultura conferre. Indulgemus etiam ut liceat vobis clericos et laicos e seculo fugientes liberos et absolutos ad conversationem vestram recipere et eos in consortio vestro sine contradictione qualibet retinere. Prohibemus insuper ut nulli fratrum vestrorum post factam in loco vestro professionem fas sit absque Abbatis sui licentia de claustro vestro discedere; discedentem vero sine communium litterarum cautione nullus audeat retinere. Inhibemus quoque, ne cui legato nisi a latere nostro directo, vel Archiepiscopo, Episcopo, Archidiacono,,Decano seu alicui[14] ecclesiastico prelato, liceat vos aut clericos vestros in procuratione hospitii onerare,[15] vel absque cause[16] cognitione et ordine iudiciario monasterium vestrum interdicto subicere,[17] aut in vos aut[18] clericos vestros degradationis, excommunicationis, suspensionis vel interdicti sententiam promulgare. Ut autem commodius[19] tam vestras quam pauperum indigentias sustentare et operibus misericordie hilariter[20] possitis deservire, solita sedis apostolice pietate[21] inducti, vobis indulgemus, ut si quis ecclesiarum patronus ius quod in ecclesiis seu capellis habuerit vobis conferre voluerit, suscepta ab Episcopo institutione, vel ab eo qui ius instituendi habuerit, liceat vobis auctoritate apostolica tam ipsas ecclesias et capellas quas in futurum prestante domino adipisci poteritis quam eas quas in presentiarum canonice adepti estis, cum eas vacare contigerit, absque cuiuslibet contradictione et impedimento in manu vestra tenere et earundem omnimodas obventiones[22] et beneficia ad sustentationem fratrum, hospitum ac pauperum in proprios usus convertere, salvis diocesano Episcopo synodalibus.[23] Ad hec auctoritate apostolica vobis indulgemus, ut terras, possessiones et decimas de iure et dominio monasterii vestri ab aliquibus possessas nomine pignoris recipiendi liberam facultatem habeatis, ne ipsi monasterio culpa possint[24] detinentium deperire, si eas per aliquem contractum alienis contingat obligari. Statuimus preterea et presentis scripti pagina prohibemus, ut nullus qui terras vel possessiones quas de monasterio vestro tenet, alii monasterio, ecclesie seu loco religioso eas possit[25] sine

---

[11] B omits conventus
[12] erased in A
[13] B, de familia vestra in aliquem donec in famulatu vestro
[14] B substitutes alii
[15] A, honerare
[16] B omits cause
[17] B, subiacere
[18] B adds in
[19] MS comodius
[20] B, hillariter
[21] A, pietati
[22] A, added in margin
[23] B, sinodalibus
[24] B, possint culpa
[25] A, possint

assensu vestro in vita vel in morte conferre sive[26] a vestro dominio quoquo modo alienare. Et si quis infra ambitum monasterii vestri seu grangiarum furtum vel[27] sacrilegium fecerit, ignem apposuerit, sanguinem fuderit, personam quamlibet ausu temerario leserit aut violentas manus in eam iniecerit, si canonice commonitus iuxta Abbatis aut Prioris arbitrium noluerit emendare, excommunicationis sententia innodetur, et sicut excommunicatus evitandus[28] denuntietur, quousque ipsi venerabili loco[29] condignam satisfactionem exhibuerit.[30] Cum autem generale interdictum terre sive episcopatus fuerit, liceat vobis ianuis clausis, exclusis excommunicatis et interdictis, non pulsatis campanis submissa voce divina officia celebrare. Sepulturam quoque ipsius loci liberam esse concedimus, ut eorum devotioni[31] et extreme voluntati qui se illic sepeliri deliberaverint, nisi forte excommunicati vel interdicti sint,[32] nullus obsistat, salva tamen iustitia ecclesiarum illarum a quibus mortuorum corpora assumuntur. Obeunte vero te nunc eiusdem loci Abbate vel tuorum quolibet successorum nullus ibi qualibet surreptionis astutia, vel[33] violentia preponatur, nisi quem fratres communi consensu[34] vel pars fratrum consilii sanioris secundum dei timorem et beati Augustini regulam providerint eligendum, habentes nunc et futuris temporibus liberam Abbatis vestri electionem, apostolice sedis privilegio[35] roboratam. Porro nulla persona ecclesiastica vel secularis conventum vestrum Abbatis sede vacante[36] impediat quominus de rebus et possessionibus suis disponendi secundum deum[37] liberam habeant facultatem. Auctoritate quoque vobis apostolica[38] indulgemus, ut[39] quotiens necessitate ingruente putantes vos in vobis aut in vestris gravari, ad Romanam ecclesiam duxeritis appellandum, libere vobis liceat eandem apostolicam sedem adire; quod si quis ausu temerario vos impedire presumpserit, hoc in periculum ordinis, honoris et beneficii sui noverit redundandum. Libertates quoque et immunitates vobis privilegiis Romanorum Pontificum seu cartis regum aut aliorum rationabiliter confirmatas, nullus impedire presumat, sed eas perpetuum robur optinere[40] sancimus.[41] Decernimus ergo ut nulli omnino hominum liceat prefatum monasterium vestrum[42] temere perturbare, aut eius possessiones auferre, vel[43] ablatas retinere, minuere, seu quibuslibet vexationibus fatigare, sed omnia integra conserventur, eorum pro quorum gubernatione ac sustentatione concessa sunt, usibus omnimodis pro futura, salva in omnibus apostolice sedis auctoritate et diocesani Episcopi canonica iustitia. Si qua igitur in futurum ecclesiastica secularisve persona hanc nostre constitutionis paginam sciens contra eam temere venire temptaverit, secundo tertiove commonita nisi reatum suum congrua satisfactione correxerit, potestatis honorisque sui[44] careat dignitate, reamque se divino iudicio

---

[26] B, seu
[28] B, devitandus
[30] B, exhibuerit satisfactionem
[32] A, sunt
[34] B, assensu
[36] B, Abbatis sede vacante conventum vestrum
[37] B omits secundum deum
[39] A omits ut
[41] MS sanccimus
[43] B substitutes aut

[27] B, s(eu)
[29] A omits loco
[31] A, devotione
[33] B, seu
[35] B, patrocinio
[38] B, apostolica vobis
[40] B omits optinere
[42] B omits vestrum
[44] B omits sui

existere de perpetrata iniquitate cognoscunt, et a sacratissimo corpore ac[45] sanguine dei ac domini redemptoris[46] nostri Jesu Christi aliena fiat[47] atque in extremo examine districte ultioni subiaceat. Cunctis autem eidem loco sua iura servantibus sit pax domini nostri Jesu Christi quatinus et[48] hic fructum bone actionis percipiant, et apud districtum iudicem premia eterne pacis inveniant. Amen.[49]

[45] B substitutes et
[47] B, fiat fiat
[49] B omits Amen

[46] B omits redemptoris
[48] B omits et

Printed: Holtzmann, i, no. 343, and Suckling ii. 437–9.
Occurs twice in the MS, A: ff 4v–9r (as inspected in no. 4), B: ff 13r–16v (as inspected in no. 9).
See Introduction, 30.

4. Archbishop Hubert Walter, 'Inspeximus' of no. 3. 1193–1205.

fo 4v Rubric: Assensus Huberti Cantuariensis Archiepiscopi de privilegio Celestini Pape.

Hubertus dei gratia Cantuariensis Archiepiscopus totius Anglie Primas, omnibus sancte matris ecclesie filiis per provinciam Cantuariensis constitutis, eternam in domino Salutem. Ad communem omnium noticiam volumus pervenire nos privilegia dilectorum filiorum nostrorum canonicorum de Leestun' a venerabili et sanctissimo patre nostro Celestino Summo Pontifice eis indulta, in hec verba inspexisse.
Celestine's privilege, no. 3, follows.
fo 8v Nos igitur hanc sacram predicti sanctissimi patris nostri paginam cum summa et debita veneratione amplectentes constitutioni ipsius in hac parte pie et rationabiliter facte, quantum in nobis est filiali favore et devoto assensu accurrimus, et ei debitam reverentiam sicut decet nos in perpetuum exhibituros promittimus, venerabiles fratres et coepiscopos nostros, universos et singulos, omnesque sancte /*fo 9r* matris ecclesie filios ad quos presens scriptum pervenerit, cum summa instantia exorantes et attentius monentes et exhortantes,[1] quatinus pro reverentia et obedientia[2] qua Romane sedi sunt obligati, omnia que in hac apostolica pagina continentur, ut ex professione sua tenentur inviolabiliter et in perpetuum tenere studeant et observare.

[1] MS exorantes, with h interlined
[2] MS obbedientia

Printed: Suckling ii. 437, 439.
See Introduction, 36.

5. Honorius III, Letter of Protection 'Iustis Petentium'. 22nd June 1224.

Honorius Episcopus, Servus Servorum Dei, dilectis filiis Abbati et conventui de Leeston' Salutem et Apostolicam Benedictionem. Iustis petentium desideriis dignum est nos facilem prebere consensum, et vota que a rationis tramite[1] non discordant effectu prosequente complere. Eapropter, dilecti in domino filii, vestris iustis precibus inclinati, personas et monasterium vestrum cum omnibus que in presentiarum rationabiliter possidet, aut in futurum iustis modis prestante domino poterit adipisci, sub beati Petri et /fo 9v nostra protectione suscipimus. Specialiter autem sancte Margarete de Leeyston', sancti Andree de Alringheam, sancte Marie de Middelton', et sancti Botulphi de Culpho ecclesias cum earum pertinentiis, nec non possessiones, nemora, prata et alia bona vestra sicut ea omnia iuste, canonice ac pacifice possidetis, vobis et per vos eidem monasterio vestro, auctoritate apostolica confirmamus, et presentis scripti patrocinio communimus. Nulli ergo omnino hominum liceat hanc paginam nostre protectionis et confirmationis infringere, vel ei ausu temerario contraire. Si quis hoc attemptare presumpserit, indignationem omnipotentis dei, et beatorum Petri et Pauli apostolorum eius se noverit incursurum. Datum Laterani x. kal' Julii pontificatus nostri anno octavo.

[1] tramite added in r. margin

See Introduction, 31.

6. Abbot Robert and the Convent of Leiston have resigned whatever rights they had in the church of Knodishall to Prior Gilbert and the Convent of Butley. c 1183–92 (possibly 1183–6).

fo 10r Omnibus sancte matris ecclesie filiis Robertus dictus Abbas de Leeston et conventus eiusdem loci Salutem. Noverit universitas vestra nos communi consensu et utilitate causa dei et intuitu pietatis concessisse et resignasse dilectis fratribus nostris, scilicet Gilberto Priori de Buttele et conventui eiusdem loci, quicquid iuris habuimus in ecclesia de Cnodeshal' cum omnibus terris et decimis, et quibuscumque aliis rebus ad eam pertinentibus ubicumque fuerint, sive in dominico nostro sive in cuiuscumque alterius, ita integre et plenarie sicut eandem predictam ecclesiam prefati canonici plenius et integrius possederunt cum omnibus suis pertinentiis ante adventum nostrum in Leeston et in ipso etiam anno quo ibi advenimus. Ne autem ista iuris nostri pretaxatis fratribus nostris canonicis de Butele facta concessio quacumque occasione urgente aliquem lesionem sustineat in posterum, eam presentis pagine litteris inscriptam et forma sigilli nostri munitam manibus nostris in eorum manus resignavimus, promittentes in verbo veritatis et fide religionis nos numquam moturos aliquam querelam vel querimoniam eis super prefata ecclesia de Cnodeshal' et quibuscumque rebus ad eam pertinentibus.

See Introduction, 2, 38.

7. Abbot Philip has confirmed no. 6, to Prior William of Butley. 1193–1213.

fo 10v Omnibus sancte matris ecclesie filiis Philippus dictus Abbas de Leeston et conventus eiusdem loci Salutem in vero salutari. Noverit universitas vestra nos communi assensu et utilitate causa dei et intuitu pietatis concessisse et resignasse dilectis fratribus nostris, scilicet Willelmo Priori de Buttele et conventui eiusdem loci concessionem quam Robertus Abbas de Leeston predecessor noster et conventus tunc temporis eis fecerunt videlicet, quicquid iuris habuerunt in ecclesia de Cnodeshal' cum omnibus terris et decimis et quibuscumque aliis rebus ad eam pertinentibus ubicumque fuerint, sive in dominico nostro sive in cuiuscumque alterius, ita integre et plenarie sicut eandem predictam ecclesiam prefati canonici plenius et integrius possederunt cum omnibus suis pertinentiis ante adventum nostrum in Leeston et in ipso etiam anno quo illuc advenimus. Ne autem ista iuris nostri pretaxatis fratribus nostris canonicis de Buttele facta concessio quacumque occasione urgente aliquam lesionem sustineat in posterum, eam presentis pagine litteris inscriptam et forma sigilli nostri munitam manibus nostris in eorum manus resignavimus.

See Introduction, 38.

8. 'Inspeximus' by Archbishop Baldwin of charter of Richard I (no. 23). October 1189 – August 1190.

Rubric: Confirmatio Ric' Cantuariensis Archiepiscopi.

fo 11r (Baldewinus)[1] dei gratia Cantuariensis[2] Archiepiscopus totius Anglie Primas, universis Christi fidelibus Salutem in domino. Noverit universitas vestra nos inspexisse et nostris manibus baiulasse cartam domini Ricardi Regis Anglie, sub hac forma.

Richard I's charter (no. 23) follows.

fo 12v Nos igitur iamdicte ecclesie quieti et securitati in posterum providere volentes, memorata sicut eidem ecclesie et canonicis in ea constitutis rationabiliter concessa sunt et collata, auctoritate[3] nostra confirmamus et sigilli nostri munimine corroboramus. Testibus Gilberto Roffensi Episcopo, Herberto Cantuariensi[2] Archidiacono, Magistro Silvestro, Magistro Ric' de Sancto Martino.

[1] MS R   [2] MS Canth'   [3] MS autorita

Printed: Monasticon, vi(ii).881, no. 5 (as Archbishop Richard).
See Introduction, 33, 35–6.

9. John of Oxford or John de Grey has inspected the Privilege of Pope Celestine. 1191–1215.

fo 12v   Rubric: Assensus bone memorie Johannis Norwicensis Episcopi de privilegio Celestini Pape.

fo 13r   Omnibus Christi fidelibus ad quos presens scriptum pervenerit, Johannes dei gratia Norwicensis Episcopus, Salutem in domino. Ad universorum volumus notitiam pervenire, nos privilegia dilectorum filiorum nostrorum canonicorum de Leyston' a venerabili et sanctissimo patre nostro Celestino Summo Pontifice eis indulta, in hac verba inspexisse.

Celestine's privilege, no. 3, follows.

fo 16v   Nos igitur sacram predicti sanctissimi patris nostri paginam cum summa et[1] debita veneratione amplectentes, constitutioni ipsius in hac parte pie et rationabiliter facte quantum in nobis est filiali favore et devoto assensu accurrimus et ei debitam reverentiam et obedientiam sicut decet in perpetuum divina annuente gratia observabimus, universos nostre iurisdictioni subiectos, cum summa instantia exorantes et propensius monentes et exhortantes eiusque firmiter iniungentes quatinus pro reverentia et obedientia qua deo et sancte Romane sedi sunt obligata, omnia que in hac apostolica pagina continentur, inviolabiliter in perpetuum tenere studeant et observare.

[1] et interlined

See Introduction, 37.

10. Archbishop Hubert has inspected Archbishop Baldwin's 'Inspeximus' of Richard I's charter (no. 8). 1193–1205.

fo 17r   Rubric: Confirmatio Huberti Cantuariensis Archiepiscopi.

Hubertus dei gratia Cantuariensis Archiepiscopus totius Anglie Primas, omnibus sancte matris ecclesie filiis ad quos presens scriptum pervenerit, eternam in domino Salutem. Ad omnium notitiam volumus pervenire nos cartam confirmationis B(aldewini) bone memorie predecessoris nostri sub huius continentie forma inspexisse. B(aldewinus) dei gratia Cantuariensis Archiepiscopus totius Anglie Primas, universis Christi fidelibus Salutem in' domino. Noverit universitas vestra nos inspexisse et nostris manibus baiulasse cartam domini Ricardi Regis Anglie sub hac forma.

Richard I's charter, no. 23, follows.

fo 19r   Nos igitur iamdicte ecclesie quieti et securitati in posterum providere volentes, memorata sicut eidem ecclesie et canonicis in ea constitutis rationabiliter concessa sunt et collata, autoritate nostra confirmamus et sigilli nostri munimine corroboramus. Testibus inscriptis. Nos itaque dignum censentes[1] et predicti domini Regis Ricardi et memorati predecessoris nostri Bal(dewini) factis in hac parte consentire et etiam securitati prenominatorum canonicorum de Leyston' in quantum possumus providere confirmationem utriusque scilicet domini Regis et predecessoris nostri predictis canonicis super hiis que in carta domini Regis Ricardi quam inspeximus continentur factam, sicut rationabiliter immo quia rationabiliter factam est, ratam habemus, et omnia prenominata predictis canonicis tamquam iuste eis collata, sicut a predicto domino nostro Rege Ricardo et B(aldewino) predecessore nostro eis concessa et confirmata, nos autoritate nostra concedimus inperpetuum et confirmamus, hanc confirmationem nostram tam presentis scripti serie et sigilli nostri appositione quam testium subscriptione munientes et robo |*fo 19v* rantes. Hiis testibus, venerabili fratre nostro Gilberto Roffensi Episcopo, Teobaldo Walteri, Ricardo cancellario, Ran(nulfo) Testra(n)u', et.[2]

---

[1] MS cencentes, altered to censentes   [2] sic in MS

See Introduction, 33, 36.

11. Form of Peace between the Abbey and the Burgesses of Dunwich. 1189–99 (probably 1193–9).

fo 19v   Rubric: Carta burgensium de Dunewico.

Hec est forma satisfactionis de violentia facta Abbati et canonicis de Leyston' per homines Dunewici, videlicet quod octo de melioribus eiusdem ville, duo clerici et duo ballivi et quatuor alii, in presentia domini Cantuariensis Archiepiscopi constituti, et literas universitatis eiusdem ville de rati habitione proferentes, solempniter iuraverunt, quod predicta universitas super dicta violentia iuri pareret ecclesie. Quo iuramento prestito et recepto, relaxata est sententia interdicti, cui autoritate domini Cantuariensis predicta villa Dunewici erat supposita. Licet igitur predicti octo viri, se et omnes meliores eiusdem ville[1] a culpa immunes esse constanter assererent, tamen ut predicto Abbati et canonicis ad honorem dei et sancte matris ecclesie super violentia predicta satisfaceret, ob reverentiam domini Cantuariensis Archiepiscopi et Episcoporum ei assidentium, coram eo fideliter promiserunt quod omnes |*fo 20r* qui predicte violentie dicebantur interesse, et predicto Abbati et suis dampna intulisse, de omni dampno eidem Abbati et suis illato et aliis etiam occasione ipsius et suorum, ad plenum satisfaciant arbitratu quatuor discretorum virorum ex parte Abbatis, et aliorum quatuor ex parte burgensium Dunewici, et noni ex parte ipsius Archiepiscopi. Si autem qui interfuisse dicebantur ad dampnum istud resarciendum de suo refundere vel noluerint vel non poterint, universitas eiusdem ville de communi errario satisfaciet. Preterea omnes qui interesse dicebantur nudis pedibus et in laneis ad ipsam abbatiam accedentes, super magno altare jurabunt, quod de cetero, nec eidem abbatie nec alicui ecclesie, nec alicui ecclesiastice persone scienter violentiam inferent, et quod predictam abbatiam et canonicos ibidem commorantes dingna veneratione pervenient et eis debitam et specialem reverentiam exibebunt, et de tanto excessu ab ipso Abbate et eo quem dominus Cantuariensis pro eodem est negotio transmissurus, penitentiam accipient. Quadraginta etiam de melioribus eiusdem ville ad predictam abbatiam accedent iuraturi, quod de voluntate eorum |*fo 20v* nunquam commissa est premissa violentia et quod ipsam ecclesiam et omnem aliam de cetero venerabuntur, et sicut decuerit, honorabunt, predicteque abbatie

63

specialem honorem inpendunt. Consequenter tota universitas Dunewici a maiore ad minimum jurabit solempniter, quod nec predictam abbatiam nec in aliam ecclesiam violenter insurget, nec in aliquam ecclesiasticam personam scienter manus iniciet violentas, sed omnem ecclesiam et predictam specialiter honorabit. Jurabit etiam omnis illa universitas in eadem solempnitate, quod perpetuam fidem et fidelitatem et pacem domino Ricardo Regi Anglie et regno servabit, et ipsi Regi Ricardo fideliter serviet contra omnes homines qui vivere et mori poterunt. Si autem de illis qui predicto maleficio interesse dicebantur in negotiis suis aliquo recesserint et presentes non fuerint, infra octo dies reversionis sue predicto modo satisfacient, quod si noluerint, universitatis eiusdem ville communionem et societatem amittent. Si qui vero, preter illos qui satisfecerint predicto Abbati, suspecti fuerint, oportebit eos vel sicut alii satisfacere, vel suam innocentiam purgare. Si que autem iniurie /fo 21r de cetero Abbati et suis ab hominibus Dunewici, vel illis per predictum Abbatem et suos deinceps irrogantur, neutra pars de iniuriis sibi illatis autoritate propria ultionem accipiet, set arbitratu duodecim virorum de Leyston' et duodecim de Dunewico, sibi invicem satisfacient. Hec autem omnia concessa sunt et ordinata, salvis in omnibus iure ecclesiastico et regia dignitate.

[1] MS will'

Date: King Richard; no Archbishop from death of Baldwin to Hubert Walter.
Notes: A summary of the events referred to: some burgesses of Dunwich committed an unspecified 'Violence' against Leiston Abbey, seemingly involving the church itself, its personnel and property, and the town was interdicted on the archbishop's authority. The 'best men' of the town must have maintained their innocence, and have been unwilling to submit to a church court; however, eight men of Dunwich bearing letters of ratification from the 'universitas' of the town, swore to submit to the law of the church whereupon the interdict was relaxed. The townsmen promised that those responsible should make amends, according to the arbitration of four men nominated by themselves, four by the Abbot, and nine by the archbishop. If those responsible were unwilling or unable to pay for the damage, the 'universitas' would do so from the common chest; furthermore, those responsible would swear on the high altar not to repeat their crime and would undergo a penance to be appointed by the abbot and someone sent by the archbishop. All the inhabitants of Dunwich would swear never to lay violent hands on the church, and forty of the 'best' of them would also swear at the Abbey that they had nothing to do with the affair. The whole 'universitas' would swear to keep faith and fidelity with King Richard, and to keep the peace. If any of those responsible should be absent at the time, they should give satisfaction in the above manner on their return, or their 'communion and society' would be avoided by the 'universitas'. If others are suspected, they should prove their innocence or give satisfaction like the others. Both sides shall promise not to take the law into their own hands in future, but to stand to the arbitration of twelve men from either side. The agreement is made saving the law of the church and the royal dignity.

The affray seems to have left no other trace.

12. Baldwin, Count of Guines, has granted freedom from toll throughout his land. 1186–9.

fo 21r   Rubric: Carta Baldewini Comitis Ginn'.

Baldewinus Comes Ginn' Omnibus amicis suis et hominibus presentibus et futuris, Salutem. Noveritis me de voluntate et assensu Enulfi filii et heredis mei dedisse et concessisse et hac mea carta confirmasse deo et ecclesie sancte Marie de Leyston' et canonicis ibidem servientibus in puram et perpetuam elemosinam, pro salute anime mee et animarum omnium antecessorum meorum, et propinquorum meorum, quietantiam de */fo 21v* paagio apud Ginnes', et per totam terram meam in eundo et redeundo, in perpetuum. Testibus, Huberto Eboracensis ecclesie Decano, Willelmo de Ganvilla, Magistro Radulfo Colecestrie[1] Archidiacono, Estachio de Digkemua, Hugone de Lanpernes, et Johanne clerico de Elinton', Stephano de Tapinton', Rannulfo et Simone clericis.

[1] MS Colestrie

Date: Hubert Dean of York.
Notes: Baldwin II was Count of Guines 1169–1205, and also lord of lands in England (Colvin, 85). In 1187 he was among the Flemish nobles who escorted Henry II, and with him Rannulf de Glanvill, from Witsand to Aumale (Eyton, 278).
See Introduction, 5.

13. Roger 'de Kedney' has received 3 acres of 'free land' of Middleton church, in Fordley, for 12d annually. c 1205–24.

Rubric: Carta Rogeri de Kedney.

Omnibus ad quos presens scriptum pervenerit Rogerus de Kedney Salutem. Sciatis me et uxorem meam Marioriam recepisse tres acras terre de libera terra ecclesie de Midelton que iacent in villa de Forl' iuxta terram que vocatur Brodedole, de Abbate de Leyston' tenendas per servitium duodecim denariorum, singulis annis reddendorum in festo sancti Michaelis quamdiu vixerimus ita, scilicet, quod post decessum nostrum prenominata terra ad abbatiam quiete de Leyston' revertetur, cum vestitura qua tunc temporis vestietur. Et ne qua discordia possit post obitum meum et uxoris mee */fo 22r* oriri inter abbatiam et heredes meos de predicta terra, presens scriptum sigillo meo roborare curavi. Testibus Rogero de Braham', Sahero de Bischele, Willelmo filio Theobaldi, Huberto Cordebof.

Date: Hubert Corndebof (see below); death of Saer de Biskele (Introduction, 11).
Notes: For the lessee, see Introduction, 12. See also 20.
Roger de Braham first occurs in 1195 (*PR 7 Richard I*, 76), and from 1198 appears frequently as seneschal of Roger Bigod (Dodwell, *Fines i.* no. 175; eg *Fines ii.* nos. 298, 482), whom he appears to have followed into rebellion against John, having to give his nephew Roger 'de Leston' as a hostage to recover his land in 1216 (*R Litt Claus* i.254; *R Litt Pat*, 171). He seems to have died in or before 1223, since his son John appears as a litigant and he himself appears no more (*CRR* xv no. 738).
Hubert Corndebof in 1205 gave 20 marks and a palfrey for seisin of 100s worth of land,

of which John his father had died seised (*R Obl et Fin* 262). Much of his lengthy trail across the records is due to his difficulty in clearing this disproportionate relief plus debts inherited from his father (eg *PR 7 John* 246, *11 John* 43). He was a small serjeanty tenant in Norfolk (*Bk Fees* i, 127, 138), with land in Suffolk as well for which his son John paid 100s relief in 1235 (*Exc e R Fin* i. 273). For Saer de Biskele see Introduction, 10–11.

14. William son of Peter of Dunwich has conceded rights over land in Leiston. 1195–c 1223.

Rubric: Carta Willelmi filii Petri de Donuwico.

Sciant presentes et futuri quod ego Willelmus filius Petri de Donuwico concessi et hac carta mea confirmavi, deo et ecclesie sancte Marie de insula de Leyston' et canonicis ibidem deo servientibus totum ius quod habui in terra Wiardi in villa de Leyston', de qua solebam annuatim accipere sex denarios, et ego et heredes mei pro posse nostro predictis canonicis guarantizabimus predictam terram contra omnes homines ad tenendum quiete et pacifice, absque omni clamore. Et ut hec mea concessio firma sit et stabilis, cartam meam sigilli appositione roboratam predictis canonicis confirmavi. Hiis testibus, Gileberto Abbate de Langel', Rogero de Braham, Willelmo filio Theobaldi, Toma fratre eius, Roberto Capellano de Leyston', Huberto filio Arnaldi, Roberto Jurdi, Nicholao filio R(oberti), et multis aliis.

Date: Foundation of Langley Abbey – death of Roger de Braham.
Notes: For the donor, see Introduction, 14. Gilbert seems to have been the first Abbot of Langley (Prem., Norfolk); most of the other witnesses come from the Leiston area.

15. Theobald de Valeines has granted to Robert de Dearneford all the land his brother Roger held in Rendham and Swefling. 1178–89.

fo 22v Theobaldus de Valeines omnibus hominibus et amicis suis francis et anglicis tam presentibus quam futuris Salutem. Sciatis me concessisse et hac presenti carta mea confirmasse Roberto de Dearneford totam terram quam Rogerus frater eiusdem Roberti tenuit de me in villa de Rindham et in Swiflinge concessu et assensu predicti Rogeri, et concessu Bartholomei senioris fratris eiusdem Roberti, illi et heredibus suis tenendam de me et de heredibus meis per servitium militis, scilicet reddendo mihi ix. denarios ad xx. solidos scutagii, et ad plus plus et ad minus minus. Et pro hac concessione et confirmatione dedit mihi predictus Robertus dimidiam marcam argenti. Hiis testibus, Ric' de Cranesford, Henrico Engaine, Baldewino de Uford', Rogero de Gimeton', Huberto Walteri, Johanne de Bures, Radulfo de Sancto Eadmundo, Bartholomeo de Norwic et multis aliis.

Date: Hubert Walter not yet Bishop of Salisbury (possibly not Dean of York either, in which case before 1186). Theobald II succeeded in 1178. See Introduction, 13–14.
Note: Baldwin de Ufford was a landholder in Ufford in 1197 (PR Soc. 1st ser., xx, no. 116), and a donor to Butley Priory (no. 153). The other witnesses are obscure, though the Engaines were a prominent Essex family.

16. Bartholomew de Dearneford has quitclaimed to Robert his brother the land Roger his brother held in Rendham. Probably 1180s.

fo 22v   Rubric: Carta Bartholomei de Dearneford.

fo 23r Notum sit omnibus tam presentibus quam futuris quod ego Bartholomeus de Dearneford quietam clamavi Roberto fratri meo totam terram cum pertinentiis quam Rogerus de Derneford frater meus tenuit de feodo Theobaldi de Valeines in Rindham. Hanc terram prenominatam cum pertinentiis quietam clamavi ego et heredes mei predicto Roberto fratri meo et heredibus suis faciendo servitium domino Theobaldo de Valeines, scilicet idem servitium quod cartha quam habeo de domino Theobaldo testatur. Et pro ista concessione et quieta clamatione dedit mihi predictus Robertus unum talentum. Hiis testibus, Roberto de Carleton, Alano fratre suo, Willelmo de Esturmi, Willelmo filio Hugonis, Nicholao de Sumerledestun', Matheo de Valeines, Helia filio Roberti et multis aliis.

Date: connected with no. 15.
Notes: See Introduction, 13–14. Sumerledestun' is presumably Somerleyton, near Lowestoft.

17. Robert de Dearneford has granted 3s 2d rent, due from Hervey son of Hunteman in Rendham and Swefling to Henry de Bosco, of which 2s 2d is to be distributed to religious houses. Early thirteenth century.

Rubric: Carta Roberti de Dearneford.

Sciant presentes et futuri quod ego Robertus de Dearneford' dedi et concessi et presenti cartha confirmavi Henrico de Bosco de Specteshale et heredibus suis tres solidos et duos denarios de censu quos */fo 23v* debet recipere de Herveo filio Hunteman de tenemento quod tenet de me in villa de Rindham et de Swefling' habendum in perpetuum in hereditate reddendo mihi annuatim pro me et uxore mea, et pro animabus antecessorum meorum duos solidos et duos denarios, scilicet ecclesie sancte Marie de Blieburg' duodecim denarios ad festum sancti Michaelis, et ecclesie sancte Marie de Leestun' duodecim denarios ad festum sancti Andree, et hospitali de Donewico duos denarios ad Pascha, pro omni servitio et consuetudine et exactione, in puram et perpetuam elemosinam. Hiis testibus, Rogero filio Osberti, Willelmo filio Gileberti, Waltero filio Osberti, Roberto de Blundeston, Roberto de Sumerletun', Henrico de Caldecotes, Johanne filio Radulfi de Burg, et aliis multis.

Date: after no. 16.
Notes: Ralf de Burgh succeeded to his serjeanty in 1166 and was still holding in 1201 (*PR 12 Henry II*, 20; *R Obl et Fin* 168) *Roger son of Osbert* occurs frequently temp. John (e.g. *PR 6 John* 245, *16 John* 170, 171; *R Litt Claus* i. 235b), as does Walter his brother (*CRR* iii. 128, 304). *Robert de Blundeston* has succeeded William by 1211 (*CRR* vi. 161; cf. ii. 153). The *Caldecotes* family can be traced in West, nos. 271–2: a Henry in 1175–6, another in c 1218 – who can be found in the 1220s too (*CRR* xi. nos. 593, 1853).

18. Henry de Bosco has granted to Leiston Abbey all his rights in Hervey son of Hunteman of Rendham which he received from Robert de Dearneford. Early thirteenth century.

Rubric: Carta Henrici de Bosco.

Sciant presentes et futuri quod ego Henricus de Bosco de Specteshale dedi et concessi et presenti carta confirmavi deo et ecclesie beate Marie de Leestun' et canonicis ordinis Premonstratensis ibidem deo servien/*fo 24r*tibus in puram et perpetuam elemosinam quicquid iuris habui vel habere debui in Herveo filio Hunteman de Rindham et in tenemento suo et in sequela sua per cartam de dono Roberti de Dearneford quam idem Robertus inde michi fecit et illam cartam quam habui de predicto Roberto reddidi predictis canonicis. Et ut hec donatio firma sit et stabilis in perpetuum eam sigilli mei appositione roborare curavi. Testibus, Godefrido de Wavere, Nicholao filio Roberti, Elia filio Roberti de Rindham, Dionisio Normanno, Ricardo de Auviliers, Hugone le Bernier, Willelmo de Wivilingeham et aliis.

Date: After no. 17.
Notes: See Introduction, 13–14.
Godfrey de Wavere was lord of Dennington under John (*PR 10 John*, 14; Dodwell, *Fines ii.* no. 491; *R Obl et Fin* 431–2), and was still alive in 1230 (*CRR* xiii. nos. 2343, 2906).
Wivilingeham is perhaps Willingham, Norfolk.
Richard de Auviliers was alive in 1230 (*CRR* xiv. nos 305, 952) and was a serjeanty tenant in Shelfanger, Norfolk, from the late 1220s (*Bk Fees* 387).

19. William de Glanvill has granted half a mark annually, from his 'camera' until he can assign rent. Late twelfth century?

Rubric: Carta Willelmi de Glamvill'.

Omnibus sancte matris ecclesie filiis ad quos presens scriptum pervenerit, Willelmus de Glamvill, Salutem in domino. Ad omnium vestrum volo pervenire notitiam me dedisse et concessisse et presenti carta confirmasse deo et ecclesie beate Marie apud Leeston constructe, et Abbati et canonicis ordinis Premonstratensis ibidem deo servientibus dimidiam marcam argenti, in puram et perpetuam elemosinam ad edificationem ecclesie, et officinarum /*fo 24v* eiusdem loci singulis annis de camera mea reddendam ad octabas sancti Michaelis, donec eandem dimidiam marcam argenti eis in certum redditum aliunde assignavero, prefate domui et canonicis in perpetuum mansurum. Hanc autem donationem feci eis pro salute anime mee, et pro animabus patris mei, et matris mee, et fratrum, et sororum, et aliorum propinquorum, et amicorum meorum. Testibus, Godwino et Gwidone capellanis, Galfrido de Glamvill', Ricardo de Briencuith, Hugone de Lega, Reginaldo de Pirho, Brien' de Hykelinge, et multis aliis.

Dates and notes: William son of Bartholomew de G. died after 1210. William son of Harvey died about 1192. This could be one of several Williams. Geoffrey de Glanville is a member of the elder branch.
Reginald de Pirho was alive temp. John (*PR 9 John*, 164; *Bk Seals*, no. 337; *R Litt Claus* i. 254b).
Brien de Hickling, son of Geoffrey, is found in the cartularies of Bromholm – fo 49v –

and Hickling – fo 9r – and seems to be a connection of the Glanvilles.
'Briencuith' may seem a mis-reading for 'Briencurt', except that a Richard 'de
Brenkuit' appears in the Bromholm cartulary, fo 52v. Perhaps the Bromholm
connections and the appearance of Geoffrey favour William son of Bartholomew,
though the evidence is hardly conclusive.

20. Pope Honorius III, Decretal Letter 'Benefaciens dominus'. 29th December 1218.

Rubric: Interpretatio Dominus Papa privilegium ordini nostro indultum.[1]

Honorius Episcopus, Servus Servorum Dei, venerabilibus fratribus Archiepiscopis Episcopis et dilectis filiis ecclesiarum prelatis, Salutem et Apostolicam Benedictionem. Benefaciens dominus bonis et rectis corde, dilectos filios fratres Premonstratensis ordinis in via mandatorum eius inoffense currentes, tamquam populum acceptabilem sibi numero et merito ampliavit, eisque de rore celi et de pinguedine terre be/*fo 25r*nedicens, dilatavit locum tentorii eiusdem ordinis et pelles tabernaculorum extendit. Sed quod dolentes referimus via in qua ambulant superbi contra laqueos extendentes, immo velud torrentes iniquitatis in eos irruentes, ipsos bonis suis que soli deo sunt dicata, non solum nequiter defraudare, cum filii huius seculi prudentiores lucis in generatione sint, verum etiam iniquitate potentes nituntur violenter spoliare, et quod gravius est, nonnulli de hiis qui eos debuerant in Christi visceribus carius amplexari et favorabilius confovere, ipsos inmanius persequentes privilegia que ipsis a sede apostolica suis exigentibus meritis sunt indulta, gestiunt penitus enervare, dicendo illa fuisse in generali concilio omnino revocata, vel alias intellectum privilegiorum ipoorum ita maligna interpretatione ad libitum pervertendo, quod nisi os loquentium iniqua obstruatur, nil restet quin predicti fratres privilegiorum suorum pene penitus fructu frustrentur, per quod illi non tam predictis fratribus quam nobis iniuriari probantur, dum contra sedis apostolice indulgentias memoratos fratres /*fo 25v* temere perturbare presumunt, molientes contra nostre plenitudinem potestatis, dum indulta nostra irreverenter impugnant. Nos igitur qui predictos fratres speciali prerogativa dilectionis amplectimur utpote qui offerentes suorum domino vitulos labiorum non solum nobis sed etiam universali ecclesie piis intercessionibus inopinabiliter suffragantur, nolentes huiusmodi vexationibus eorum sabbati amaricari quietem quos omnimodis tenemur consolari; universitatem vestram monemus et hortamur attente ac per apostolica scripta percipiendo mandamus, quatinus predictos fratres ob reverentiam divinam et nostram habentes in visceribus caritatis eis privilegia et indulgentias apostolice sedis concessas, inviolabiliter conservetis et faciatis ab aliis conservari, salva moderatione concilii generalis, videlicet ut de alienis terris a tempore predicti concilii adquisitis et de cetero adquirendis exsolvant decimas ecclesiis quibus antea ratione prediorum solvebantur, nisi aliter cum eis duxerint componendum. Alias quoque dilectos fratres ab incursibus malignorum taliter defendatis, quasi defensores iustitie ac pietatis probemini amatores, deumque vobis propitium /*fo 26r* et nos favorabiles et benignos inveniatis. Data Laterani iiii kal' Januar' pontificatus nostri anno tertio.

[1] recte, . . . domini Pape privilegii . . . indulti?

See Introduction, 20, 31.

21. Pope Honorius III, Decretal Letter 'Contingit interdum'. 18th February 1219.

Rubric: Item alia interpretatio.

Honorius Episcopus, Servus Servorum Dei, dilectis filiis Abbati Premonstratensi et universis coabbatibus eius et fratribus sub eodem ordine deo servientibus, Salutem et Apostolicam Benedictionem. Contingit interdum quod nonnulli propriis incumbentes affectibus dum sanctionum sensum legitimum ad sua vota non haberent accomodum, superadducunt adulterinum intellectum in temporali compendio eternum dispendium non timentes. Sane quia sicud audivimus quidam suo nimis inherentes ingenio nimiumque voluntarii concilii generalis interpretes de novalibus post idem concilium adquisitis a vobis intendunt decimas extorquere. Ne super hiis contingat vos indebita molestatione vexari, nos interpretationem illorum intellectium constitutionis predicti concilii super Premonstratensium decimis edite asserimus peregrinam in ipsa quidem expresse cavetur ut de alienis terris a tempore dicti concilii adquisitis et amodo adquirendis, si eas /*fo 26v* propriis manibus aut sumptibus colueritis, decimas ecclesiis persolvatis quibus ratione prediorum antea solvebantur. Unde si ad prope positum aciem discretionis extenderent, advertentes nichilominus de quibus novalibus apostolice sedis intelligant indulgentiam super talibus piis locis concessam, non sic circa novalia nove interpretationis ludibrio ingenia fatigarent. Inhibemus igitur autem presentium aut nullus a vobis de novalibus a tempore concilii excultis vel in posterum propriis manibus aut sumptibus excolendis, decimas exigere aut extorquere presumant. Nulli ergo omnino hominum liceat hanc paginam nostre inhibitionis infringere vel ei ausu temerario contraire. Si quis autem hoc attemptare presumpserit, indignationem dei omnipotentis et beatorum Petri et Pauli apostolorum eius se noverit incursurum. Datum Laterani xii kal' Martii pontificatus nostri anno iii.

Calendared: Potthast no. 5991.
Printed: Suckling ii. 439.

22. Inspeximus by Simon, Prior of Norwich (27th February 1243), of inspeximus by William Ralegh, Bishop of Norwich (10th February 1243), of Leiston's papal and episcopal documents.

fo 27r Omnibus Christi fidelibus ad quos presens scriptum pervenerit, Symon Prior ecclesie Christi Norwicensis et eiusdem loci conventus, Salutem in domino. Ad communem omnium notitiam volumus pervenire, nos cartam et confirmationem dilectorum nostrorum P. Abbatis et conventus de Leyston' a venerabili patre nostro Willelmo dei gratia Norwicensis Episcopo eis concessam et confectam, in hec verba inspexisse.

Omnibus Christi fidelibus ad quos presens scriptum pervenerit, Willelmus dei gratia Episcopus Norwicensis Salutem in domino. Universitati vestre notum facimus quod cum inspexerimus privilegia Romanorum pontificum felicis memorie Lucii, Celestini, Innocentii, et Honorii tertii in quibus

70

indultum est dilectis filiis nostris in Christo Abbati et conventui de Leyston', ut habeant et teneant ecclesias et capellas suas in proprios usus ad sustentationem fratrum, pauperum et hospitum, et quod etiam deservire possint in ecclesiis et capellis suis per proprios canonicos si velint: postea inspeximus et propriis manibus nostris contrectavimus cartas et confirmationes predecessorum nostrorum Episcoporum /fo 27v Norwicensium bone memorie Johannis primi et Johannis secundi in quibus concesserunt et confirmarunt dictis Abbati et conventui de Leyston' ecclesiam sancte Margarete de Leyston cum capella de Alringham et cum decimis de dominico suo de Leystona et ecclesiam beate Marie de Middelton' et ecclesiam sancti Botulphi de Culpho cum omnibus pertinentiis suis in usus proprios, ad sustentationem fratrum, pauperum et hospitum perpetuo possidendas. Nos igitur in suprascriptis articulis privilegiis felicis recordationis dictorum Romanorum pontificum ut apostolice convenit dignitati obedire volentes, necnon cartas et confirmationes predictorum Episcoporum Norwicensium conprobantes, pietatis intuitu et favore religionis de assensu et voluntate capituli nostri concedimus et presenti pagina confirmamus prenominatis dilectis nostris P. Abbati et conventui de Leystona et successoribus eorum in perpetuum supradictas ecclesias videlicet ecclesiam sancte Margarete de Leyston' cum capella de Alrinham et cum capella de Syswelle de novo constructa, et cum decimis de dominico suo de Leystona, et ecclesias beate Marie de Middelton' et sancti Botulphi de Culpho cum omnimodis /fo 28r obventionibus suis et pertinentiis in usus proprios ad sustentationem fratrum, pauperum et hospitum, salva dignitate, reverentia et obedientia nobis et successoribus nostris et sancte Norwicensi ecclesie debita et consueta et salva competenti et honesta sustentatione capellanorum temporallum qui pro voluntate dictorum Abbatis et conventus de Leystona in prenominatis ecclesiis et capellis ministrabunt. Ut autem hec nostra concessio et confirmatio perpetuam optineat firmitatem, eam presenti scripto et sigilli nostri appositione roboravimus. Datum apud Suthelmham iiij. idus Februarii pontificatus nostri anno quarto.

Nos igitur prenominatam cartam et confirmationem prenominatis Abbati et conventui de Leyston' a venerabili patre nostro confectam, pio et devoto assensu concedimus et quantum in nobis est confirmamus et sigilli nostri inpressione communimus. Datum apud Norwic' tertio kal' Martii pontificatus domini Willelmi de Raleg' Norwicensis Episcopi anno quarto.

See Introduction, 22, 37–8

23. General Confirmation Charter of Richard I. 14th October 1189.

Ricardus dei gratia Rex Anglie, Dux Normannie et Aquitanie, Comes Andegavie, Archiepiscopis, Episcopis, Abbatibus, Comitibus, Baronibus, Iustic', Vicecomitibus, Ministris, et omnibus Ballivis[1] et fidelibus suis totius Anglie, francis, et anglis,[2] presentibus et futuris, Salutem. Sciatis nos ad

---

[1] B adds suis   [2] B, anglicis

petitionem fidelis nostri Rannulfi de Glanvill'[3] concessisse et hac presenti carta nostra confirmasse donationem quam idem Rannulfus fecit deo et[4] ecclesie in honore beate Marie apud Leestun'[5] constructe, et canonicis ordinis Premonstratensis ibidem deo servientibus ad abbatiam ibidem construendam, ad ministrandum[6] ibi in perpetuum. De toto manerio de Leestun' possidendo in libera et pura et perpetua elemosina,[7] cum omnibus pertinentiis suis, et cum ecclesia sancte[8] Margarete de Leestun', et cum ecclesia sancti Andree de Alringeham,[9] quas ecclesias prefatus Rannulfus prius dederat canonicis de Buttele, unde ipsi habent cartam ipsius Rannulfi et cartam confirmationis nostri patris, quas ipsi canonici de Butthele[10] resignaverunt ipsis canonicis de Leestun', quod manerium pater noster prius dederat memorato Rannulfo de Glanvill' fideli suo[11] pro bono servitio suo. Concedimus etiam et confirmamus concessionem et promissionem quam prefati canonici de Leestun' fecerunt eidem Rannulfo quando eos ibidem fundavit,[12] scilicet quod nullam villam vel terram ement, vel in vadium vel ad firmam vel aliquo alio modo recipient, nisi que eis gratis collata fuerint in libera elemosina, et quod non capient vel auferent ab aliquo hominum, qui tunc temporis quando eos fundavit in eadem villa manserunt, vel a successoribus eorum aliquid de aliquo tenementorum suorum quod tunc temporis tenuerunt, set omnia tenementa sua eis et successoribus eorum permittent tenere bene et in pace, per servitia que ad ipsa tenementa pertinent.[12] Preterea concessimus et presenti carta[13] confirmamus deo et ecclesie sancte[14] Marie de Leestun' et canonicis ibidem deo servientibus omnes donationes terrarum et hominum et elemosinarum que eis rationabiliter facte sunt, in ecclesiis et omnibus aliis rebus et possessionibus. Quare volumus et firmiter precipimus quod predicti canonici et eorum homines omnes terras et possessiones, et elemosinas suas habeant et teneant cum socha et sacha, et thol et theam,[15] et infangenetheof,[16] et cum omnibus aliis libertatibus et liberis consuetudinibus et quietantiis[17] suis, in bosco et plano et pratis et pascuis, in aquis et molendinis, in viis et semitis, in stagnis[18] et vivariis, et mariscis et piscariis, et grangiis et virgultis, infra burgum et extra, et in omnibus rebus, et in omnibus locis, solutas liberas[19] et quietas de sectis schirarum et hundredorum et placitis et querelis, et de pecunia danda pro forisfacturo de murdro, et de wapentachio et scutagio,[20] et geld et denegeld,[21] et hidagiis, et assisis, et de operationibus castellorum et parcorum et pontium et calcearum, et de ferdwita[22] et de hengwita,[23] et de flemmenesfrenthe,[24] et de hamsocha,[25]

[3] B, Ganulla, C Glanwill' throughout
[4] C adds sancte
[5] B and C, Leyston' throughout
[6] B administrandum, C ad administrandum
[7] C, elemosina et perpetua
[8] B, C, beate
[9] B, Aldringeh', C, Aldringh'
[10] B, C, Buttele
[11] B, C, nostro
[12]....[12] erased in A, complete in B and C, but B has 'fuerit' for C's 'fuerint' and 'eo' for C's 'eos'. B is clearly the worst of the three copies.
[13] B adds nostra
[14] B omits sancte
[15] B and C, soca et saca et tol et team
[16] B, invangenetheof, C, invangenethef
[17] B, quetantiis
[18] B, stangnis
[19] B, solitas libertates
[20] B, et wapentac et de, C, et de wapentac et de
[21] B, de geld et denegeld, C, de geld et de denegeld
[22] B, fredwite
[23] B, C, hengenewita
[24] B, C, flemenesfrenta
[25] B, hamsoca

et de warpeni,[26] et de averpeni,[27] et de blodwita,[28] et de fictwita,[29] et de leirwita[30] et de hundredpeni,[31] et de thenthingpeni,[32] nisi in introitu, et sint quieti ipsi et homines sui per totam terram nostram de omni theloneo et de omnibus rebus quas ipsi canonici vel homines sui poterunt[33] assecurare quod emant vel vendant eas ad proprios usus ipsorum canonicorum[34] vel hominum suorum absque venditione ulterius facienda, et de passagiis, et de pontagiis, et de stallagio et de lestagio,[35] et de omni seculari servitio et opere servili et exactione, et omnibus aliis occasionibus et consuetudinibus secularibus, excepta sola iustitia mortis et membrorum. Hec omnia eis concessimus in perpetuam elemosinam pro dei amore et salute anime mee[36] et anime domini[37] Regis patris nostri Henrici et omnium antecessorum[38] et successorum nostrorum. Testibus Hugone Episcopo Dunelmensi, Ricardo Londoniensi, Godefrido Wintoniensi, Huberto Sareberiensi electis, Willelmo Comite de Arundel, Willelmo de Sancto Johanne, Galfrido filio Petri, Hugone Bard(ulfi), Willelmo Ruffo, Michaele Beleth.[39] Datum apud Arundel' per manum Willelmi de Longo Campo cancellarii nostri Eliensis electi, quartodecimo die Octobris regni nostri anno primo.

[26] B, C, warpani
[27] B, C, averpani
[28] B, blodwite
[29] B, fiedwita, C, ficthwit'
[30] B, legwit, C, leg(er)wit
[31] B, hunderedepan', C, hundred' pan'
[32] B, tetingpan', C, tethingpan'
[33] B, poterunt
[34] B, C, canonicorum ipsorum
[35] B, C, lestagio et stallagio
[36] B, C, nostre (correctly?)
[37] B, C, omit domini
[38] B adds suorum
[39] B, Belet   [40] B, C, xiiii
Occurs three times in the MS: A, ff 29r–31r (taken as basic text)
    B, ff 11r–12v (see no. 8)
    C, ff 17r–19v (see no. 10)

Printed: Monasticon, vi(ii).881, no. 5; Suckling ii. 434–5.
See Introduction, 33–4.

24. Henry II confirms the Abbey's possessions. December 1184–May 1185.

fo 31r   Rubric: Carta Henrici Regis de manerio de Leeston.

Henricus dei gratia Rex Anglorum et Dux Normannorum et Aquitanorum et Comes Andegavorum, Archiepiscopis, Episcopis, Abbatibus, Comitibus, Baronibus, Iustic', Vicecomitibus, Ministris, et omnibus Ballivis et fidelibus suis totius Anglie francis et anglis presentibus et futuris, Salutem. Sciatis me ad petitionem fidelis mei Rannulfi de Glamvill' concessisse et hac presenti carta mea confirmasse donationem quam idem Rannulfus fecit deo et ecclesie in honore beate Marie apud Leestun' */fo 31v* constructe, et canonicis ordinis Premonstratensis ibidem deo servientibus ad abbatiam ibidem construendam ad ministrandum ibi in perpetuum, de toto manerio de Leestun' possidendo in libera et pura elemosina, cum omnibus pertinentiis suis, et cum ecclesia beate Margarete de Leestun', et cum ecclesia sancti Andree de Alringeham', quas ecclesias prefatus Rannulfus prius dederat canonicis de Buttele, unde ipsi habent cartam ipsius Rannulfi et cartam confirmationis mee, quas ipsi canonici de Buttele resignaverunt ipsis canonicis de Leestun'; quod manerium ego prius dederam memorato Rannulfo de Glamvilla fideli meo

73

pro bono servitio suo. [1]Concedo etiam et confirmo concessionem et promissionem quam prefati canonici de Leestone fecerunt eidem Ranulpho quando eos ibidem fundavit scilicet quod nullam terram ement vel in vadium vel ad firmam vel aliquo alio modo recipient nisi que eis gratis collata fuerit in libera elemosina et quod non capient vel auferent ab aliquo hominum *|fo 32r* qui tunc temporis quando eos fundavit in eadem villa manserunt vel a successoribus eorum aliquid de aliquo tenemento suorum quod tunc temporis tenuerunt sed omnia tenementa sua eis et successoribus eorum permittent tenere bene et in pace per servitia que ad ipsa tenementa pertinent.[2] [1] Hanc autem concessionem et confirmationem eis feci pro salute anime mee, et omnium antecessorum et successorum meorum. Quare volo et firmiter precipio quod prefati canonici totum manerium prefatum de Leestun' habeant et teneant in libera et pura et perpetua elemosina bene et in pace, libere et quiete integre et honorifice et plenarie cum omnibus pertinentiis suis, scilicet in bosco et plano, in pratis et pascuis, in stangnis et molendinis, in piscariis et turbariis, in mariscis et iuncariis, in viis et semitis et in omnibus aliis locis et rebus, cum sach et soch et tol et them et infangenethef, et cum omnibus aliis libertatibus et liberis consuetudinibus ad ipsum maner*|fo 32v*-ium pertinentibus. Testibus Baldewino Wigornensi Episcopo Cantuariensi electo, Johanne Norwicensi, Galfrido Eliensi, Hugone Dunelmensi, Reginaldo Bathonensi et Seffrido Cicestrensi Episcopis, et Godefrido de Luci.

[1]....[1] erased, but rewritten in gold in a different hand
[2] Pertinent in right margin

See Introduction, 2, 32.

25. Henry II's 'Charter of Liberties'. May 1185 – July 1189.

Rubric: Carta Henrici Regis de libertatibus.

Henricus dei gratia Rex Anglorum, et Dux Normannorum et Aquitanorum et Comes Andegavorum, Archiepiscopis, Episcopis, Abbatibus, Comitibus, Baronibus, Iustic', Vicecomitibus, Ministris, et omnibus fidelibus suis francis, et anglis, Salutem. Sciatis me concessisse et presenti carta confirmasse deo et ecclesie beate Marie de Leestun', et canonicis ibidem deo servientibus omnes donationes terrarum et hominum, et elemosinarum que eis rationabiliter facte sunt in ecclesiis, et omnibus aliis rebus et possessionibus. Quare volo et firmiter precipio quod predicti canonici et eorum homines omnes terras et possessiones suas, et elemosinas suas habeant et teneant cum soca et saca et tol et theam et infan*|fo 33r*genetheof, et cum omnibus aliis libertatibus, et liberis consuetudinibus, et quietantiis suis, in bosco et plano et pratis et pascuis, in aquis et molendinis, in viis et semitis, in stangnis et vivariis et mariscis et piscariis et grangiis et virgultis, infra burgum et extra, et in omnibus rebus, et in omnibus locis solutas, liberas, et quietas de sectis scirarum et hundredorum, et placitis et querelis, et de pecunia danda pro forisfacto de murdro, et de wapentach, et scutagio, et geldo et denegeldo et hidagio et assisis, et de operationibus castellorum et parcorum et pontium et calcearum, et de ferdwita, et de hengewita et de flemennefrenthe et de hamsoca et de warpeni et de averpeni et de blodwitha et de fichtwita et de leerwitha et de hunr(ed)peni, et de thiethingpeni, nisi in introitu, et sint quieti ipsi et homines sui per totam terram meam de omni theloneo et de omnibus rebus quas ipsi canonici vel */fo 33v* homines sui poterunt assecurare quod emant vel vendant eas ad proprios usus ipsorum canonicorum vel hominum suorum absque venditione ulterius facienda, et de passagio et leestagio et stallagio et de omni seculari servitio et opere servili et exactione et omnibus aliis occasionibus et consuetudinibus secularibus, excepta sola iustitia mortis et membrorum. Hec omnia eis concessi in perpetuam elemosinam pro dei amore, et salute anime mee et omnium antecessorum et successorum meorum. Testibus Baldewino Cantuariensi Archiepiscopo, Johanne Norwicensi, Galfrido Eliensi, Hugone Dunelmensi Episcopis,[1] R(eginaldo) Bathoniensi, Seur' Cicestrensi Episcopis, Herberto Cantuariensi Archidiacono, Godfrido de Lucy Rychmundensi Archidiacono, Huberto Walteri, Hamelino Comite Warenne, Willelmo Comite de Suthsexia, Comite Albr', Ricardo Comite de Clara, Bernardo de Sancto Walerico, Waltero filio Roberti, apud Westmonasterium.

[1] cartulary omits remainder – supplied from Charter Rolls.

Printed: CChR, iii. 199.
See Introduction, 33–4.

26. Henry II has granted Loieton manor and other gifts to Rannulf de Glanville. 1175–6.

Rubric: Carta Regis Henrici quam fecit Rannulfo de Glanvill'.

Henricus dei gratia Rex Anglorum, Dux Normannorum et Aquitanorum et Comes Andegavorum, Archiepiscopis, Episcopis, Abbatibus, Comitibus, Baronibus, Iustic', Vicecomitibus, Ministris, et omnibus fidelibus suis francis et anglis totius Anglie, Salutem. Sciatis me dedisse et concessisse et presenti carta confirmasse, Rannulfo de Glamvill' manerium de Le-*/fo 34r*estun' cum omnibus pertinentiis suis, et Uptonam cum iis[1] que ad eam pertinent, et lii. solidos quos Willelmus filius Hervei solebat reddere mihi annuatim de terra de Selfleta sibi et heredibus suis ad tenendum de me et de heredibus meis per servitium dimidii militis. Quare volo et firmiter precipio quod ipse Randulfus et heredes sui post eum omnia predicta habeant et teneant de me et de heredibus meis per prenominatum servitium, bene et in pace, libere et quiete, integre et plenarie et honorifice, in bosco et plano, in pratis et pasturis, in aquis et molendinis, in vivariis et stagnis, et in donationibus ecclesiarum et in viis et semitis et omnibus aliis locis et aliis rebus ad ea pertinentibus et cum omnibus libertatibus et liberis consuetudinibus suis, sicut ipsa dedi eis et concessi et hac carta mea confirmavi. Testibus, Ricardo de Luci, Hugone de Cressi, Roberto de Stutewill', Rogero de Stutevill', Willelmo de Stutevill', et aliis. Apud Westmonasterium.

[1] iis omitted in MS

Printed: Monasticon, vi(ii).880, no. 3; and Suckling ii. 423, no. 3.
See Introduction, 32–3.

Domino Ranulpho de Glanvilla, memorandum quod dominus Henricus secundus dedit manerium suum de Leyston' cum omnibus libertatibus et liberis consuetudinibus cum portu de Mismere et medietatem portus de . . . demuth cum omnibus que inter eas sunt, tenendum de domino Rege per servitium dimidii militis. Dominus vero Ranulphus postquam per multos annos dictum manerium tenuisset examinata conscientia sua volens se deo reconciliare in dicto manerio abbatiam ordinis Premonstratensis de consensu domini Regis construxit et dominus Rex dictum manerium Abbati et conventui et suis successoribus liberum in perpetuum concessit solutum de omni servitio seculari, ut patet in cartis dicti domini Regis et successorum suorum.

27. Rannulf de Glanvill has endowed Leiston Abbey. 1186–9.

fo 34v   Rubric: Carta Rannulfi de Glamvill' de manerio de Leeston.

Omnibus sancte matris ecclesie filiis presentibus et futuris Rannulfus de Glamvilla Salutem. Noverit universitas vestra me dedisse et concessisse deo et ecclesie in honore beate Marie apud Leestun' constructe, et canonicis ordinis Premonstratensis professis ibidem deo servientibus, ad abbatiam ibidem construendam ad ministrandum ibi deo in perpetuum, totum manerium de Leeston possidendum in libera et pura et perpetua elemosina, cum omnibus pertinentiis suis, et cum ecclesia beate Margarete de Leestun' et cum ecclesia sancti Andree de Aldringeham, quas ecclesias prius dederam canonicis de Buttele, unde ipsi habent cartam meam et confirmationem domini mei Henrici Regis secundi, quas ipsi canonici de Buttele resign-averunt ipsis canonicis de Leestun' coram domino Johanne Norwicensi Episcopo, et coram me, et Walkelino Archidiacono et Galfrido capellano, Huberto Walteri, Magistro Reinero de Hecam, et Magistro Roberto de Waxton', et Jordano de Ros, et Magistro Lam/*fo 35r*berto, et Simone de Scales, et Magistro Waltero de Calna, et Rogero de Glamvill', et Osberto et Gerardo, et Galfrido filio Petri et Alano de Valeines, et aliis multis, quod manerium venerabilis dominus meus Rex Anglorum Henricus secundus mihi dedit pro servitio meo. [1]Quando autem eosdem canonicos ibidem fundavi concesserunt et in veritate promiserunt quod nullam terram ement vel in vadium vel ad firmam vel aliquo alio modo recipient nisi que eis gratis collata fuerit in libera elemosina et quod non capient vel auferent ab aliquo hominum qui tunc temporis quando eos ibidem fundavi in eadem villa manserunt vel a successoribus suis aliquid de aliquo tenementorum suorum quod tunc temporis tenuerunt sed omnia tenementa sua eis et successoribus eorum permittent tenere bene et in pace per servitia ad ipsa tenementa sua pertinentia.[1] Hanc autem donationem feci eis pro salute memorati domini mei illustris Regis Henrici et pro salute anime mee /*fo 35v* et Berthe uxoris mee, et omnium antecessorum et successorum nostrorum. Quare volo et concedo quod prefati canonici totum prefatum manerium de Leestun' cum omnibus pertinentiis suis, et cum prefatis ecclesiis habeant et teneant in libera et pura et perpetua elemosina bene et in pace, libere et quiete, integre et honorifice et plenarie, in boscis et plano, in pratis et pascuis, in stagnis et molendinis, in piscariis et turbariis et mariscis et iuncariis, in viis et semitis et

76

omnibus aliis locis et aliis rebus, cum omnibus libertatibus et liberis |
consuetudinibus ad ipsum manerium pertinentibus. Testibus hiis, Johanne
filio domini Regis, Willelmo de Aubervill', Radulfo de Ardene, Rogero de
Glamvill', Osberto de Glamvill', Willelmo de Valeines, Radulfo Murdac,
Rannulfo de Gedinge, Alardo filio Willelmi, Teobaldo Walteri, Ricardo
Malebise, Willelmo de Basingeham, Rogero Walteri, Willelmo filio Willelmi
de Aubervill', Thoma de Ardene.

^{|···|} Erased, but rewritten in gold in different hand.

Printed: Monasticon, vi(ii).880–1, no. 4; and Suckling, ii.431–2.
See Introduction, 2, 3, 33.

28. General Confirmation by King John. 14th May 1201.

fo 36r   Rubric: Carta Johannis Regis.

Johannes dei gratia Rex Anglie, Dominus Hybernie, Dux Normannie (et)
Aquitanie, Comes Andegavie, Archiepiscopis, Episcopis, Abbatibus, Comitibus, Baronibus, Iustic', Vicecomitibus, Prepositis, Ministris, et omnibus
Ballivis, et fidelibus suis, Salutem. Sciatis nos concessisse, et presenti carta
nostra confirmasse deo et ecclesie sancte Marie de Leestun' et canonicis
ibidem deo servientibus omnes donationes terrarum et hominum et
elemosinarum que eis rationabiliter factae sunt in ecclesiis et omnibus aliis
rebus et possessionibus. Quare volumus et firmiter precipimus quod predicti
canonici, et eorum homines, omnes terras et possessiones suas et elemosinas
suas habeant et teneant, cum soca et saka et thol et theam, et infangeneth(ef),
et cum omnibus aliis libertatibus et liberis consuetudinibus et quietantiis
suis, in bosco et plano, in pratis et pascuis, in aquis et molendinis, in viis et
semitis, in stagnis et vivariis et mariscis et piscariis et grangiis/*fo 36v* et
virgultis, infra burgum et extra, et in omnibus rebus et in omnibus locis,
solutas, liberas et quietas de sectis scirarum et hundredorum et placitis et
querelis et de pecunia danda pro forisfacto de murdro, et de wapentacio[1] et
scutagio et geld et denegeld et hidagio et assisis, et de operationibus
castellorum et parcorum et pontium et calcearum et de ferdwita et de
hengewitha et de flemenefreth', et de hamsoca et de wardpeni et de averpeni
et de blodwitha et de fithwitha et de leerwitha et de hundr(ed)peni et de
thethingepeni, nisi in introitu, et sint quieti ipsi et homines sui per totam
terram nostram de omni theloneo et de omnibus rebus quas ipsi canonici vel
homines sui poterunt assecurare quod emant vel vendant eas ad proprios usus
ipsorum canonicorum vel hominum suorum absque venditione ulterius
facienda, et de passagio et pontagio et lestagio et stallagio et de omni seculari
ser/*fo 37r* vitio et opere servili et exactione, et omnibus aliis occasionibus et
consuetudinibus secularibus excepta sola iustitia mortis et membrorum. Hec
omnia eos concessimus in perpetuam elemosinam pro dei amore, et salute
anime Henrici Regis patris nostri et omnium antecessorum et successorum
suorum sicut carta ipsius Regis Henrici patris nostri rationabiliter testatur.
Testibus Huberto Cantuariensi Archiepiscopo, Willelmo Londoniensi,
Johanne Norwicensi Episcopis, Galfrido filio Petri Comite Essex', Hugone[2]

Bard(ulfi), Willelmo Briwerr', Hugone de Nevill'. Datum per manum Simonis Archidiaconi Wellensis apud Porecestr', xiiij. die Maii, anno regni nostri tertio.

¹ MS wapentat'   ² MS Hugo

See Introduction, 34–5.

29. Confirmation charter of John, Count of Mortain. October 1189 – March 1190.

Rubric: Confirmatio Comitis Johannis de Moret'.

Johannes Comes Moret' omnibus hominibus et amicis suis francis et anglis, Salutem. Sciatis me concessisse et hac mea carta confirmasse donationem quam Rannulfus de Glamvill' fecit deo et ecclesie in honore beate Marie apud Leestun' construc/*fo 37v* te, et canonicis ordinis Premonstratensis ibidem deo servientibus ad abbatiam ibidem deo construendam ad ministrandum ibi in perpetuum, de toto manerio de Leestun' possidendo in libera et pura et perpetua elemosina cum omnibus pertinentiis suis, et cum ecclesia beate Margarete de Leestun', et cum ecclesia sancti Andree de Alringeham. Quare volo et firmiter precipio quod prefati canonici totum prefatum manerium de Leestun' habeant et teneant bene et in pace, libere et quiete, integre et honorifice et plenarie, cum omnibus pertinentiis suis in bosco et plano, in pratis et pascuis, in stangnis et molendinis et piscariis et turbariis et mariscis et iuncariis, in viis et semitis et omnibus aliis locis et rebus cum soch et sach et tol et them, et infongenethef, et cum omnibus aliis libertatibus et liberis consuetudinibus ad ipsum manerium pertinentibus sicut Henricus Rex Anglie pater meus et Ricardus frater meus Rex Anglie eis concesserunt, et cartis suis confir/*fo 38r* maverunt. Testibus Huberto Saresberiensi Episcopo, Hugone de Malaln', Theobaldo Walteri, Rogero de Plan(es), Willelmo de Buch', <u>Radulfo de Ardene</u>, Roberto Picoth, Willelmo Brit', Magistro Petro de Litlebr'. Apud Everam.

See Introduction, 35.

30. Agreement in the County Court between Abbot Philip and Robert 'de Woodcroft', over meadow in Aldringham. 1204; or 1206–9.

Rubric: Conventio inter Abbatem et Robertum de Wdecrofft.

Hec est conventio facta inter Philippum Abbatem et conventum de Leestun' tenentes, et Robertum filium Rogeri de Burend' parcarium petentem, de prato in Alringeham', quod Willelmus de Malevill' ut dicitur tenuit. Scilicet quod Robertus parcarius tenebit quattuor acras dicti prati, et tertiam partem dimidie acre que iacent iuxta domum Roberti cognomine Decani quoad vixerit de Abbate et conventu de Leestun per servitium sex denariorum singulis annis ad festum sancti Michaelis reddendorum sub tali conditione scilicet, quod si predictus Robertus habuerit heredem de uxore sua Emma, filia scilicet Walteri Flandrensis, predicte quattuor acre prati cum tertia parte dimidie acre remanebunt /fo 38v illi heredi et heredibus eiusdem heredis in perpetuum per predictum servitium. Si vero contigerit prenominatum Robertum ex predicta Emma uxore sua heredem non habere, prenominate quattuor acre prati cum tertia parte dimidie acre revertentur post obitum sepedicti Roberti ad abbatiam de Leestun', integre et quiete, absque reclamatione consanguineorum, vel aliquorum quocumque modo eidem Roberto succedentium. Et sciendum quod sepedictas quattuor acras prati cum tertia parte dimidie acre sive fodiendo, sive alio aliquo modo irrationabiliter non vastabit, sed tantummodo animalia sua ibidem pascet, vel fenum falce secatum ex inde asportabit. Hec autem conventio facta est in pleno comitatu coram Johanne de Cornherd' tunc temporis Vicecomite Suffolch', et coram istis militibus ei assidentibus, scilicet Roberto de Novill', Willelmo de Cretingeham', Willelmo de Henle, Ada de Bedingefeld, Rogero de Braham, Huberto de Brumford', Rogero de Horshag', Johanne de Westh'.

Date: John of Cornard sheriff.
Notes: Other examples of concords made in shire courts are cited by Dodwell (*Fines ii.* xxxiii). There is another, 'in comitatu Norwic'', between Langley Abbey and St Benet's in BL Add. MS 5948, ff 15r–16r.
The witnesses are all to be found in legal records temp. John.

31. Agreement between Butley and Leiston over the parish churches of Leiston and Aldringham, and the demesne tithes of Leiston. c 1183–9.

fo 39r Rubric: Carta Gilberti Prioris de Buttele.

Omnibus sancte matris ecclesie filiis Gilbertus Prior de Buttele et conventus eiusdem loci Salutem in vero salutari. Noverit universitas vestra nos communi consensu et utilitate causa dei et intuitu pietatis concessisse[1] et resignasse fratribus nostris videlicet Roberto Abbati de Leestun' et conventui eiusdem loci totum ius quod habuimus in duabus ecclesiis de Leestun', scilicet in ecclesia sancte Margarete de Leestun', et in ecclesia sancti Andree de Alringham, et totum illud ius quod nobis vendicavimus in decimis monachorum de Heya de dominico prefate ville de Leestun' reddendo nobis nomine prefatarum decimarum de dominico de Leestun' x. solidos in festo sancti Michaelis, ita tamen quod adquietabimus prefatos canonicos de Leestun' apud monachos de Heya, et promisimus in verbo veritatis et fide religionis nos nunquam moturos aliquam querelam vel querimoniam eis super prefatis ecclesiis et decimis. Hiis testibus, Rannulfo de Ganvill' et Huberto Walteri, Adam de Wellebec Abbate, Rogero de Tykehil' canonico, Nicholao de Butteleia.

[1] MS concesse

Date: Approximate beginning of Leiston's foundation; Hubert Walter not yet Bishop of Salisbury – possibly not Dean of York, in which case before 1186.
See Introduction, 2, 20, 38; also no. **6**.

32. Prior William of Butley has confirmed the arrangements of nos. 6 and 31. 1192–1213.

fo 39v   *Rubric:* Carta Willelmi Prioris de Butteleia.

Omnibus sancte matris ecclesie filiis[1] Willelmus Prior de Butteleia et universalis eiusdem loci conventus Salutem in vero salutari. Noverit universitas nos communi consensu et utilitate causa dei et intuitu pietatis concessisse et resignasse dilectis fratribus nostris videlicet Philippo Abbati de Leestun' et conventui eiusdem loci concessionem quam Gilbertus Prior de Buttele predecessor noster et conventus tunc temporis eis fecerunt, scilicet totum ius quod habuimus in duabus ecclesiis de Leestun', videlicet in ecclesia sancte Margarete de Leeston' et in ecclesia sancti Andree de Alringham', et totum illud ius quod nobis vendicavimus in decimis monachorum de Eya de dominico prefate ville de Leestun', reddendo nobis nomine prefatarum decimarum de dominico de Leestun' decem solidos singulis annis in festo sancti Michaelis, ita tamen quod acquietabimus prefatos canonicos de Leestun' apud monachos de Eya et promisimus in verbo veritatis et fide religionis nos nunquam moturos aliquam querelam vel querimoniam eis super prefatis ecclesiis et decimis. Et ut ista concessio predictis canonicis /*fo 40r* firma et stabilis in perpetuum permaneat, eam sigilli nostri appositione roborare curavimus.

[1] MS omits filiis

See Introduction, 38.

33. Prior Robert of Butley has confirmed the arrangements of nos 6, 31 and 32. Probably before 1213.

Rubric: Carta Roberti Prioris de Butteleia.

Omnibus sancte matris ecclesie filiis Robertus Prior de Butteleia et universalis eiusdem loci conventus Salutem in vero salutari. Noverit universitas nos communi consensu et utilitate causa dei, et intuitu pietatis concessisse et presenti carta confirmasse dilectis fratribus nostris Philippo Abbati de Leeston et eiusdem loci conventui, concessionem et resignationem quas Gilbertus et Willelmus Priores de Butthele predecessores nostri et conventus tunc temporis eis fecerunt, scilicet totum ius quod habuimus in duabus ecclesiis de Leestun', scilicet in ecclesia sancte Margarete de Leestun' et in ecclesia sancti Andree de Alringeham, et totum ius illud quod nobis vendicavimus in decimis monachorum de Eya de dominico prefate ville de Leestun' reddendo nobis nomine prefatarum decimarum de dominico de Leestun' decem solidos singulis annis in festo sancti Michaelis, ita tamen quod adquietabimus prefatos canonicos de /*fo 40v* Leestun' apud monachos de Eya et promisimus in verbo veritatis, et fide religionis nos nunquam moturos aliquam querelam vel querimoniam eis super prefatis ecclesiis et decimis. Et ut ista concessio predictis canonicis firma et stabilis in perpetuum permaneat eam sigilli nostri appositione roborare curavimus. Hiis testibus.

See Introduction, 38.

34. Solemn charter of John of Oxford, Bishop of Norwich, confirming gifts to Leiston Abbey. 1187.

Rubric: Confirmatio Johannis Norwicensis Episcopi.

Omnibus Christi fidelibus ad quos presens scriptum pervenerit, Johannes dei gratia Norwicensis Episcopus Salutem in domino. Ad episcopalis officii sollicitudinem pertinere dinoscitur, ecclesiastica beneficia quibus canonice sunt concessa, auctoritatis sue munimine firmare, ne que iuste collata sunt alicuius possint temeritate vel malicia possidentibus avelli. Eis autem promptius et propensius protectionis tenetur impendere patrocinium, quorum artioris vite regula constringit, quorum honeste conversationis meritum, sacre relligionis bonum emittit odorem. Ea propter omnibus notum esse volumus, nos confirmasse deo et ecclesie sancte Marie de Leestun' et Abbati et canonicis ibidem deo servientibus, locum ipsum in quo predicta constituta est *|fo 41r* ecclesia quam vir illustris Rannulfus de Glanvilla pia devotione fundavit, ubi sicut discreta provisione constitutum est, ordo Premonstratensis iuxta regulam beati Augustini firmius observetur, et ad honorem et laudem dei sub Abbate presente et eius successoribus canonice substituendis, vigeat et floreat in perpetuum. Nichilominus etiam eisdem canonicis confirmamus totum manerium de Leestun' cum omnibus perti-` nentiis ex donatione memorati Rannulfi de Glanvill' consentiente domino nostro illustrissimo Rege Anglorum Henrico secundo, in puram et perpe-tuam elemosinam, sicut eorum carte testantur. Similiter ecclesiam sancte Margarete de Leestun' et ecclesiam sancti Andree de Aldringham, quas ecclesias post spontaneam resignationem prioris et canonicorum de Butteleia qui eas prius habuerunt in manu nostra factam, canonicis de Leestun' ad presentationem sepedicti Rannulfi canonice concessimus et dedimus. Hec quidem et alia que memorati canonici de Leestun' sive in presentiarum *|fo 41v* possident vel futuris temporibus annuente domino iustis modis poterunt adipisci ipsis firmare constare volumus et illibata, salvo in omnibus iure sancte Norwicensis ecclesie subiectione et obedientia. Hanc itaque confirmationis nostre paginam ut perpetue firmitatis robur optineat, sigilli nostri appositione communimus districtius inhibentes, ne quis contra eam temeraria presumptione venire presumat. Eam autem observantibus et suprascripte ecclesie caritatis intuitu aliqua bona conferentibus sit pax et salus eterna. Datum ab incarnatione domini m. c. lxxxvii. Testibus.

See Introduction, 3, 37.

35. John de Grey, Bishop of Norwich, has inspected a document of his predecessor John of Oxford (i.e. no. 36), 1200–c.1206.

Rubric: Carta Johannis Episcopi secundi Norwicensis.
Left margin: Johannis secundi.

Omnibus sancte matris ecclesie filiis ad quos littere presentes pervenerint, Johannes dei gratia Norwicensis Episcopus Salutem in domino. Inspeximus cartam Johannis Episcopi bone memorie predecessoris nostri cuius talis est continentia.

No. 36 follows.

fo 42r Nos itaque confirmationem predecessoris nostri Johannis Norwicensis Episcopi ratam habentes */fo 42v* ecclesiam sancte Margarete de Leestonia cum capella de Alringham et pertinentiis suis Philippo Abbati et canonicis de Leestun' ibidem deo servientibus confirmamus, eorum usibus in perpetuum profuturam. Hiis testibus, Magistro Willelmo de Len, Magistro Thoma.

Date: Master William of Lynn ceases to occur in 1205/6.
See Introduction, 37.

36. John of Oxford, Bishop of Norwich, has confirmed Leiston and Aldringham churches to Leiston Abbey. 13th January, 1186.

Rubric: Confirmatio Johannis primi Norwicensis Episcopi.
Left margin: Johannis primi.

Omnibus Christi fidelibus Johannes dei gratia Norwicensis Episcopus Salutem in domino. Universitati vestre notum esse volumus, Gilbertum Priorem de Butteleia ex assensu et voluntate conventus eiusdem loci in manu nostra sponte resignasse ecclesiam de Leestun' cum capella de Alringeham et pertinentiis suis[1] liberam et quietam quam predicto Priori et conventui confirmaveramus, similiter et decimas de dominico de Leestun' quas de monachis de Eya tenebant annuatim decem solidos solvendo. Hanc itaque ecclesiam liberam et vacantem cum predicta capella et pertinentiis Roberto Abbati sancte Marie de insula de Leestun' et canonicis ibidem deo servientibus et servituris concessimus et dedimus ad presentationem illustris viri Rannulfi de Glanvilla eiusdem ecclesie patroni. Hanc itaque ecclesiam prefatis canonicis eorum usibus in perpetuum profuturam, presenti scripto et sigilli nostri appositione confirmamus, salvo[2] iure et obedientia sancte Norwicensis ecclesie et salva honesta sustentatione eius qui in eadem ecclesia ministrabit. Facta sunt autem hec anno ab incarnatione domini m. c. lxxxv. apud Hoxham[3] in die sancti Hilarii, presente Rannulfo de Glanvill', Walkelino Archidiacono, Huberto Waltero[4].

[1] A omits suis
[2] B adds in omnibus
[3] presumably Horham
[4] B omits Hubert Walter, adds et pluribus aliis

Notes: occurs twice in the ms., A ff 42v–43r
B ff 41v–42r (see no. 35.)
See Introduction, 19, 36–7.

37. John of Oxford has confirmed the gift of Middleton church. 1186–1200.

fo 43r *Rubric:* Confirmatio Johannis primi Norwicensis Episcopi de ecclesia de Middeltun.
Right margin: Johannis primi de Middeltun.

Omnibus Christi fidelibus ad quos presens scriptum pervenerit Johannes dei gratia Norwicensis Episcopus Salutem in domino. Universis notum esse volumus, nos concessisse dilectis filiis nostris viro venerabili Roberto Abbati et canonicis de Leeston', pietatis intuitu et favore religionis, ecclesiam de Middeltun' in usus proprios perpetuo[1] habendam, salva possessione Rogeri clerici quamdiu vixerit. Et ut hec nostra concessio perpetuam optineat firmitatem, eam presenti scripto et sigilli nostri appositione confirmamus. Testibus[2] Galfrido Archidiacono, Eustachio capellano, Magistro Rogero.

[1] B omits perpetuo
[2] B, Hiis testibus, Galfrido Archidiacono et pluribus aliis.

Date: Last appearance of Archdeacon Geoffrey's predecessor is no. 36, and the Bishop is John of Oxford, d 1200.
Notes: Occurs twice in the MS, A: fo 43r, B: fo 43v (see no. 38).
See Introduction, 19.

38. John de Grey, Bishop of Norwich, has inspected no. 37. 1200–6.

fo 43v Left margin: Carta Johannis Episcopi secundi.

Omnibus Christi fidelibus ad quos presens scriptum pervenerit Johannes dei gratia Norwicensis Episcopus Salutem in domino. Inspeximus cartam Johannis Episcopi Norwicensis bone memorie predecessoris nostri cuius talis est continentia.
No. 37 follows.
Nos igitur confirmationem predecessoris nostri ratam habentes predictam ecclesiam de Middelton' dilectis filiis nostris Philippo Abbati et canonicis de Leeston' in usus proprios habendam confirmamus salva honesta sustentatione eius qui in eadem ecclesia ministrabit. Hiis testibus, Magistro Willelmo de Len'.

Date: as no. 35.
See Introduction, 37.

39. Roger de Glanvill has granted Middleton church. c 1183–90.

Rubric: Carta Rogeri de Glamvill' de Ecclesia de Middelton.
fo 44r Right margin: Carta Rogeri de Glanvilla.

Universis sancte matris ecclesie filiis presentibus et futuris Rogerus de Glanvilla Salutem. Universitati vestre notum fieri volo me concessisse et dedisse et hac mea carta confirmasse deo et ecclesie sancte Marie de Leestun' et canonicis ibidem servientibus, ecclesiam sancte Marie de Middeltun' que est de feodo meo libere et quiete et integre cum omnibus pertinentiis suis in puram et perpetuam elemosinam pro salute anime mee et anime Comitisse Gundrede uxoris mee et patris mei et matris mee et uxoris mee Christiane et pro salute anime Hervei fratris mei et omnium parentum meorum et amicorum. Huius mee concessionis et donationis sunt testes, Thoma Archidiacono, Magistro Reinero.

Date: approximate foundation of Leiston abbey; the donor left for the crusade and does not reappear in England.
Printed: Monasticon, vi(ii).881, no. 6.
Notes: see Introduction, 8. Archdeacon Thomas (of Norwich) had been succeeded by 1200 (*Fasti* ii. 64).

40. Roger Bigot, Earl of Norfolk, has confirmed the gift of Middleton church. c 1190–1221.

Rubric: Confirmatio Rogeri Comitis de ecclesia de Middeltun'.
Right margin: Carta Rogeri Comitis.

Omnibus Christi fidelibus ad quos presens scriptum pervenerit Rogerus Bigot Comes Norfolch' Salutem. Noverit universitas vestra me pro salute anime mee et Comitis Hugonis patris mei et Comitisse Juliane matris mee, et Comitisse Ide uxoris mee, et omnium antecessorum et successorum meorum concessisse deo */fo 44v* et ecclesie beate Marie de Leestun' et canonicis ibidem deo servientibus ecclesiam beate Marie de Middelton' que pertinet ad feodum meum quod Robertus de Crec tenet de me in eadem villa habendam et tenendam in puram et perpetuam elemosinam cum omnibus ad eam pertinentibus, sicut carta eiusdem Roberti ecclesie eiusdem patroni quam eis inde fecit, testatur. Et ut hec mea concessio perpetue firmitatis robur optineat, eam presenti scripto et sigilli mei appositione confirmavi in perpetuum valituram. Testibus, Willelmo de Fraxino, Henrico et Galfrido de Grimilies.

Date: Robert de Crek may have succeeded to Roger de Glanville's fee in 1190, or possibly not until a fine with Robert de Glanville (Dodwell, *Fines* ii. no. 422) in 1203. See Farrer, iii. 428–31; Robert de Crek was dead in 1232 (*Exc e R Fin* i. 223). Roger Bigod, second earl, d. 1221.
Printed: Monasticon, vi(ii).881–2, no. 7.

41. Robert de Crek has confirmed the gift of Middleton church. c 1190–1221.

Rubric: Confirmatio Roberti de Crek de ecclesia de Middeltun.
Left margin: Carta Roberti de Crek.

Universis sancte matris ecclesie filiis ad quos presens scriptum pervenerit, Robertus de Crec Salutem in domino. Noverit universitas vestra me pro salute anime mee et Agnetis uxoris mee et antecessorum nostrorum concessisse deo et ecclesie beate Marie de Leestun' et canonicis ibidem deo servientibus, ecclesiam sancte Marie de Middeltun' cum omnibus pertinentiis suis in puram et perpetuam elemosinam sicut carta Rogeri de Glanvill quam eis fecit de donatione eiusdem ecclesie testatur. Et ut hec */fo 45r* mea concessio perpetuam habeat firmitatem, presenti scripto et sigilli mei appositione eam confirmavi. Test(e) Comite Rogero.

Date: as no. 40.

42. William son of Alan has quitclaimed two men and their families. Before 1221.

Rubric: Carta Willelmi filii Alani.
Right margin: Carta Willelmi filii Alani.

Sciant presentes et futuri quod ego Willelmus filius Alani quietum clamavi Abbati et conventui de Leestun', Alexandrum et Thomam filios Elene uxoris Rogeri Wuluardi cum tota sequela eorum tanquam nativos natos de nativa non desponsata predicti Abbatis et conventus de Leestun'. Et ut hec concessio et quietantia stabilis et firma in perpetuum maneat, eam sigilli mei appositione roboravi, quia nihil iuris in predictis Alexandro et Thoma habui. Hiis testibus, Hamfrido de Criketot.

Date: Hemfrid d. 1221. The beginnings of his and William's active lives are not precisely datable.
See Introduction, 28.

43. William de Valeines has granted the church of Culpho. Before 1208.

Rubric: Carta Willelmi de Valeines de ecclesia de Culfou.
Right margin: Carta Willelmi de Valeines.

Sciant presentes et futuri quod ego Willelmus de Valeines dedi et concessi et hac presenti carta mea confirmavi deo et ecclesie sancte Marie de insula de Leestun' et canonicis ordinis Premonstratensis ibidem deo servientibus pro salute anime mee et omnium antecessorum meorum et successorum meorum */fo 45v* ecclesiam de Culfou cum omnibus pertinentiis, in puram et perpetuam elemosinam, et ut ista donatio firma et rata habeatur, eam sigilli mei appositione roboravi. Hiis testibus, Willelmo capellano.

Date: William d. 1208.
Printed: Monasticon, vi(ii).882, no. 8.
See Introduction, 19.

44. Osbert de Wachesham has confirmed the gift of Culpho church. Before 1209.

Rubric: Confirmatio Osberti de Wachesham de ecclesia de Culpho.[1]

Sciant presentes et futuri quod ego Osbertus[2] de Wachesham concessi et presenti carta[3] confirmavi deo et ecclesie sancte Marie de insula de Leeston'[4] et canonicis ordinis Premonstratensis ibidem deo servientibus donationem et concessionem quam Willelmus de Valeines illis fecit videlicet ecclesiam sancti

Botulfi de Culfo in puram et perpetuam elemosinam, pro salute anime mee et omnium antecessorum meorum et successorum meorum, et ut hec concessio et confirmatio rata et inconcussa habeatur in perpetuum sigilli mei appositione roboravi. Hiis testibus,[5] Johanne et Roberto capellanis, Theobaldo de Valeynes, Hamone de Valeines, Rannulfo de Onhus, Matheo de Valeines et ceteris.

[1] A, Culfou   [2] B, Osseb'
[3] A adds mea   [4] A, Leestun'
[5] A omits witness-list.

Date: Theobald II de Valeines d. 1209. William d. 1208, but this charter need not necessarily date from after his death.
Notes: Occurs twice in the MS, A: fo 45v, B: fo 69v.

45. Osbert de Wachesham has granted 3s rent in Bruisyard. Before 1235.

Rubric: Carta Osberti de Wachesham.
Left margin: Item carta eiusdem Osberti.

Sciant tam presentes quam futuri quod ego Osbertus de Wachesham concessu uxoris mee Ysabel dedi et concessi et presenti carta confirmavi deo et ecclesie beate Marie de Leestun' tres solidos sterlingorum in villa Burgeswerd */fo 46r* in liberam puram et perpetuam elemosinam, quos videlicet solidos Abbas vel canonici de Leestun' recipient singulis annis ab homine meo Ricardo Coterel et ab heredibus eius in perpetuum ad tres terminos per annum, scilicet xii d. ad festum sancti Michaelis, et xii d. ad Purificationem sancte Marie, et xii d. ad Pentecosten. Hanc autem donationem feci predictis canonicis pro anima patris mei, et pro anima Willelmi de Valeines, et pro animabus omnium predecessorum meorum et successorum meorum. Testibus, Hamone de Valeines.

Date: Osbert d. 1235. William de Valeines d. 1208, and this may date from after then.

46. Hemfrid de Criketot has granted 20 acres of his demesne in Kelsale. Before 1221.

Rubric: Carta Hamfridi de Criketot de xx. acris terre.
Right margin: Carta Hamfridi de Criketot.

Omnibus sancte matris ecclesie filiis Hamfridus de Criketot, Salutem in domino. Ad omnium volo pervenire notitiam me dedisse et concessisse et hac presenti carta confirmasse deo et ecclesie sancte Marie de Leestun', et canonicis ordinis Premonstratensis ibidem deo servientibus viginti acras terre de dominico meo de Fordleha(n)g que iacent apud villam de Keleshale concessu Marie uxoris mee, et Willelmi heredis mei in puram et perpetuam elemosinam pro salute */fo 46v* anime mee et pro salute uxoris mee et pro animabus patris et matris mee et omnium antecessorum et successorum meorum. Quare volo et devote exopto ut predicti canonici habeant et teneant prenominatam terram libere et quiete et honorifice absque omni consuetudine et exactione seculari. Et ut hec donatio firma et stabilis in perpetuum habeatur, eam sigilli mei appositione munire curavi. Hiis testibus, Waltero Malet.

Date: Hemfrid d. 1221.

47. William son of Theobald has quitclaimed his rights in the soke of Leiston, and land and rent, to the abbey; two of his men shall help the abbot with the 'common aids' of the vill. In return, his knight's fee within the soke is confirmed to him, together with some land and men, except for 8 acres. 1193–1205.

Rubric: Carta Willelmi filii Theobaldi.
Left margin: Carta Willelmi filii Theobaldi.

Willelmus filius Theobaldi omnibus amicis suis et hominibus presentibus et futuris Salutem. Sciatis me de propria voluntate mea quietum clamasse domino meo Roberto Abbati de Leestun' et conventui eiusdem loci quicquid iuris habui vel habere debui adquisiti in socha de Leestun' per antecessores meos, vel aliquo alio modo; et Walterum prepositum et omnes pueros suos, et vi. acras terre in Torresdale, et xiiii. denariatos redditus de Roberto Mercatore quos predictus Theobaldus pater meus dedit ecclesie sancte Marie de Leestun' in perpetuam elemo/*fo 47r*sinam. Concessi etiam quod Haldanus Palmarus et Rogerus filius Ulf homines mei adiuvabunt dominum meum Abbatem ad communia auxilia ville. Pro hac concessione et confirmatione confirmaverunt mihi dominus Abbas et universalis conventus carta sua omnes alias terras, et omnes alios redditus et omnia alia tenementa et omnes alios homines cum tota sequela sua quos pater meus Theobaldus tenuit in socha de Leestun' die qua fuit vivus et mortuus, vel quando unquam illa melius tenuit. Confirmaverunt etiam mihi dominus meus Abbas et omnis conventus vi. acras terre et unam gravam in Tidbertunia et in Fordleia omnes pueros Suatman cum omnibus terris [1] suis, et cum omnibus redditibus suis et omnibus tenementis suis, et cum omni sequela quos mihi reddiderunt sicut ius meum quod appendit ad militiam meam in socha de Leestun', preter viii. acras terre quas Willelmus frater Roberti tenet de domino meo Abbate et de conventu in Fordleia. Et ego Willelmus domino meo Roberto Abbati et conventui firmiter promisi, et tactis sacrosanctis euuangeliis iuravi, quod de illo /*fo 47v* die et deinceps quo fuit carta ista facta super vendicatione si quam habui vel habere debui in socha de Leestun' nullam moverem questionem vel calumpniam. Hiis testibus, Huberto Cantuariensi Archiepiscopo.

[1] illegible erasure overwritten

Date: Archbishop Hubert.
See Introduction, 25.

48. Exchange between the Abbey and Theobald son of William. Before 1205.

Rubric: Compositio inter Robertum Abbatem et Theobaldum filium Willelmi.
Left margin: Cirographum Theobaldi de Leeston.

Sciant omnes ad quorum notitiam hoc scriptum pervenerit quod hec est compositio inter Robertum Abbatem de Insula Sancte Marie de Leestun' et conventum eiusdem loci et Theobaldum filium Willelmi, scilicet prefatus Abbas concessit Theobaldo filio Willelmi terram quandam quam Gudiva uxor Ulf tenuit de Abbate, et Theobaldus in excambium dedit Abbati totam terram suam de Chilteril. Hiis testibus, Arnaldo filio Petri.[1]

[1] illegible erasure

Date: Theobald is presumably the father of the William of no. 47, who must have succeeded by 1205. But in all probability this dates from the early years of the foundation.

49. Gerard 'Parker' of Dennington grants the mill-site of 'Holyoak'. Before 1225.

Rubric: Carta Girardi parcarii de situ molendini qui dicitur Holyoc.
Left margin: Carta Girardi parcarii.

Sciant tam presentes quam futuri quod ego Girardus parcarius de Dinheue-tun' dedi et concessi et presenti carta confirmavi deo et ecclesie sancte Marie de Leestun' et canonicis ibidem deo servientibus totum situm molendini qui dicitur */fo 48r* Holyoc in liberam puram et perpetuam elemosinam, quem Galfridus persona de Dinheuetun' quandoque tenuit de me. Hunc vero predictum situm eis warantizabo contra omnes homines. Hanc donationem feci predictis canonicis pro salute anime mee et pro salute animarum omnium antecessorum et successorum meorum. Hiis testibus, Galfrido Archidiacono.

Date: Archdeacon Geoffrey de Burgh of Norwich was made Bishop of Ely in 1225; Archdeacon Geoffrey de Bocland of Norfolk probably died in office in 1225; Geoffrey Archdeacon of Suffolk had been superseded by 1214 (Dennington is in his archdeaconry).
Marginal note, fo 47v:
C. de transactionibus L'. Si quis maior triginta s. annorum adversus pacta vel transactiones quamque[1] invocato omnipotentis nomine nullo cogente imperite[1] sacramenta religionis solidivit minend'[1] esse putaverit vel interpellando iudices vel supplicando potentioribus vel promisso non adimplendo non solum infamia notatur verum etiam actione privatur, et pena restitutur q' peccatis probatur inserta et re careat de qua lis est et emolumento quo eo peccato consecuturus esset, privetur. Hiis omnibus ad eum devoluend' q' iura peccati[1] intemerata servavit.

[1] reading uncertain

88

50. Oliver de Vaux has granted land in Chediston. Before 1235.

Rubric: Carta Oliveri de Vaus.
Right margin: Carta Oliveri de Vallibus.

Omnibus Christi fidelibus ad quorum audientiam presens carta pervenerit, Oliverus de Vaus Salutem in domino. Ad omnium vestrum volo pervenire notitiam me dedisse et presenti carta confirmasse deo et ecclesie beate Marie de Leestun', et canonicis ibidem deo servientibus unam dimidiam acram terre que appellatur Hegrone, et undecim acras terre et unam rodam que iacent in Derhage, et tres rodas que iacent ex orientali parte domus Radulfi Wine quas Driu de Chedestan tenuit de me reddendo annuatim duodecim denarios mihi pro omni servitio. Hanc donationem feci predictis canonicis in puram et perpetuam elemosinam pro salute anime mee et pro salute anime uxoris mee Olive /fo 48v et pro animabus antecessorum et successorum nostrorum; et ut hec donatio tam a me quam ab heredibus meis firma et stabilis in perpetuum habeatur, eam sigilli mei appositione roboravi. Hiis testibus, Henrico de Grimill'.

Date: no. 88 assumes the Abbey's possession of this land, and dates before c 1235. (It also locates the land in Chediston).
See no. 88 below.
Henry de Grimilies first appears in 1199 (Palgrave, ii. 136), and occurs fairly frequently until 1229 (*CRR* xiii. no. 1737). A charter to Rumburgh by a man of this name (PRO Ancient Deed A 7622) looks too old to be this Henry: possibly it is of an ancestor of his.

51. Hemfrid de Criketot has granted a woman and her children to the Abbey for 2 marks. Before 1209 (possibly 1206).

Rubric: Carta Henfridi de Criketot.
Left margin: Carta Hemfridi de Criketot.

Notum sit omnibus sancte matris ecclesie filiis quod ego Heinfridus de Criketot concessi Roberto Abbati de Leestun' humagium Thedild filie Nigelli et liberorum eius. Pro qua concessione predictus Abbas dedit mihi duas marcas. Hiis testibus, Roberto Jurdi.

Date: Abbot Robert.

52. William son of Alan has granted 2 acres of his demesne next to 'Newalesclade'. Early thirteenth century.

Rubric: Carta Willelmi filii Alani.
Left margin: Carta Willelmi filii Alani.

Omnibus sancte matris ecclesie filiis ad quos presens scriptum pervenerit, Willelmus filius Alani Salutem. Noverit universitas vestra me dedisse et hac presenti carta mea confirmasse deo et ecclesie beate Marie de Leestun' et canonicis ordinis Premonstratensis ibidem deo servientibus duas acras terre de dominico meo que iacent iuxta Newalesclade in puram et liberam et perpetuam elemosinam, pro salute anime mee et uxoris mee et pro animabus omnium liberorum /fo 49r meorum et pro animabus patris et matris mee et omnium predecessorum meorum. Et ut concessio ista firma sit et stabilis[1] in perpetuum, sigilli mei appositione eam munire curavi. Hiis testibus, Willelmo filio Theobaldi,[2] Thoma fratre eius, Roberto filio Alani, Mattheo de Kelesh(ale), et ceteris.

[1] A omits et stabilis
[2] A ends here

Date: Approximate known lifetime of donor is c 1189–1223, and it is unlikely to be very much longer.
Notes: Occurs twice in MS, A: ff 48v–49r, B: fo 71v.

53. Saer de Biskele has granted two men, their tenements and families. Before c 1223.

fo 49r   Rubric: Cartha Seaeri de Biskele.

Sciant presentes et futuri quod ego Seaerius de Biskele filius Galfridi dedi et concessi et presenti carta confirmavi deo et ecclesie beate Marie de Leestun' et canonicis ordinis Premonstratensis ibidem deo servientibus totum tenementum quod Walterus Garleach tenuit de me vel de matre mea Alpasia; et ipsum Walterum Garleach cum tota sequela sua, et Willelmum King cum tota sequela sua, et totum tenementum ipsius Willelmi quod de me vel de matre mea Alpasia tenuit, in liberam puram et perpetuam elemosinam pro salute anime mee, et Ade uxoris mee et pro animabus omnium antecessorum et successorum meorum. Hanc donationem et concessionem et confirmationem predictis canonicis ego et heredes mei warantizabimus in perpetuum, nec de cetero ego vel heredes mei possumus aliquid servitii vel consuetudinis, vel exactionis exigere a predictis hominibus vel eorum tenementis. Ut autem /fo 49v hec donatio et concessio et confirmatio firma et stabilis in perpetuum permaneat eam sigilli mei appositione roborare curavi. Hiis testibus, Rogero de Braham.

Date: Roger de Braham (see no. 13, notes).

54. Saer de Biskele has granted land in Leiston, plus the tenements which the Abbey's men held of him in Leiston. Before c 1223.

Rubric: Carta Seari de Biskele.

Sciant tam presentes quam futuri quod Searius de Biskele filius Galfridi dedi et concessi et presenti carta confirmavi deo et ecclesie beate Marie de Leestun' et canonicis ibidem deo servientibus duas acras terre, cum duobus curtilagiis iuxta mariscum ubi abbatia predictorum canonicorum sita est; et

90

omnes terras, et omnia tenementa quas homines predictorum canonicorum tenuerunt de me vel de matre[1] Alpasia in liberam, puram et perpetuam elemosinam pro salute anime mee et uxoris mee Ade et pro animabus patris mei et matris mee et omnium antecessorum et successorum meorum. Hec sunt nomina hominum eorum qui de me et de matre mea tenuerunt: Petrus Soikors, Adam Mercator, Rogerus filius Ordmari, Radulfus Mengi, Willelmus Ruffus, Rogerus filius Bernardi, Willelmus Cate, Stephanus Holming. Ut autem hec donatio /fo 50r et concessio predictis canonicis firma et stabilis in perpetuum permaneat eam sigilli mei appositione roboravi. Hiis testibus, Rogero de Braham.

[1] mea omitted?

Date: as no. 53.

55. Saer de Biskele has granted two woods in Theberton, and a man and his family. Before c 1223.

Rubric: Carta Seaeri de Biskele.

Sciant presentes et futuri quod ego Saerius de Biskele filius Galfridi dedi et concessi et presenti carta confirmavi deo et ecclesie beate Marie de Leestun' et canonicis ordinis Premonstratensis ibidem deo servientibus duos boscellos meos quos habui in parrochia de Theburtun', quorum unus vocatur Uphalheg et alius Wimundesheg iacentes iuxta boscum Abbatis et canonicorum de Leestun' qui vocatur Chiltre et Rogerum Caretarium cum tota sequela sua in liberam, puram et perpetuam elemosinam pro salute anime mee et Ade uxoris mee, et pro animabus omnium antecessorum meorum et successorum. Hanc donationem et concessionem et confirmationem ego et heredes mei predictis canonicis in perpetuum warantizabimus. Ut autem hec donatio et concessio et confirmatio /fo 50v stabilis in perpetuum permaneat, eam sigilli mei appositione roborare curavi. Hiis testibus, Rogero de Braham.

Date: as no. 53.

56. Jocelin de Hispania has granted 2s annual rent in Glevering. Early thirteenth century.

Rubric: Carta Gocelini de Hispania.
Trace of left margin note.

Omnibus sancte matris ecclesie filiis ad quos presens scriptum pervenerit, Goscelinus de Hispania Salutem. Noverit universitas vestra me dedisse et concessisse et presenti carta confirmasse deo et ecclesie sancte Marie de Leestun' et canonicis ordinis Premonstratensis ibidem deo servientibus annuum redditum duorum solidorum de tenemento quod Johannes de la Batalie tenet de me in Gleveringe ad luminaria ecclesie in liberam puram et perpetuam elemosinam, quos duos solidos predictus Johannes et heredes eius annuatim solvent predicte ecclesie in perpetuum ad duos terminos, scilicet ad festum sancti Michaelis xii. denarios, et ad Pentecosten xii. denarios. Hanc autem donationem feci deo et predictis canonicis pro salute anime mee, et pro animabus antecessorum et successorum meorum. Ut autem hec donatio mea in perpetuum rata sit et stabilis eam presenti scripto et sigilli mei appositione roboravi. Hiis testibus.

Date: the donor occurs in 1205 and 1210.

57. Saer de Biskele has quitclaimed a man and his family. Before 1223.

fo 51r Rubric: Carta Saeri de Biskele.
Right margin: Item de Saerio.

Sciant tam presentes quam futuri quod ego Saerius de Biskele filius Galfridi quietum clamavi Abbati et conventui de Leestun' Warinum filium Willelmi Crispini et Basilie Claude cum tota sequela eiusdem Warini in puram et perpetuam elemosinam. Ut autem hec donatio firma sit et stabilis, sigilli mei appositione roboravi. Hiis testibus, Rogero de Braham.

Date: as no. 53.

58. Robert de Crek has given William son of Adric, his family and tenement, except two acres and one rood which William gave back to Robert. Before 1221.

Rubric: Carta Roberti de Crek de quodam homine cum sequela sua et terra.[1]

Omnibus ad quos presens carta pervenerit, Robertus de Crek[2] Salutem. Sciatis me dedisse et concessisse et presenti carta confirmasse deo et ecclesie beate Marie de Leestun' et canonicis ibidem deo servientibus, Willelmum filium Edrici[3] cum tota sequela sua et cum toto tenemento suo quod tenuit de Rogero de Glamvill', exceptis duabus acris et una roda terre quas reddidit domino suo Roberto de Crek[4] et quietas clamavit. Hanc donationem et concessionem feci predictis canonicis in liberam[5] puram et perpetuam elemosinam, pro anima Agnetis uxoris mee, et pro salute antecessorum et successorum meorum. Hanc donationem et concessionem ego et heredes mei warantizabimus predictis canonicis in perpetuum. Ut autem hec donatio et concessio firma et stabilis sit,[6] eam sigilli mei appositione roboravi. Hiis testibus, Hemfrido de Criketot,[7] Rogero de Kethneto, Bartholomeo de Glamvill', Johanne filio eius, Willelmo filio Alani, Ric' de Sybetun', Galfrido[8] senescallo.

[1] A, Carta Roberti de Crek   [2] A, Crec
[3] A, Adric   [4] A, Creck
[5] A omits liberam   [6] A, sit et stabilis
[7] A ends here   [8] MS Garfr'

Date: Hemfrid de Criketot, d. 1221.
Note: occurs twice in MS, A: fo 51r–v, B: fo 58r.

59. Roger de Cheney has granted his land and marshes, in an unidentified village. Before 1225.

fo 51v Rubric: Carta Rogeri de Kedney.
Left margin: Carta Rogeri de Cheney.

Sciant ,tam presentes quam futuri quod ego Rogerus de Cheney dedi et concessi et presenti carta confirmavi deo et ecclesie sancte Marie de Leestun' et canonicis ibidem deo servientibus terram que dicitur Sueft croft hegd et unum mariscum ad domum Roberti Gobert, et alium mariscum qui dicitur Hemmingesfen, quos Robertus le Brun aliquando tenuit de me. Hos mariscos et predictam terram dedi predictis canonicis in puram et perpetuam elemosinam, libere et honorifice in perpetuum possidendum. Hiis testibus, G(alfrido) Archidiacono.

Date: 'Archdeacon Geoffrey', as no. 49.

60. John son of Robert of Dunwich has granted half an acre of his demesne in Middleton. Early thirteenth century.

Rubric: Carta Johannis filii Roberti de Dunewico.
Left margin: Carta Johannis filii Roberti.

Omnibus sancte matris ecclesie filiis ad quos presens scriptum pervenerit Johannes filius Roberti de Donewico Salutem in domino. Ad omnium vestrum volo pervenire notitiam me dedisse et concessisse et hac carta confirmasse deo et ecclesie beate Marie */fo 52r* de Leestun' et canonicis ordinis Premonstratensis ibidem deo servientibus dimidiam acram prati de dominico meo que iacet in villa de Middeltun' quam Hunteman aliquotiens tenuit in puram et perpetuam elemosinam, pro anima Ernaldi filii Edwardi et pro salute animarum patrum et matrum nostrarum et pro animabus omnium antecessorum et successorum nostrorum. Quare volo et devote exopto ut predicti canonici habeant et teneant prenominatam dimidiam acram prati libere et quiete absque omni consuetudine et exactione seculari. Et ut hec donatio firma in perpetuum habeatur, eam sigilli mei appositione roboravi. Hiis testibus, Henrico de Grimill'.

Date: see Introduction, 14, for donor, and no. 50, notes, for witness.

61. Master Richer has granted all his holding of William de Falesham in Dunwich. Before 1214.

Rubric: Carta Magistri Richeri de redditu in Donewic'.

Sciant tam presentes quam[1] futuri quod ego Magister Richerius filius Alexandri dedi et concessi et hac presenti carta confirmavi deo et ecclesie sancte Marie de Leeston'[2] et canonicis ibidem deo servientibus totum tenementum quod tenui de domino meo Willelmo de Falesham in Donewico, in liberam et[3] puram et perpetuam elemosinam, ecclesie sancte Marie de Leeston' salvo servitio prenominati Willelmi de Falesham, videlicet xvi. denariis per annum ad festum sancti Michaelis pro omni servitio. Hanc donationem et concessionem feci prenominate ecclesie et canonicis eiusdem loci[4] pro anima mea et pro animabus patris et matris mee et omnium antecessorum et successorum meorum. Hiis testibus, Abbate de Sibetona,[5] Abbate de Langeleia, Galfrido Archidiacono de Gippewico, Priore de Butteleia, Priore de Snapes, Willelmo Decano de Dunewico, Eustachio filio Walteri, Johanne filio Ulphi, Rogero de Braham', Willelmo filio Theobaldi, Roberto filio Ricardi, Haldano filio Lefrici, Waltero filio Haldani, Willelmo filio Petri, Alexandro filio Walteri, Nicholao filio Roberti, Waltero filio Eustachii et plurimis aliis.

[1] A et	[2] A, Leestun'
[3] A omits et	[4] A, feci after loci
[5] A ends here	

Date: Geoffrey's successor as Archdeacon of Ipswich first apears in 1214.
Notes: Occurs twice in the MS, A: fo 52r–v, B: ff 60v–61r.

62. William de Falesham has confirmed no. 61. Before 1214.

Rubric: Confirmatio Willelmi de Falsham de dicto redditu.

Sciant tam presentes quam futuri quod ego Willelmus de Falesham concessi et hac presenti carta confirmavi concessu uxoris mee Aliz et heredis mei Willelmi donationem quam Magister Richerius filius Alexandri fecit deo et ecclesie sancte Marie de Leestona[1] et canonicis ordinis Premonstratensis ibidem deo servientibus, videlicet totum tenementum quod idem Richerius tenuit de me in villa Dunewici,[2] salvo servitio meo, scilicet xvi. denarios per annum pro omni servitio, sicut carta quam prenominati canonici habent de predicto Richerio testatur. Hiis testibus, Abbate de Sibetona,[3] Abbate de Langeleia, Galfrido Archidiacono Gippuici, Priore de Butteleia, Priore de Snapes, Willelmo Decano de Dunewico, Eustachio filio Walteri, Johanne filio Ulphi, Rogero de Braham, Willelmo filio Theobaldi, Roberto filio Ricardi, Haldano filio Leverici, Waltero filio Haldani, Willelmo filio Petri, Alexandro filio Walteri, Nicholao filio Roberti, Waltero filio Eustachii et multis aliis.

[1] A, Leestun'	[2] A, Donewici
[3] A ends here	

Date: as no. 61.
Notes: Occurs twice in the MS, A: fo 52v, B: fo 61r.

63. Rannulf de Onehouse has granted a mill with appurtenant rights. Before 1212.

fo 52v   Rubric: Carta Rannulfi de Onhus.
Traces of left margin note.

Sciant tam presentes quam futuri quod ego Rannulfus de Onhus concessu uxoris mee Petronille dedi et concessi et presenti /*fo 53r* carta confirmavi deo et ecclesie sancte Marie de Leeston' et canonicis ibidem deo servientibus molendinum meum de Lag Wade cum toto ripario meo et stagno, et cum Smithespol et cum alneto eidem ripario adiacenti, et cum terris versus orientem et occidentem prefato ripario adiacentibus, et cum ceteris aisiamentis et communibus et omnibus consuetudinibus ad idem molendinum pertinentibus in liberam, puram et perpetuam elemosinam, exceptis duabus marcis argenti quas Normannus de Pesehale dedit mihi de eodem molendino cum filia sua in maritagium, quas ego Rannulfus de Onhus et heredes mei recipiemus singulis annis de abbatia de Leestun'. Et ego Rannulfus et heredes mei warantizabimus sepedictum molendinum cum omnibus pertinentiis prenominatis canonicis de Leestun' contra omnes homines et feminas qui vivere et mori poterunt, et si ita contigerit quod ego et heredes mei predictum molendinum sepedictis canonicis warantizare non poterimus dabimus eis, quadraginta marcas sterlingorum ad opus ecclesie sancte Marie de Leeston pro animabus nostris et pro animabus omnium antecessorum nostrorum et successorum. Test' domino Abbate Laurentio de Sibeton.

See no. 64.

64. Norman de Peasenhall has granted the same mill as in no. 63. Before 1212.

fo 53v   Rubric: Carta Normanni de Pesehale.

Sciant presentes et futuri quod ego Normannus de Pesehale concessu heredis mei Radulfi dedi et concessi et presenti carta confirmavi deo et ecclesie sancte Marie de Leestun' et canonicis ibidem deo servientibus totum molendinum meum de Langwade cum toto ripario meo et stagno, et cum Smithespol et cum alneto eidem ripario adiacenti et cum terris versus orientem et occidentem prefato ripario adiacentibus et cum ceteris aisiamentis et communibus et omnibus consuetudinibus ad idem molendinum pertinentibus, in liberam, puram et perpetuam elemosinam exceptis duabus marcis argenti quas dedi Rannulfo de Onhus cum filia mea in maritagium de eodem molendino, quas ipse Rannulfus de Onhus' et heredes sui recipient singulis annis[1] de abbatia de Leestun'. Et ego Normannus et heredes mei warantizabimus iamdictum molendinum cum omnibus pertinentiis predictis canonicis de Leeston contra omnes homines et feminas qui vivere et mori possunt. Et si ita contigerit quod predictum molendinum ego et heredes mei prenominatis canonicis warantizare non poterimus, /*fo 54r* dabimus eis quadraginta marcas argenti ad opus ecclesie sancte Marie de Leestun' pro animabus nostris et animabus omnium antecessorum et successorum nostrorum. Testibus domino Laurentio Abbate de Sibetun', Galfrido Archidiacono Suff' et multis aliis.

[1] annis omitted

Date: Alexander, abbot of Sibton, Laurence's successor, is found in 1212 (Knowles, Brooke & London, 142).
Note: in Easter term 1221 the abbot of Leiston vouched Rannulf de Anhus to warranty, since he was being sued by William Russell who claimed the mill of Langwade against him; Rannulf duly came and vouched it to him (*CRR* x. 46; cf 220). In Hilary 1223 William Russell was seeking the mill against Rannulf de Anhus, who vouched Petronilla to warrant, having himself vouched it to the abbot. Rannulf and Petronilla then vouched Norman de Peasenhall to warrant (*CRR* xi. nos. 39, 996). In 1234 Petronilla began to sue the abbot for the mill, claiming it as her *maritagium*, the abbot having entry only through her husband: the mill was in the king's hands. After that, the case disappears from view (*CRR* xv. no. 939). It transpires that the mill is in Farnham.

65. William son of Theobald has granted one acre of pasture. Before 1224.

Rubric: Carta Willelmi filii Theobaldi de pastura de Wagefen.

Sciant presentes et futuri quod ego[1] Willelmus filius Theobaldi de Leestun'[2] dedi et concessi et presenti carta confirmavi deo et ecclesie beate Marie de Leeston' et canonicis ordinis Premonstratensis ibidem deo servientibus unam acram pasture que iacet inter fontem de Wagefen et aliam pasturam quam prenominati canonici de me habent, in puram et perpetuam elemosinam, libere et honorifice in perpetuum possidendam, et ut hec donatio et concessio et confirmatio firma sit et stabilis in perpetuum eam sigilli mei appositione roboravi. Hiis testibus, Willelmo filio Alani, Saero de Biskele,[3] Huberto Cordebof, Johanne filio eius,[4] Willelmo Fukelin, Dionisio cementario, Willelmo de Wiveligham et multis aliis.

[1] B omits ego
[3] A ends here
[2] A, C, Leeston'
[4] C ends here

Date: Saer de Biskele.
Notes: Occurs three times in the MS, A: fo 54r, B: fo 60r, C: ff 71v–72r.

66. Saer de Biskele has granted six acres of his demesne. Before 1224.

fo 54v Sciant presentes et futuri quod ego Saerus de Biskele filius Galfridi dedi et concessi et presenti carta confirmavi deo et ecclesie beate Marie de Leeston' et canonicis ordinis Premonstratensis ibidem deo servientibus, sex acras terre de dominico meo, iacentes iuxta domum Hervei Koket tenendas de me et de heredibus meis libere et quiete, pacifice et honorifice per servitium sex denariorum mihi et heredibus meis singulis annis solvendorum in festo sancti Michaelis pro omnibus servitiis et consuetudinibus et demandis. Pro hac autem donatione et concessione et confirmatione dederunt mihi predicti canonici unam marcam argenti in gersumam et ego et heredes mei warantizabimus predictam terram prenominatis canonicis contra omnes homines in perpetuum. Ut autem hec donatio et concessio et confirmatio firma sit et stabilis in perpetuum, eam sigilli mei appositione roboravi. Hiis testibus, Henrico de Grimill'.

Date: Saer de Biskele.

67. Saer de Biskele has granted land near 'Kaldham', in Theberton, plus tenant land, for two gold pieces. Before 1222.

Rubric: Carta Saeri de Biskelle.

Sciant presentes et futuri quod ego Saerus de Biskele filius Galfridi dedi et concessi et presenti carta confirmavi deo et ecclesie beate Marie de Leeston' et canonicis ordinis Premonstratensis ibidem deo servientibus totam terram meam que iacet inter domum meam /fo 55r de Kaldham et domum Walteri de Kaldham, ubi estimantur tres acre vel plus, et duas acras terre quas Johannes parmentarius tenuit de me et dimidiam acram terre quam Petrus Soikors tenuit de me, et totam terram quam Bernardus Helle tenuit de me, et ipsum Bernardum et uxorem eius cum tota sequela sua tenendas de me et de heredibus meis libere et quiete, pacifice et honorifice, per servitium unius libre cimini, mihi et heredibus meis singulis annis in festo sancti Michaelis solvende, pro omnibus servitiis et consuetudinibus et demandis. Pro hac autem donatione et concessione et confirmatione dederunt mihi predicti canonici duos aureos in gersumam. Ut autem hec donatio et concessio et confirmatio firma sit et stabilis in perpetuum, eam sigilli mei appositione roboravi. Hiis testibus, Heinfrido de Criketot, Willelmo filio eius, Adam de Bedigfeld.

Date: Hemfrid de Criketot.
Notes: Adam de Bedingfeld, an early member of a family famous in Norfolk and Suffolk, was a tenant of the honor of Tickhill in Notts. and Derby as well as at Bedingfield (*PR 9 Richard I* 154; *2 John* 19). From litigation in 1230 the following tree can be reconstructed:

Adam(2) = Gundrada de Mustiers = (1)Stephen Mallovel

Adam   daughter = Robert le Enveyse

Adam the father (d. 1226–30) gave land to his son 'quadam die post prandium' in the presence of the lord of the fee, who took young Adam's homage 'pro una supertunica' and 1*d* 'de arreragio servitii' owed by the father; but Adam then gave the land with his daughter to Robert le Enveyse (*CRR* xiv. no. 457; Palgrave i. 47).

68. Roger, Prior of Eye, has confirmed the arrangements concerning the tithes of Leiston, as in nos. 31, 32 and 33. c 1210–19.

Rubric: Confirmatio Rogeri Prioris de Eya de decimis de dominico de Leeston'.

Omnibus sancte matris ecclesie filiis, Rogerus Prior de Eya et eiusdem loci conventus Salutem in domino. Noverit universitas vestra nos inspexisse cartas pie recordationis Priorum de Butteleia decessorum, videlicet Gileberti et Willelmi, necnon et Roberti Prioris presentis de Butteleia et eiusdem loci conventus, quibus /*fo 55v* communi assensu et intuitu pietatis concedunt et resignant ac confirmant dilectis fratribus nostris in Christo Philippo Abbati de Leeston' et eiusdem loci conventui, inter alia in eisdem cartis expressa, totum ius illud quod vendicabant in decimis de dominico aule de Leeston' provenientibus. Nos igitur eandem concessionem et resignationem ac confirmationem gratam et ratam habentes, quia prenominate decime ad nos pertinent sicud et iamdicte carte testantur, de communi consensu et intuitu divine pietatis concedimus et presenti carta confirmamus dictis Abbati et conventui de Leeston' prefatas decimas de dominico aule de Leeston' pacifice in perpetuum habendas salvis nobis decem solidis singulis annis in perpetuum inde percipiendis, per manum Prioris de Butteleia, sicud sepedicte carte testantur Priorum et conventus de Butteleia. Ut autem hec concessio et confirmatio firma sit et stabilis in perpetuum, presentem cartam sigilli nostri appositione roboravimus. Hiis testibus, domino S. Abbate de Sibeton, Magistro Roberto Archidiacono Suff'.

See Introduction, 38–9.

69. Letter from Edward III to the pope requesting approval of the removal of Leiston abbey, in the diocese of Norwich, under the patronage of Robert of Ufford, earl of Suffolk, which had already been begun with the patron's permission and the king's, from the present site near the sea where the canons, their men and livestock are in constant risk of their lives from flooding at each high tide, to a safer site inland. Given under the privy seal, 12 October (no year).

fo 56v In French.
Note: the addressee is almost certainly the pope, as the most appropriate recipient both of the title *très-saint père*, and of the information given.
See Introduction, 7–8.

70. Birchard Burdun has granted a man, his family and tenement, in Middleton. Before 1221.

fo 57r Rubric: Carta Burkardi Burdun de quodam homine cum sequela sua in Middeltune.

Sciant presentes et futuri quod ego Birchardus Burdun dedi et concessi, et presenti carta confirmavi deo et ecclesie beate Marie de Leestun et canonicis ordinis Premonstratensis ibidem deo servientibus in liberam, puram et

98

perpetuam elemosinam, totum tenementum Semanni filii Radulfi quod de me tenuit in parochia sancte Marie de Middeltun' et ipsum Semannum cum tota sequela sua pariter cum una acra que iacet iuxta Brunsiesheg, quam dedi predicto Semanno in escambio pro quadam terra que vocatur Sortelond, ad pratum absque ullo retenemento mihi et heredibus meis. Et ego Burchardus et heredes mei acquietabimus predictum predictis canonicis contra omnes homines in perpetuum. Ut autem hec donatio et concessio et confirmatio firma sit et stabilis in perpetuum, eam sigilli mei appositione roboravi. Hiis testibus, Adam de Bedingefled, Ricardo de Kalstun', Henfrido de Criketoth, Willelmo filio eius, Henrico de Grimil', Willelmo filio Alani, Huberto Cordebof, Willelmo filio Theobaldi, Thoma fratre eius, et multis aliis.

Date: Hemfrid de Criketot.

71. John de Hopton has granted four acres in Hopton. Before 1221.

fo 57r   Rubric: Carta Johannis de Hopetun de iiii. acris terre in Hopetun'.

fo 57v   Sciant presentes et futuri quod ego Johannes filius Alicie filie Rogeri de Hopetun' dedi et concessi et presenti carta confirmavi deo et ecclesie sancte Marie de Leeston' et canonicis ibidem deo servientibus pro salute anime mee et meorum quatuor acras terre in Hopetun' scilicet duas acras in Wrabesheg iacentes, et duas acras que iacent in Benecroft, habendas et tenendas illas in liberam, puram et perpetuam elemosinam, quietas ab omni seculari servitio, consuetudine et exactione, in perpetuum. Et ut hec mea concessio et donatio firma sit et stabilis in perpetuum perseveret, eam presenti scripto et sigilli mei appositione roboravi. Hiis testibus, Henrico de Grimil', Hemfrido de Criketot, Sahero de Biskele, Reginaldo de Pyrhowe, Roberto Jurdi, Willelmo filio Theobaldi, Galfrido Jurdi, Willelmo Fukelin et aliis pluribus.

Date: Hemfrid de Criketot.

72. William, son of William de Falesham, confirms Master Richer's gift (no. 61). Before 1221.

fo 58v   Rubric: Carta Willelmi de Falesham.

Omnibus Christi fidelibus ad quos presens scriptum pervenerit Willelmus filius Willelmi de Falsham, Salutem. Noverit universitas vestra me concessisse et presenti carta confirmasse deo et ecclesie beate Marie de Leestun' et canonicis ordinis Premonstratensis ibidem deo servientibus, totum tenementum quod Magister Richerus illis dedit, et concessit et carta sua confirmavit in Donewico, unde habent cartam patris mei, quam eis concedo et warantizo. Hiis testibus, Henrico de Grimil', Henfrido de Criketot, Willelmo filio Alani, et multis aliis.

Date: Hemfrid de Criketot. Cf no. 62; this is a confirmation by the son.

73. William, son of William fitz Roscelin, has granted 10s annually from the fee-farm of Sutton. Before 1221.

Rubric: Carta Willelmi filii Roscelini de redditu x. solidorum in Suttun'.

Sciant presentes et futuri quod ego Willelmus filius Willelmi filii Rocelini concessi et dedi et presenti carta confirmavi deo et ecclesie beate Marie de Leestun', et canonicis ordinis Premonstratensis ibidem deo servientibus pro salute anime mee, et pro animabus patris mei et matris mee et antecessorum et parentum et heredum meorum, decem solidos sterlingorum annuatim ad Pascha de Rogero de Holesle et heredibus suis, nomine redditus percipiendos, scilicet de quindecim marcis quas mihi dictus Rogerus debuit pro villa de Suttun' nomine feodefirme habendos et tenendos in liberam puram et perpetuam elemosinam, cum omni integritate in perpetuum. Volo autem et concedo ut dicti canonici distringant dictum Rogerum et heredes suos et alios qui pro tempore dictam villam tenuerint, per ipsum feodum cum necesse distringere fuerit pro defectu redditus sui, sine contradictione et inpedimento mei et heredum meorum. Et ego et heredes mei warantizabimus predictis canonicis predictum redditum decem solidorum contra omnes. Hiis testibus, Thoma de Arden', Hemfrido de Criketot, Henrico de Grimil', Willelmo filio Alani et multis aliis.

Date: Hemfrid de Criketot.

74. Herbert de Alencun has confirmed gifts of Saer de Biskele. Before 1221.

fo 59r Rubric: Confirmatio Herberti de Alencun de terra de Caldham.

Sciant presentes et futuri quod ego Herbertus de Alencun concessi et presenti carta confirmavi deo et ecclesie beate Marie de Leestun', et canonicis ordinis Premonstratensis ibidem deo servientibus illud tenementum quod Saherus de Biskele predictis canonicis dedit, et carta sua confirmavit, in puram et perpetuam elemosinam, videlicet septem acras terre que vocantur Mikelappeltun', et boscellum de eodem feodo qui vocatur Wimundesheg, iacentes iuxta nemus predictorum canonicorum quod vocatur Chiltre, in parochia de Thebertun'. Hanc concessionem et confirmationem feci predictis canonicis pro salute anime mee, et pro animabus omnium antecessorum et successorum meorum. Ut autem tam concessio et confirmatio mea, quam donatio et concessio et confirmatio predicti Saheri perpetuam obtineant firmitatem, eas sigilli mei appositione roboravi, quia predictum tenementum pertinet ad feodum militie mee. Testibus, Henrico de Grimil', Hemfrido de Criketot, Henrico de Hosa, et aliis.

Date: Hemfrid de Criketot.
Note: The gifts confirmed are in nos. 55 and 92.

75. William son of Alan has granted Theberton church. September 1189– 90.

Rubric: Carta Willelmi filii Alani de ecclesia de Thebertun'.

Omnibus sancte matris ecclesie filiis presentibus et futuris, Willelmus filius Alani Salutem. Universitati vestre notum fieri volo, me concessisse et dedisse, et hac mea carta confirmasse deo et ecclesie sancte Marie de Leeston' et canonicis ibidem deo servientibus ecclesiam sancti Petri de Thebertun' que est in feodo meo, libere et quiete, et integre /fo 59v cum omnibus pertinentiis suis, in puram et perpetuam elemosinam, pro salute anime mee et anime patris mei, et matris mee, et pro animabus omnium parentum meorum et amicorum. Hiis testibus, Huberto Episcopo Saresberiensi,[1] Radulfo Archidiacono Colecestrie, Rannulfo clerico, Wim' et Symone clericis, Radulfo de Ardene, Willelmo de Glamwill', Osberto de Glamvill, et multis aliis.

[1] MS Sarr'
Date: Hubert, Bishop of Salisbury from Sept. 1189, left for the crusade in 1190 (certainly before August).
Note: See Introduction, 17–19.

76. Receipt from Walter le Neve for the repayment of 120 marks deposited in the Abbey during the reign of John. 6th May, 1219.

Rubric: Carta Walteri le Neve de solutione debiti sui.

Sciant presentes et futuri quod ego Walterus le Neve tradidi Abbati de Leestun' quandam summam pecunie videlicet sexies viginti marcas argenti sterlingorum in custodia tempore Regis Johannis, quando fui in eius servitio apud Dunwic. Et idem Abbas plenarie satisfecit mihi de tota predicta summa pecunie, et perpacavit eandem mihi existenti in propria persona apud domum suam de Leestun' ad festum sancti Johannis Ewangeliste ante portam latinam anno primo legationis domini Pandulphi Norwicensis electi. Unde predictus Abbas de Leestun' et eiusdem loci conventus omnino remanent quieti in perpetuum de tota predicta pecunia erga me et heredes meos. Et in huius rei testimonium ego Walterus le Neve tradidi ipsi Abbati de Leestun' propria manu mea hanc cartam quietantie sigillo meo munitam. Hiis testibus, Willelmo, Gileberto, Roberto, Michaele, canonicis eiusdem domus de Leestun', Magistro Nicholao, Dionisio, Roberto de Snap' cementariis,

Philippo de Bedingefeld, et multis aliis.

Notes: Walter le Neve is perhaps the Walter 'de Neves', a knight of Girard d'Athies, used as a royal messenger in 1209 (*R Lib* 127), who went to Ireland in 1210 (*ibid.*, 181, 205, 225). He was given the manor of Wissett (nr Southwold), in Dec. 1215 (*R Litt Claus* i. 240): and so must have returned to royal service after a lapse in the summer of 1214 (*ibid.*, 169).

Monasteries were not infrequently used as storehouses by the king and his servants: cf *R Litt Pat* 144b, 148–9 (list of jewels returned by Welbeck). Philip de Ulecotes deposited money at Welbeck (*R Litt Claus* i. 439). The money seems more likely to have been Walter's own than the King's, from the personal terms of the receipt.

The witness of canons can be explained by the Statutes (Lefèvre, 43): 'Nullus abbas a quoquam recipiat depositum, nisi sub duorum vel trium testimonio de senioribus domus sue'.

77. Michael de Orford has granted a meadow in Grundisburgh, and a messuage in Orford. Early thirteenth century.

fo 60r   Rubric: Carta Michaelis de Orford.

Omnibus Christi fidelibus ad quos presens scriptum pervenerit, Michael filius Reginaldi de Orford' Salutem. Noverit universitas vestra me dedisse et concessisse et hac presenti carta confirmasse, deo et ecclesie beate Marie de Leeston' et canonicis ibidem deo servientibus in puram et perpetuam elemosinam pro anima mea et pro animabus antecessorum meorum et successorum meorum unum pratum in parochia de Grundesburg, scilicet in villa Boytun' et dicitur Holemeduue quantum ibi habeatur de feudo meo, ubi predecessores mei solebant habere unum molendinum, et unum mesagium in villa de Orford' ad calceam Catfoth versus orientem iacens inter terram Walteri le Poier et terram Jordani filii Aluredi habens centum pedes in longitudine et tantum in latitudine. Ut autem hec donatio mea stabilis et firma perseveret eam sigilli appositione roboravi. Testibus, Roberto capellano de Orford', Ricardo filio Ranulfi, Hakun filio Willelmi, Roberto filio Aliz, Gileberto filio Bringuuam, Willelmo Smal, Rogero de Petereste, Hugone filio eius, Johanne de Staunpes de Tudeham, Roberto filio Widonis de Beliges, Johanne filio Rogeri senescalli, Oseberto de Tudeham, Fulcone filio Symonis de Alduluestun', Roberto de Bernesheg, Fulcone fratre eius.

78. William son of Theobald and the Abbey have exchanged two acres. Before 1221.

fo 60v   Rubric: Carta Willelmi filii Theobaldi.

Sciant presentes et futuri quod ego Willelmus filius Theobaldi de Leeston' dedi et concessi et presenti carta confirmavi deo et ecclesie beate Marie de Leeston' et canonicis ibidem deo servientibus duas acras terre de feodo meo que iacent iuxta le Westhus in escambium pro duabus acris terre de dominico

Abbatis et conventus, que iacent iuxta Picacespet in villa de Leeston'. Ita scilicet quod ego Willelmus warantizabo prenominato Abbati et conventui illas duas acras quas de me receperunt in escambium, et illi warantizabunt mihi et heredibus meis illas duas acras quas de illis suscepi. Et ut huius scambii confirmatio firma sit et stabilis in perpetuum eam presenti carta et sigilli mei appositione roboravi. Testibus, Henrico de Grimill', Rogero de Braham, Hemfrido de Criketot, Willelmo filio Alani, Willelmo de Falesham, Roberto Jurdi, Nicholao filio Roberti, Huberto Cordebof, Thoma filio Theobaldi et multis aliis.

Date: Hemfrid de Criketot.

79. Hugh de Rickinghall has granted all his marsh, meadow and pasture in Playford. Before 1233.

Rubric: Carta Hugonis de Rikinhale de marisco et prato et pastura de Plaiford.

Sciant presentes et futuri quod ego Hugo de Rikingehale concessi et dedi et presenti carta confirmavi deo et ecclesie sancte Marie de Leestun' et canonicis ordinis Premonstratensis ibidem deo servientibus totum mariscum meum cum prato et pastura que habui in villa de Plaiford cum omnibus pertinentiis suis, in liberam et puram et perpetuam elemosinam. Et ego et heredes mei acquietabimus prefatum mariscum cum supradictis contra omnes homines in perpetuum. Ut autem hec donatio mea firma sit et stabilis in perpetuum, eam sigilli mei appositione roboravi. Hiis testibus, Henrico de Grimill', Hugone de Gosebech, Eadmundo de Tudeham, Willelmo filio Alani, Waltero de Hetfeld, Henrico de Batesford, Johanne de Stampes, Johanne de Culfo, Adam de Wereden' et multis aliis.

Date: Edmund de Tudeham.
Notes: Hugh de Gosbeck occurs in 1203 (*CRR* ii. 308), and in the 1230s as juror and justice (*CPR* iii. 164; *CRR* xiv. nos. 457).
Edmund de Tudeham (Tuddenham) was the son of John de T. who gave two parts of the tithes of his demesne in T. to Holy Trinity Ipswich (*R Chart* 116). He held of the Raimes fee in Norfolk and Suffolk, and of the earl of Devon in Devon (*Bk Fees* i, 136, 233; *CCR* i. 120). Edmund succeeded his father between 1200 and 1210 (after *CRR* i. 314), and was dead by Dec. 1233 (*Exc e R Fin* i, 253).
John de Culpho is probably the same as in nos. 106, 107.

80. Hugh de Rickinghall has granted a man, his family and tenement in Playford. Before 1233.

Rubric: Carta Hugonis de Rikingehale de Edwardo Gesth.

Sciant presentes et futuri quod ego Hugo filius Roberti de Rikingehale concessi et dedi et presenti carta confirmavi deo et ecclesie beate Marie de Leestun' et canonicis ordinis Premonstratensis ibidem deo servientibus, Edwardum Gesth qui fuit homo meus in villa de Plaiford cum tota sequela sua et tenemento suo quod tenuit de me in eadem villa in liberam puram et perpetuam elemosinam, salvo servitio domini feodi duodecim videlicet denariis pro omni servitio consuetudine et exactione. Et ego et heredes mei pacem faciemus dictis canonicis de dicto homine et sequela sua et tenemento suo, et warantizabimus eum eis cum sequela sua et tene/*fo 62r*mento contra omnes homines in perpetuum. Ut autem hec donatio mea firma et stabilis in perpetuum perseveret, presens scriptum sigilli mei appositione roboravi. Hiis testibus, Henrico de Grimill', Hugone de Gosebech, Eadmundo de Tudeham, Willelmo filio Alani, Waltero de Hetfeld, Henrico de Batesford, Johanne de Stampes, Johanne de Culfo, Adam de Wereden', et multis.

Date: as no. 79.

81. William de Winderville has granted 3 acres for 6 years from Michaelmas 1220.

Rubric: Carta Willelmi de Windervile de tribus acris in villa de Tudeham.

Sciant presentes et futuri quod ego Willelmus de Windervill' dedi et concessi et presenti carta confirmavi deo et ecclesie beate Marie de Leeston', ad fabricam eiusdem ecclesie tres acras terre et dimidiam in villa de Tudeham, que iacent inter terram Abbatis et conventus de Leeston' et terram Theobaldi de Tudeham, in liberam et puram elemosinam, per sex annos habendas complendos a festo sancti Michaelis proximo preterito ante consecrationem domini Elyensis Episcopi quondam Abbatis de Funtain'. Quod si infra predictum terminum prefatam terram ego warantizare non potero prenominate ecclesie de Leeston' ego et heredes mei dabimus ad fabricam sepedicte ecclesie de Leeston', tantam terram de terra mea de Gleruing, ad valentiam predicte terre usque ad predictum terminum completum possidendam. Ut autem hec donatio et concessio ac confirmatio quam feci predicte ecclesie de Leeston pro salute anime mee, et omnium antecessorum meorum rata sit et stabilis infra predictum terminum, eam me observaturum affidavi et sigilli mei appositione roboravi. Hiis testibus, Willelmo filio Alani, Saero de Biskele, Willelmo filio Theobaldi, Baldewino de Poteford', Johanne de Eston'.

Date: John of Fountains, bishop of Ely 1220–5.

82. Roger de Culpho has granted 8 acres which he had bought, to his daughter Margaret. Before 1233.

Sciant tam presentes quam futuri quod ego Rogerus de Culpho filius Terri dedi et concessi et hac presenti carta confirmavi Margarete filie mee pro homagio et servitio suo octo acras terre de terra Berd', quam tenui de Johanne de Tudeham et de Eadmundo filio suo /*fo 62v* de emptu meo, et de mea adquisitione, illi et heredibus suis tenendas de me et de heredibus meis hereditarie libere et quiete et honorifice, per duos solidos annuatim reddendos

104

et ad quattuor terminos, scilicet ad festum sancti Andree vi. denarios, ad
Pascham vi. denarios, et ad festum sancti Johannis vi. denarios, et ad festum
sancti Michaelis vi. denarios, pro omnibus servitiis et exactionibus, salvo
servitio domini Regis, scilicet ad xx. solidos octo denariis, et ad plus plus et
ad minus minus; et pro hac donatione et confirmatione predicta Margareta
filia mea inde fecit mihi homagium suum. Et ego et heredes mei predicte
Margarete et heredibus suis contra omnes warantizabimus illam predictam
terram. Hiis testibus, Galfrido de Clopton', Rogero de Stampes, Osberto de
Tudeham.

Date: Edmund de Tudeham (no. 79).

83. John, son of Roger the Seneschal of Culpho has granted Leiston his land of 'Gosepeth' in Culpho, with 3d rent. Early thirteenth century.

Rubric: Carta Johannis senescalli de Culfo de quattuor acris terre.[1]

Sciant presentes et futuri quod ego Johannes filius Rogeri Senescalli de Culfo
concessi et dedi et presenti carta confirmavi deo et ecclesie sancte Marie de
Leeston' et canonicis ordinis Premonstratensis ibidem deo servientibus totam
terram meam que vocatur Gosepeth, in villa de Culfo, ubi estimantur
quattuor acre et plus et redditum iii. denariorum quos Theobaldus de Culfo
solebat reddere mihi annuatim, in liberam et puram et perpetuam elemosinam. Preterea concessi et dedi predictis canonicis totum pratum meum et
totam pasturam meam quam habui apud Gosepeth, reddendo inde domino
Willelmo de Verdun et heredibus suis xii. denarios per annum ad quattuor
terminos, scilicet ad festum sancti Andree iii. denarios, ad Pascham iii.
denarios, ad festum sancti Johannis Baptiste iii. denarios, ad festum sancti
Michaelis iii. denarios pro omnibus servitiis, consuetudinibus et demandis.
Et ego Johannes et heredes mei adquietabimus et warantizabimus predictam
terram et prefatum redditum prenominatis canonicis in perpetuum. Ut
autem hee concessiones et donationes stabili firmitate in perpetuum
perseverent, eas sigilli mei appositione roboravi. Hiis testibus, domino R.
capellano de Saxlingh(am), Ric' persona de Theburton', Henrico de Grimill',
Willelmo filio Theobaldi.

[1] remainder illegible

Date: rough lifetimes of William de Verdun (probably II), and Grimilies.

84. Martin de Beaufo has confirmed the donations from Saer de Biskele made of his fee. Before 1221.

fo 63r   Rubric: (Carta) Martini de Beaufo de terra et redditu Saeri de Biskele.

Sciant presentes et futuri quod ego Martinus de Beaufo assensu Egidie uxoris
mee concessi et confirmavi ac quietum clamavi in perpetuum pro me et pro
heredibus meis deo et ecclesie beate Marie de Leeston et canonicis ordinis
Premonstratensis ibidem deo servientibus omnes donationes tam terrarum
quam hominum et reddituum quas Saerus de Biskele fecit predictis canonicis

de Leeston, videlicet in parochia de Theburton' xl. acras terre arabilis et duos boscellos iuxta nemus de Ciltre, et unum pratum ac redditum x. solidorum in homagio et omnes alias donationes, quas predictus Saerus de Biskele fecit prefatis canonicis de Leeston' de eodem feodo, sicut carte eiusdem Saeri testantur. Hanc autem concessionem et confirmationem ac quietam clama-tionem feci deo et predicte ecclesie beate Marie de Leeston et canonicis eiusdem loci pro salute anime mee et omnium antecessorum et successorum meorum. Et ut firma sit et stabilis in perpetuum, presentem cartam sigilli mei appositione roboravi. Hiis testibus, Henrico de Grimill', Hemfrido de Criketot, Willelmo filio Alani.

Date: Hemfrid de Criketot.
Notes: The rent is possibly that of the 8 men of no. 54; the woods are in no. 55, one of them also confirmed by Herbert de Alencun in no. 74. The meadow is in no. 92. The forty acres are possibly Caldham (no. 92).

85. Egidia de Beaufo has confirmed Saer de Biskele's gifts. Before 1221?

Rubric: (Carta) Egidie de Beaufo.

Sciant presentes et futuri quod ego Egidia uxor Martini de Beaufo assensu eiusdem Martini viri mei, concessi et confirmavi et quietum clamavi in perpetuum pro me et pro heredibus meis deo et ecclesie beate Marie de Leeston et canonicis ibidem deo servientibus omnes donationes tam terrarum quam hominum et redditum quas Saerus de Biskele fecit predictis canonicis de Leeston, videlicet in parochia de Theberton' xl. acras terre arabilis, et duos boscellos iuxta nemus de Ciltre, et unum pratum ac redditum x. solidorum in homagio et omnes alias donationes quas predictus Saerus de Biskele fecit prefatis canonicis de Leeston' de eodem feodo, sicut carte eiusdem Saeri testantur. Hanc autem concessionem etc. ut supra.

Date: presumably close to no. 84.

86. William son of Alan has granted the tenements of some men in Theberton. Early thirteenth century.

Rubric: Carta Willelmi filii Alani de Henrico filio Haldan et tenemento suo et sequela sua et de aliis tenementis, et heredes sui debent warantizationem unde (scriptum) est.[1]

fo 63v Sciant presentes et futuri quod ego Willelmus filius Alani concessi et dedi et presenti carta confirmavi deo et ecclesie sancte Marie de Leeston' et canonicis ordinis Premonstratensis ibidem deo servientibus pro salute anime mee et meorum totum tenementum Henrici filii Haldani quod de me tenuit in villa de Tebertun', scilicet unam acram terre cum mesagio suo et uxore sua, et tota sequela eiusdem uxoris sue, et unam acram terre que fuit Alani filii Oki cum mesagio. Et preterea unam acram[2] terre que iacet in mora. Et totum tenementum quod Hamo filius Osberti Uni tenuit de me, scilicet duas acras terre in eadem villa de Tebertun', et totum tenementum quod Galfridus filius Euerwak' de Thornes tenuit de me, videlicet unam acram[2] que iacet iuxta domum dicti Galfridi, et unam acram macilentissimam que iacet in dicta villa iuxta domum Osmundi de Sureia, cum omnibus reditibus et consuetudinibus ad prefata tenementa spectantibus, in liberam, puram et perpetuam elemosinam. Et ita contingat, quod deus avertat, quod ego vel heredes mei non possimus warantizare dictis canonicis predicta tenementa, dabimus eis de dominio nostro in villa de Cretinges in terris vel reditibus vel in utriusque ad valentiam sepedictorum tenementorum; et ut hec concessio mea et donatio firma sit et stabilis.[3]

[1] remainder illegible   [2] acram omitted – possibly rodam
[3] incomplete in MS

Date: donor's approximate lifetime.
See Introduction, 17–18.

87. Ralph de Cookley has granted 10d rent. Early thirteenth century?

Sciant presentes et futuri quod ego Radulfus filius Willelmi de Cukeleie dedi et concessi et presenti carta confirmavi deo et ecclesie beate Marie de Leestun'[1] et canonicis ordinis Premonstratensis ibidem deo servientibus in liberam et puram et perpetuam elemosinam, redditum decem denariorum eis annuatim ad festum sancti Michaelis in perpetuum solvendorum per manum Johannis de Dernicford' hominis mei et heredum eius, quos denarios predictus Johannes et heredes eius solvent predictis canonicis in perpetuum ad predictum terminum[2] de annuo censu suo quem mihi reddere consueverat ad festum sancti Michaelis, pro feodo quod de me tenet in villa de Cukel'. Concessi etiam et[3] confirmavi prenominatis canonicis ut distringant predictum Johannem et heredes suos cum necesse fuerit per feodum quod de me tenet in predicta villa de Cukel' ad solvendum predictum redditum decem denariorum. Hanc donationem, concessionem et confirmationem ego Radulfus filius Willelmi de Cukel' feci sepedictis canonicis de Leestun' pro salute anime mee et Rohaisie[4] uxoris mee, et Willelmi primogeniti mei et ceterorum liberorum meorum, et pro anima Willelmi patris mei et Sare matris mee et pro animabus omnium antecessorum meorum,[5] et successorum meorum. Et ego sepedictus Radulfus filius Willelmi et heredes mei warantizabimus predictum redditum decem denariorum predictis canonicis contra omnes homines et feminas in perpetuum. Ut autem hec donatio, concessio et confirmatio firma sit et stabilis in perpetuum, presentem cartam sigilli mei appositione roboravi. Hiis testibus, Roberto Malet, Michaele de Beavent,[6] Radulfo de Melles,[7] Baldewino filio eius, Roberto de Estune, H. de Chedeston, Toma fratre eius, Ricardo filio Osberti, Oliverio filio eius, et multis aliis.

[1] B, Leeston' throughout   [2] B, terminum predictum
[3] B omits et   [4] B, Rohusie
[5] B omits meorum   [6] B, Bauuent
[7] B ends here

Date: see Introduction, 12.
Notes: occurs twice in MS, A: ff 63v–64r, B: fo 73v.

88. William Lenveise agrees to rent the land granted in no. 50 (for 28d a year). Before c 1235.

fo 64r   Rubric: Carta W. Lenueise de xxviii. denariis annui redditus . . .[1]

Sciant presentes et futuri quod ego Willelmus Lenueise et heredes mei debemus solvere singulis annis viginti octo denarios nomine redditus ad duos terminos, scilicet ad Pascha quatuordecim denarios et ad festum sancti Michaelis quatuordecim denarios Abbati et conventui de Leestun' de terra quam Driu de Chedestan tenuit quondam de eis in villa de Chedestan et quam dicti canonici habuerunt ex dono Oliveri de Vallibus in liberam et puram et perpetuam elemosinam, scilicet undecim acras terre et unam rodam que iacent in Derhage, et unam dimidiam acram que appellatur Hegrone, et tres rodas que iacent ex orientali parte domus Radulfi Lewine. Cum vero contigerit, quod deus avertat, */fo 64v* quod ego Willelmus Lenueise vel heredes mei defecerimus solvere dictum redditum dictis Abbati et conventui de Leestun' ad prefatos terminos, ego prefatus Willelmus concedo pro me et pro heredibus meis ut sepedictus Abbas et conventus de Leestun' distringant tam me quam heredes meos cum necesse fuerit per predictum feodum quousque eis plena facta fuerit solutio. Et in huius rei testimonium hanc prescriptam cartam meam eis feci et sigilli mei appositione roboravi. Hiis testibus, Henrico de Grimill', Johanne de Braham, Willelmo filio Alani, Huberto Cordebof, Galfrido Jurdi, Willelmo filio Theobaldi, Toma fratre eius.

[1] remainder illegible

Date: Hubert Corndebof d. c 1235 (see no. 13n). John de Braham is the son of Roger, succeeding his father c 1223 – which would not prevent him from witnessing a charter before then.
Note: the Lenveise family were related by marriage to the Glanvilles. Various Lenveises are to be found in *Cartulary of the Abbey of Old Wardon* (ed G. H. Fowler, Bedfordshire Hist. Rec. Soc. xiii, 1930) eg nos. 298, 391. Another can be found in Bedingfeld, nos. 26. 27).

89. Agreement between Leiston Abbey and Butley Priory over the tithes of Knodishall. 18th November 1235.

Hec est forma puralee facte inter Philippum Abbatem et conventum de Leystona et Willelmum Priorem et conventum de Buttele tempore relaxationis generalis interdicti de terris infra parochiam de Cnoteshal' de quibus dicti Abbas et conventus decimas percipere debent tam maiores quam minores omnibus aliis decimis maioribus et minoribus omnium parochianorum dicte ecclesie de Cnoteshal prefatis Priori et conventui de Buttele in pace perpetuo remanentibus. Specificaciones autem decimarum terrarum secundum formam puralee memorate sunt hee. Videlicet decime de tota terra Walrami Rufi (Henricus Faber) ubicumque iacuerit, de terra Hugonis de

Bruerio (Roberto Lutewine) scilicet de Dreystoc, et de terra que iacet sub curia Johannis le Sopere de feodo Willelmi filii Theobaldi, scilicet de quatuor acris de Akerheg (Julic' de Braham) et de duabus acris et dimidia que terminant super Akerheg (Ric' Lunetild et Adam le Paumer), de terra Petri filii Walteri (Willelmi Perres) scilicet duabus partibus que sunt de libera terra ecclesie de Leystona, de duabus acris et dimidia (Roberti Hurt) que vocantur Aylemerestoft, de terra Willelmi Side /fo 65r scilicet tribus rodis que iacent ultra Hallecroft, et de tribus rodis que iacent iuxta altam divisam, et de una roda ad Hahemere, de terra que vocatur Grimestoft, de terra que vocatur Margareteswelle, de terra que vocatur Hahemere (Prior de B.) excepta acra quam Walter Godcnape tenet que pertinet ad ecclesiam de Cnoteshal', de tota terra Odonis Palmarii (Walter Ode) quam tenet de Willelmo filio Theobaldi et de terra que vocatur Aspes (Johannes Orgar), de Calkiacre et de tribus rodis (Prior de B.) que terminantur super Calkiacre, de duabus acris que vocantur Dirilond (Ric' Bert) et de tribus rodis Walteri Godcnape (Edward Godcnape) quas tenet de libera terra ecclesie de Leyston, de terra Edric Gripun (Robertus Gripun) quam tenet de ecclesia de Leystun, de novem partibus terre quas Willelmus Harlepin (Ranulphus Harlepin) tenet pro quinque acris, de tota terra Rogeri Bellehus (Mirine Bellus[1]) ubicumque iacuerit, de duabus partibus terre Rogeri filii Herberti (Prior de B.), de dimidia parte de Hallecroft que iacet in uno continenti ubi estimantur septem acre, de tota terra que dicitur Leshestoft, de Orgaresacre (Ric' Lunetild), de tota terra Walthef (Gerardi clerici), de terra Roberti mercatoris scilicet tribus acris et dimidia (Robertus de Rindham) quas tenet de Willelmo filio Theobaldi, item de tenemento Willelmi filii Theobaldi scilicet duabus acris et tribus rodis (Willelmus Ode) iuxta Prestelund, de terra Roberti filii Alcredi (Ric' Roberti) scilicet una acra iuxta Blakelond, de terra Rogeri filii Ulfi (Willelmus Wlmer) ubicumque iacuerit, de terra Willelmi filii Theobaldi que dicitur Erburestoft (Prior de B.), de tota terra de Wahefen (Theobaldi de Leystun') a termino usque ad terminum, de duabus acris quas Andreas de Keleshale tenuit (Robertus Bacheler) medietatem habebimus, de tota terra Walteri Rufi, de tota terra que dicitur Wivelesfeld (Theobald de Leystun), de terra Walteri prepositi scilicet duabus acris et dimidia (Ric' Lunetild) iuxta le Stonrenneles, de terra Roberti le Waleys (Willelmus le White) ubicumque iacuerit, de terra Walteri Wlmer ubicumque (Rogerus Elyot et Cokeman) /fo 65v iacuerit, de terra Odonis Same (Johannes Ode et Ric' Ode) ubicumque iacuerit, de terra Radulphi filii Gunnore ubicumque iacuerit, de terra Halden Brun (Johannes Cole) ubicumque iacuerit, de terra Roberti Palmarii (Thomas clericus) ubicumque iacuerit, de tota terra de Landelund (Willelmus Theobald), de una acra Gerardi le Gleuman (Alicia Corn' de Bob') quam tenet de Willelmo filio Theobaldi pertinet ad nos, de terra Wlfrici de le Westhus (Thomas de Ubestune et participes sui) scilicet duabus partibus ultra Wdissemor et de duabus partibus que iacent ex orientali parte eiusdem domus. Et ut hec puralea stabilis et inconcussa perpetuo permaneat hinc instrumento ad modum cirographi confecto, tam Abbas et conventus quam Prior et conventus sigilla sua apposuerunt. Actum apud Buttele in octabis sancti Martini anno gratie millesimo ducentesimo tricesimo quinto.

[1] reading uncertain

Note: the bracketed names are interlined in the MS. See Introduction, 21.

90. Final 'Actum' (18th November 1235) by papal judges delegate, on mandate of Gregory IX (28th July 1234), in suit between Leiston Abbey and Butley Priory over tithes in Knodishall.

Omnibus has litteras inspecturis, Thomas dei gratia Norwicensis Episcopus, Decanus Norwicensis et Prior sancte Fidis de Horsford, Salutem eternam in domino. Noverit universitas vestra nos mandatum domini Pape suscepisse in hec verba.

Gregorius Episcopus, Servus Servorum Dei, venerabili fratri Episcopo et dilectis filiis Decano Norwicensi et Priori sancte Fidis Norwicensis diocesis, Salutem et Apostolicam Benedictionem. Querelam Prioris ac conventus de Buttele recepimus continentem quod Abbas et conventus de Leyston', Premonstratensis ordinis, et quidam alii Norwicensis, Lincolniensis et Londoniensis diocesis super terris, decimis, debitis et rebus aliis iniuriantur eisdem. Ideo discretioni vestre per apostolica scripta mandamus, quatinus partibus convocatis audiatis causam et apellatione remota fine debito decidatis, facientes quod decreveritis per censuram ecclesiasticam firmiter observari. Testes autem qui fuerint nominati si se gratia, odio vel timore subtraxerint, per censuram eandem apellatione cessante cogatis veritati testimonium perhibere. Quod si non omnes hiis exequendis, /fo 66r potueritis interesse tu, frater Episcope, cum eorum altero ea nichilominus exequaris. Datum Reatum quinto kal' Augusti pontificatus nostri anno octavo.

Huius igitur auctoritate mandati Priore et conventu de Buttele in contentionem suam contra Abbatem et conventus de Leystune sub hac forma proponente, dicunt Prior et conventus de B. quod cum ecclesia de Cnoteshale fuisset in possessione minimarum decimarum provenientium de domo eorum qui dicitur le Westhus in parochia de Cnoteshale et oblationum et obventionum servientium secularium in dicta domo commorantium, Abbas et conventus de Leyston' eas iniuste detinent et reddere contradicunt. Partibus in iure coram nobis constitutis, exceptionibus ex parte dictorum Abbatis et conventus propositis et rationibus utriusque partis auditis et intellectis tandem lis inter partes in presentia nostra hoc fine conquievit. Videlicet quod dicti Prior et conventus renunciaverint omni iuri parochiali tam in decimis quam in omnibus aliis rebus quod habuerunt vel habere potuerunt in dicta grangia vel servientibus secularibus ibidem commorantibus, salvis oblationibus et obventionibus et omnibus provenientibus parochianorum dictorum Prioris et conventus de quacumque sua parochia provenientibus, in dicta grangia pro quocumque tempore commorantium, Abbati[1] et conventui memoratis. Si vero parochiani alicuius ecclesie que pro aliquo tempore non fuerit dictorum Abbatis et conventus vel Prioris et conventus in dicta grangia fuerint commorantes, unusquisque eorum libere propriam adeat ecclesiam, Abbate et conventui prenominatis nullum impedimentum procurantibus quo minus dictam ecclesiam de Cnoteshale adeat si voluerit, et iura ibidem percipiat ecclesiastica. Item renunciaverunt dicti Prior et conventus omni iuri parochiali quod habuerunt vel habere potuerunt in dominicis de Westhus et de Leystun' cultis et incultis que dicti Abbas et conventus habuerunt tempore relaxationis generalis interdicti de quibus decime ecclesie prefate de

110

Cnoteshale tunc temporis non fuerant persolute, et decimis /fo 66v terre de Keleshalelond iacentis sub bosco de Grendelheg et campi qui vocatur Oldelond et duarum acrarum terre que vocantur Radismere quas dicti Abbas et conventus tenent in dominico, puralea etiam inter dictas ecclesias de Leyston' et de Cnoteshale tempore Philippi Abbatis et conventus et Willelmi Prioris et conventus dictorum facta, et sigillis utriusque domus roborata, in suo robore perdurante. Et ut inter dictas domus de Leyston' et de Buttele pax perpetua firma et inconcussa in posterum permaneat, dicti Abbas et conventus decimas terre que vocantur Erburestoft, et duarum acrarum terre quas Willelmus Fukeman tenuit, et sex peciarum terre quas Walter Rakebald et Galfridus frater eius tenent, et unius rode terre de feodo Ade de monasterio, iacentis versus occidentem de le Stablecroft pro bono pacis Priori et conventui in perpetuum concesserunt memoratis. Nos autem compositionem prenominatam ratam et gratam habentes, eam autoritate domini Pape nobis commissa confirmamus et sigillorum nostrorum munimine roboramus. Actum apud Buttele in octabis sancti Martini anno gratie m. cc. tricesimo quinto.

[1] MS Priori

See Introduction, 20–1, 32.

91. Pope Honorius III frees the Abbot and Prior of Leiston from serving as papal judges delegate. 14th March 1225.

Rubric: Ne simus iudices delegati.

Honorius Episcopus Servus Servorum Dei, dilectis filiis Abbati et Priori monasterii de Leyston', Premonstratensis ordinis, Salutem et Apostolicam Benedictionem. A nobis humiliter postulastis ut cum non habeatis iuris peritiam et propter commissiones que vobis ab apostolica sede fiunt monasterii vestri negligantur negotia, ac gravia idem monasterium subeat onera expensarum, exinde vos ab ipsarum commissionum sollicitudine dignaremur. Nos ergo vestris supplicationibus annuentes, advocationi vestro auctoritate presentium indulgemus, ne per commissiones nostras quas ad vos de cetero impetrari contigerit, procedere teneamini, nisi de indulgentia huiusmodi fecerint mentionem. Nulli ergo omnino hominum liceat hanc paginam nostre concessionis infringere, vel ei ausu temerario contraire. Si quis autem hoc attemptare presumpserit, indignationem omnipotentis dei et beatorum Petri et Pauli apostolorum eius se noverit incursurum. Datum Laterani ii. id' Martii pontificatus nostri anno nono.

See Introduction, 31–2.

92. Saer de Biskele has granted land at 'Caldham' and 'Apeltun' (Theberton), and repeats previous gifts. Before 1221.

fo 67r   Rubric: Carta Saeri de Biskele de terra de Caldham.

Sciant presentes et futuri quod ego Saerus de Biskele filius Galfridi dedi et concessi et presenti carta confirmavi pro salute anime mee et Ade uxoris mee, et omnium antecessorum et successorum meorum deo et ecclesie beate Marie de Leestun', et canonicis ordinis Premonstratensis ibidem deo servientibus viginti quattuor acras terre circa mesagium meum quod vocatur Caldham in villa de Thebertun', et totum ipsum mesagium cum pomerio et omnibus curtillagiis, et cum boscello iacente iuxta mesagium, et septem acras terre cum fossato infra et extra que vocantur Apeltun', et duas acras terre cum duobus curtillagiis ubi abbatia predictorum canonicorum sita est, et preterea duos boscellos in predicta villa de Thebertun', quorum unus vocatur Wimundesheg, et alter Uphalheg, et totam pasturam meam que iacet inter nemus prefatorum canonicorum quod vocatur Hiltre, et domum quondam Walteri de Caldham in longitudine et latitudine, et unam acram prati que iacet in Bolecroft in tres partes iuxta pratum predictorum canonicorum, et totum tenementum Rogeri caretarii, et eundem Rogerum cum uxore sua et tota sequela */fo 67v* eorum, et totum tenementum Walteri Garleach et eundem Walterum cum uxore sua et tota sequela eorum, et quicquid iuris habui vel habere debui vel potui, in mariscis et turbariis, iuncariis et pasturis in villa de Thebertun', in liberam, puram et perpetuam elemosinam. Et ego Saerus de Biskele et heredes mei prefatas terras et dicta tenementa, et omnia superius memorata prenominatis canonicis acquietabimus, erga omnes homines de omni seculari servitio, consuetudine et exactione in perpetuum. Hiis testibus, Henfrido de Criketoth, Henrico de Grimill'.

Date: Hemfrid de Criketot.
Note: this repeats previous gifts (nos. 53–55 and 67) as well as adding more.

93. Jocelin de Hispania has granted all his land, with messuage, in Glevering. Early thirteenth century.

fo 68r   Top margin: Sancti Spiritus assit nobis gratia Amen.
Rubric. Carta Jocelini de Yspania de villa de Gleruing'.

Sciant presentes et futuri quod ego Jocelinus de Yspania dedi et concessi et presenti carta confirmavi deo et ecclesie beate Marie de Leeston' et canonicis ordinis Premonstratensis ibidem deo servientibus in liberam puram et perpetuam elemosinam totam terram cum mesagio quam habui in villa de Gleruing cum omnibus pertinentiis, in terris scilicet, et hominibus ac redditibus, in pratis et pasturis in boscis et planis ac alnetis, in aquis et molendinis, in viis et semitis et omnibus rebus que pertinuerunt ad me et heredes meos in villa de Gleruing, vel pertinere debuerunt per me vel per antecessores meos, salvis michi et heredibus meis duabus marcis ex predicta terra singulis annis percipiendis, scilicet ad mediam Quadragesime,[1] unam marcam, et ad Nativitatem beate Marie i. marcam, et salvo servitio forinseco, scilicet servitio dimidii militis, et ego et heredes mei warantizabimus prefatis canonicis totam predictam terram cum pertinentiis contra omnes homines. Hanc autem donationem et concessionem ac confirmationem feci prenominatis canonicis de Leeston' pro salute anime mee et omnium antecessorum meorum et pro anima Rannulfi de Glanvill' avunculi mei, qui eosdem canonicos fundavit. Ut ergo eadem donatio et concessio ac confirmatio firma sit et stabilis in perpetuum, presentem cartam sigilli mei appositione roboravi. Hiis testibus.

[1] MS xl

Date: cf **94**.

94. Jocelin de Hispania has granted land and his messuage at Glevering with adjacent woods, and his share in the mill. Before 1235.

fo 68v   Rubric: Item alia carta Jocelini de Grervinge.

Sciant presentes et futuri quod ego Jocelinus de Hyspania concessi et dedi et hac carta confirmavi deo et ecclesie sancte Marie de Leeston' et canonicis ordinis Premonstratensis ibidem deo servientibus totum mesagium meum de Gleruing cum edificiis et omnibus alnetis adiacentibus et cum tota terra que dicitur Hallecroft et cum omnibus pratis meis et cum tota parte mea molendini in Gleruing, scilicet parte media, in liberam, puram et perpetuam elemosinam. Hanc autem donationem feci prenominatis canonicis pro salute anime mee et anime Rannulfi de Glanvill', et omnium antecessorum et successorum meorum. Et ego Jocelinus et heredes mei adquietabimus omnia superius memorata predictis canonicis in perpetuum. Ut autem hec concessio mea et donatio firma et stabilis perpetuo perseveret eam sigilli mei appositione roboravi. Hiis testibus, Waltero de Ribo, Henrico de Grimill', Godefrido de Wavere, Huberto Cordebof, Willelmo filio Alani, Nicholao filio Roberti, et ceteris.

Date: Hubert Cordebof.

95. Hugh le Rus has granted a man and an acre of land, and confirmed the man's gift of 6 acres and a messuage. Before 1231.

Rubric: Carta Hugonis Rusi de quadam terra in Culfo.

Sciant presentes et futuri quod ego Hugo le Rus concessi et presenti carta confirmavi pro salute anime mee et omnium antecessorum meorum in liberam et puram et perpetuam elemosinam, deo et ecclesie beate Marie de Leeston et canonicis ordinis Premonstratensis ibidem deo servientibus Willelmum filium Hervei de Bernesh(eg) et sex acras terre cum uno mesagio quas idem Willelmus habuit in Alduluest(on) et dedit predictis canonicis sicut carta eiusdem /fo 69r Willelmi testatur, quarum una acra vocatur Horland et una acra et dimidia iacent ad Suotwalle et due acre et dimidia iacent ad Wulfrichescroft et una acra iacet ad Godieveswude; tenendas illis pacifice et quiete absque omni impedimento et contradictione quod per me vel per heredes meos in perpetuum eis poterit inferri. Preterea concessi et confirmavi predictis canonicis de Leeston' unam acram terre quam predictus Willelmus habuit in Aldulueston, iacentem in campo qui vocatur Bergh, inter terram[1] Fukonis fratris predicti Willelmi et terram Gileberti capellani de Bernesheg, tenendas illas absque omni contradictione et impedimento quod per me vel heredes meos eis poterit inferri, et habendas in perpetuum de Roberto fratre sepedicti Willelmi et de heredibus suis libere et quiete ac pacifice per servitium sex denariorum singulis annis solvendorum et unum obolum ad scutagium domini Regis, quos prefatus Willelmus reddidit annuatim prenominato Roberto de Bernesheg fratri suo pro tota terra sua quam tenuit de eo in Adldulueston' pro omni servitio, consuetudine et exactione ac demanda. Ut autem hec concessio et confirmatio firma sit et stabilis in perpetuum, presentem cartam sigilli mei appositione roboravi. Hiis testibus, Ada de Bedingfeld, Ricardo de Kaleston, Oseberto de Tudeham, Huberto Cordebof, Nicholao filio Roberti etc.

[1] MS interam

Date: Hugh le Rus succeeded his father 1209–12, and was dead by 1231. See Introduction, 10.

96. William de Verdun has confirmed the gift of Culpho church. Early thirteenth century.

fo 69v   Rubric: Confirmatio Willelmi de Verdun de ecclesia de Culpho.

Sciant presentes et futuri quod ego Willelmus de Verdun, ad petitionem Matilde uxoris mee concessi et hac presenti carta mea confirmavi deo et beate Marie et canonicis ordinis Premonstratensis de Leeston' donationem ecclesie sancti Botulfi de Culfo quam fecit eis Willelmus de Valeines pater predicte uxoris mee et quia proprium sigillum non habui eam sigillo Wydonis patris mei roboravi. Hiis testibus, Wydone de Verdun', Johanne de Verdun', Willelmo de Holcham, Matheo de Stokes, et ceteris.

Date: approximate lifetime of donor.
Printed: Monasticon, vi(ii). 882, no. 9.

97. William Meus has granted an assart in Tuddenham. Before 1233.

Rubric: Carta Willelmi Meus de quodam essarto in Tudeham.

Sciant presentes et futuri quod ego Willelmus Meus dedi et concessi et presenti carta confirmavi deo et ecclesie sancte Marie de Leeston' et canonicis ibidem deo servientibus totam brutiam meam in Tudeham que iacet ad capud bosci Eadmundi de Thudeham versus aquilonem et proceditur usque ad /fo 70r viam, in liberam puram et perpetuam elemosinam pro salute anime mee et meorum habendam et tenendam libere et quiete absque omni seculari servitio et exactione in perpetuum. Et ut hec mea concessio et confirmatio firma sit et stabilis in perpetuum, eam sigilli mei appositione roboravi. Hiis testibus, Ada de Bedigfeld, Henrico de Grimill', Eadmundo de Tudeham, Huberto Cordebof et ceteris.

Date: Edmund de Tudeham.

98. Walter of Culpho has granted a piece of land in Culpho. Before 1224.

Rubric: Carta Walteri filii Alani de quadam pecia terre in Culpho.

Sciant presentes et futuri quod ego Walterus filius Alani filii Sikarii de Culfo dedi et concessi et presenti carta confirmavi pro salute anime mee et omnium antecessorum meorum deo et ecclesie beate Marie de Leeston, et canonicis ordinis Premonstratensis ibidem deo servientibus in puram et perpetuam elemosinam, unam peciam terre mee que iacet inter terram Simonis de Lafuntaine et terram Serlonis de Lafuntaine, proxima domui Rogeri Grim in Culpho. Ut autem hec donatio, concessio et confirmatio et cetera. Hiis testibus, Willelmo filio Alani, Saero de Biskele, Waltero filio Theobaldi, Johanne de Stampes et ceteris.

Date: Saer de Biskele.

99. William son of Hervey de Bernesheg has granted six acres and a messuage. Before 1231.

Rubric: Carta Willelmi filii Hervei de vi. acris terre in Culfo.

Sciant presentes et futuri quod ego Willelmus filius Hervei de Bernesheg' dedi et concessi et presenti carta confirmavi deo et ecclesie beate Marie de Leeston et canonicis ordinis Premonstratensis ibidem deo servientibus, vi. acras terre cum uno mesagio quas habui in Aldulueston quarum i. acra vocatur Horland' ubi mesagium fuit et i. acra et dimidia iacet ad Suotwalle, et ii. acre et dimidia iacent ad Wlurikescroft, et i. acra ad Godievewde, in liberam et puram et perpetuam elemosinam pro salute anime mee et omnium antecessorum meorum. /fo 70v Ut autem hec donatio et concessio et confirmatio firma sit etc. Hiis testibus, Ada de Bedingfeld, Ricardo de Kaleston, Huberto Cordebof etc.

Date: confirmed in no. 95.

100. William son of Hervey de Bernesheg has granted one acre to Leiston abbey. Before 1231.

Rubric: Carta predicti Willelmi.

Sciant tam presentes quam futuri quod ego Willelmus filius Hervei de Bernesheg dedi et concessi et presenti carta confirmavi Abbati et conventui de Leston unam acram terre in Aldulueston iacentem in campo qui vocatur Berg inter terram Fulkonis fratris mei et terram Gileberti capellani de Bernesheg, tenendam illam in perpetuum de Roberto fratre meo de Bernesheg', et de heredibus suis libere et quiete et pacifice per servitium vi. denariorum singulis annis reddendorum et pro uno obolo ad scutagium domini Regis, quos reddidi eidem Roberto pro tota terra mea quam tenui de eo in Aldulueston pro omni servitio, consuetudine et exactione ac demanda. Preterea dedi et concessi eidem Abbati et conventui totum ius meum quod habui vel habere debui in totis tenementis patris mei Hervei et matris mee Matilde et omnium antecessorum meorum tam in Aldulueston' quam in Bernesheg, et ubicumque sint salvis omnibus forinsecis servitiis dominorum. Ut autem hec donatio etc. Hiis testibus, Ada de Bedingfeld, Ricardo de Kaleston', Huberto Cordebof, Nicholao filio Roberti etc.

Date: confirmed in no. 95.

101. Robert de Bernesheg has confirmed the gifts of his brother William. Before 1231.

Rubric: Confirmatio Robertii de Bernesheg de dono predicti Willelmi.

Sciant presentes et futuri quod ego Robertus de Bernesheg concessi et hac presenti carta mea confirmavi donum quod Willelmus frater meus fecit deo et ecclesie sancte Marie de Leeston' et fratribus ibidem deo servientibus, scilicet de vi. acris terre cum pertinentiis quas idem Willelmus tenuit de me in Aldulueston cum vi. denariis red/*fo 71r*ditus quos ipse debuit mihi de eadem terra in puram et perpetuam elemosinam, quietam et solutam ab omni seculari servitio et demanda et salvo servitio domini Regis, scilicet ad scutagium domini Regis quando evenerit unum obolum domino Hugoni Rufo et heredibus suis reddendum, et pro hac concessione et huius carte mee confirmatione concessit et remisit et omnino quietum clamavit mihi et heredibus meis predictus Willelmus totum ius et clamium quod ipse habuit et habere potuit vel aliquis occasione sui in tota terra que fuit Hervei patris nostri in Clopton' et Aldulueston'. Hiis testibus, Hugone Rufo, Eadmundo de Tudeham, Thoma de Oteleie, Osseberto de Tudeham, Johanne de Staunpes etc.

Date: Hugh Ruffus (see Introduction, 10).

102. William son of Alan has quitclaimed a man, his family and chattels. Early thirteenth century.

Rubric: Carta Willelmi filii Alani.

Sciant presentes et futuri quod ego Willelmus filius Alani quietum clamavi Girardum filium Selvie cum tota sequela sua et cum omnibus catallis suis domino Philippo Abbati et conventui de Leeston', in puram et perpetuam elemosinam. Et ut hec donatio mea firma sit et rata sigilli mei appositione eam roboravi. Testibus, Willelmo filio Theobaldi, Willelmo de Glamvill', Waltero filio eius, etc.

Date: Abbot Philip.
See Introduction, 17–18.

103. William son of Theobald has granted 10 acres which he has in pledge from Saer de Biskele, until the pledge is redeemed. Before 1221.

Rubric: Carta Willelmi filii Theobaldi.

Sciant presentes et futuri quod ego Willelmus filius Theobaldi de Leeston' dedi et concessi et presenti carta confirmavi deo et ecclesie beate Marie de Leeston et canonicis[1] ibidem deo servientibus ad fabricam eiusdem ecclesie in puram elemosinam, decem acras terre que vocantur Middeldole, quas habeo de Saero de Biskele in vadio, habendas usque ad terminum prefixum inter Saerum et me, sicut carta sepedicti /fo 71v Saeri testatur, nisi idem Saerus vel heredes eius illam terram infra dictum terminum adquietare voluerit; quod si ego et heredes mei non poterimus warantizare prefatis canonicis predictam terram usque ad prenominatum terminum, dabimus eis decem acras terre de proprio tenemento meo ad Wagefen iacentes iuxta terram sepedictorum canonicorum habendas usque ad supradictum terminum. Ut autem hec donatio et concessio et confirmatio firma sit et stabilis, presentem cartam, etc. Hiis testibus, Henfrido de Criketot, Willelmo filio eius, Henrico de Grimill', Willelmo filio Alani, etc.

[1] ordinis expunged

Date: Hemfrid de Criketot.

104. Hemfrid de Criketot has granted all his rights over a man, his family and chattels. Before 1221.

fo 72r Rubric: Carta Hemfridi de Criketoth de Bernardo de Stodhaghe.

Sciant presentes et futuri quod ego Hemfridus de Criketoth concessi et dedi et presenti carta confirmavi deo et ecclesie sancte Marie de Leeston', et canonicis ordinis Premonstratensis ibidem deo servientibus, pro salute anime mee et antecessorum et successorum meorum Bernardum de Stodhage cum tota sequela sua et omnibus catallis suis, et quicquid iuris habui vel habere debui ego et heredes mei in eisdem, in liberam, puram et perpetuam elemosinam. Ut autem hec donatio mea et concessio firma sit et stabilis in perpetuum perseveret, eam presenti scripto et sigilli mei appositione roboravi. Hiis testibus, Henrico de Grimil', Waltero de Valeines, Willelmo filio Alani, etc.

Date: Hemfrid de Criketot.

105. Margaret, daughter of Roger the Seneschal, has granted land in Grundisburgh. Before 1233.

Rubric: Carta Margarete filie R. senescalli de Culpho de tribus acris terre in parochia de Grundesburch.

fo 72v Sciant presentes et futuri quod ego Margareta filia Rogeri senescalli de Culfo dedi et concessi et presenti carta confirmavi pro salute anime mee et omnium antecessorum meorum deo et ecclesie beate Marie de Leeston' et canonicis ordinis Premonstratensis ibidem deo servientibus in liberam, puram et perpetuam elemosinam, tres acras terre mee in parochia de Grundesburg, que abutant super le Broc versus austrum, et terram meam que vocatur Gandresacre ubi estimantur tres rode que abutat super predictum Broc, et unam rodam terre mee in eodem campo. Ut autem hec concessio, donatio et confirmatio firma sit et stabilis in perpetuum, presentem cartam sigilli mei appositione roboravi. Hiis testibus, Hugone le Rus, Eadmundo de Tudeham, Willelmo de Verdun, Oseberto de Wachesham.

Date: Edmund de Tudeham.

106. John, son of Roger the Seneschal, has confirmed his sister's gifts. Before 1233.

Rubric: Carta Johannis filii R. senescalli de Culfo de vii. acris terre in Grundesburg.

Sciant presentes et futuri quod ego Johannes filius Rogeri senescalli de Culfo concessi et presenti carta confirmavi pro anima Rogeri patris mei deo et ecclesie beate Marie de Leeston', et canonicis ordinis Premonstratensis ibidem deo servientibus in liberam et puram et perpetuam elemosinam totum donum illud quod Margareta soror mea dedit predictis canonicis sicut carte predicte Margarete testantur, quas prefati canonici habent, scilicet septem acras terre et dimidiam in parochia de Grundesburg que sunt de feodo meo, quarum tres acre abutant super le Broc versus austrum, et tres rode vocantur Gandresacre et abutant super predictum Broc et una roda iacet in eodem campo. Tres vero alie acre vocantur la Rode, et dimidia acra abutat super easdem. Salvo mihi et heredibus meis servitio meo quod debet fieri de tribus illis acris que vocantur la Rode et de dimidia acra que abutat super easdem,

118

videlicet viginti et uno denariis pro omni servitio, consuetudine et demanda, annuatim solvendis ad terminos qui in carta sepedicte Margarete sororis mee continentur quam sepedicti canonici de Leeston habent de ea. Ut autem hec concessio et confirmatio firma sit et stabilis in perpetuum, presentem |fo 73r cartam sigilli mei appositione roboravi. Hiis testibus, Hugone le Rus, Eadmundo de Tudeham, Willelmo le Verdun.

Date: as no. 105.
Note: the confirmation is of land granted in no. 105, and of 'la Rode', for which there is no charter in the cartulary.

107. John, son of Roger the Seneschal, has granted part of the 7 acres granted by his sister. Before 1233.

Rubric: Carta Johannis filii R. senescalli de Culfo de una acra et una roda.

Sciant presentes et futuri quod ego Johannes filius Rogeri senescalli de Culfo dedi et concessi et presenti carta confirmavi deo et ecclesie beate Marie de Leeston' et canonicis ordinis Premonstratensis ibidem deo servientibus, in liberam puram et perpetuam elemosinam, unam acram terre et unam rodam in parochia de Grundesburg que pertinebant ad septem acras terre quas Margareta soror mea dedit predictis canonicis sicut carta predicte Margarete sororis mee els inde facta testatur.[1] Et ego Johannes et heredes mei warantizabimus prefatis canonicis predictam acram cum una roda contra omnes homines in perpetuum. Ut vero hec mea donatio firma et stabilis perpetuo perseveret eam sigilli mei appositione roboravi. Hiis testibus, Osberto de Wachesham, Eadmundo de Tudeham, Willelmo de Verdun.

[1] MS testantur.

Date: as no. 105.

108. Alan de Witherdale has confirmed the gift of Hugh de Rickinghall in Playford. Before c 1229.

Rubric: Carta Alani de Witherdale de dono Hugonis de Rikinhale de marisco de Plaiford et de Adwardo Gest.

Sciant presentes et futuri quod ego Alanus de Witherdale concessi, et presenti carta confirmavi deo et ecclesie beate Marie de Leeston et canonicis ordinis Premonstratensis ibidem deo servientibus pro salute anime mee et meorum, totum donum quod dedit illis Hugo de Rikingehale in Plaiford, scilicet totum mariscum suum cum prato et pastura que habuit in Plaiford cum omnibus pertinentiis et sunt de feodo meo in liberam, puram et perpetuam elemosinam. Et cum Edwardo Gest qui fuit homo predicti Hugonis cum tota sequela sua, et tenemento eiusdem Edwardi, quod tenuit de dicto Hugone in villa de Plaiford, quod tenementum similiter est de feodo meo, salvis |fo 73v duodecim denariis pro predicto Edwardo et eius sequela et tenemento domino feodi annuatim solvendis pro omni servitio, consue-

119

tudine, et exactione, sicut carte sepedicti Hugonis quas prefati canonici de Leestun' habent testantur. Ut autem hec concessio et confirmatio firma sit et stabilis presentem cartam sigilli mei appositione roboravi. Hiis testibus, Henrico de Grimil', Adam de Bedingefeld et aliis.

Date: Henry de Grimilies – see no. 50 n.
Note: the grants confirmed are in nos. 79 and 80.

109. (i) The abbot of Leiston   (ii) Edmund de St Clere (*de Sancto Claro*), **concerning service from a tenement in Coddenham. 1288–9.**

fo 74r–v   A. Pleading at Westminster before Thomas de Wayland, 30th May 1288.
(ii) was summoned to answer (i) on the following plea: that (ii) should acquit (i) of the service which Alexander de Criketot exacts of (i) for a free tenement held by (i) of (ii) in Coddenham, which service (ii) ought to acquit. (i) asks why Alexander is distraining him for 12*d* annual rent from the tenement, whence he has sustained 100*s* damages, since he holds 4 acres plus appurtenances in Coddenham in free, pure and perpetual alms by gift of (ii)'s grandfather Robert de St Clere, and produces a charter of Robert concerning such acquittance.
   (ii) through his attorney cannot deny liability to acquit (i) of the service.
   Judgement: that (ii) acquit (i) of the service. The sheriff is ordered to distrain (ii) to acquit (i) in future; (i) recovers damages, (ii) is in mercy, and the sheriff is to hold an inquest into damages.
   Note that if enrolment needs to be found, it is in Trinity, 16 Edward I, no. 11.[1]

fo 74v   B. Writ, witnessed Thomas Weyland, Westminster 8th June 1289, to sheriff of Suffolk, ordering distraint of (ii) in case of future failure to acquit (i) of service as above, and an inquest into (i)'s damages, paying them out of (ii)'s lands and chattels.

[1] De Banco Roll no. 73 (Trinity 16 Edward I) m.7

110. (i) The abbot of Leiston   (ii) William and Isabella Cumyn, concerning service from a tenement in Buxlow. 1288–9.

A. Pleading at Westminster, 3rd November 1288.
fo 75r–v   (ii) were summoned to answer (i) on the following plea: that (ii) should acquit (i) of the service which Roger de Huntingfield exacts of (i) for a free tenement which (i) holds of (ii) in Buxlow (*Buckeslowe*), which service (ii) ought to acquit. (i) asks why Roger is distraining him for an annual rent of 5*s*, and one pound of cummin or 8*d*, whence he has sustained damages of £20; since he holds of (ii) 40 acres with appurtenances in Buxlow for an annual service of 5*s*, plus 2*s* per 40*s* scutage; and (i) produces suit.
   (ii) through their attorney deny force and tort, admit liability to acquit (i) of the said service, but deny that (i) has been distrained for lack of their acquittance. Both parties request a jury, which the sheriff is ordered to

120

assemble on the quindene of Easter. On 4th October 1289 (ii) do not appear: a day appointed for their essoiners.

The jurors (no date given) say (i) was distrained for lack of (ii)'s acquittance.

Judgement: (i) awarded 100s damages; (ii) in mercy.

fo 75v B. Writ, copy incomplete, ordering distraint of (ii) to acquit (i) henceforward, and recovery of 50s from lands and chattels of (ii) of the 100s which (i) recovered, unless (ii) had acquitted (i) previously.

111. (i) Adam Ostechirche of Knodishall, and Adam Skil of Westleton (ii) Michael son of John of Dunwich, John le Fulur, and Henry Ringulf, concerning unjust imprisonment. 1293.

A. Pleading before Gilbert de Torintone, 31st May 1293.
fo 75v–77r (ii) were summoned to answer (i) on the plea that on 3rd February 1293, while returning the king's writ to (ii) concerning replevin of the abbot of Leiston's chattels unjustly detained by (ii), (i) were unjustly taken and imprisoned for 8 days by (ii), whence damages are £10[1] to themselves, and £100 for contempt of the king; and (i) produce suit.[2]

(ii) deny force and tort.

Augustine le Clerc, bailiff of the town of Dunwich, produces a royal charter of Edward I, given by the king's own hand, Westminster, 28th June 1285, confirming to the men of Dunwich that they should neither plead nor be summoned outside their town. He says (ii) are burgesses of Dunwich, and asks for their liberty to be allowed.

(i) say they were bearing a royal writ, under the seal of Norwich castle, that is, the sheriff's seal, valid throughout the county; being thus royal messengers, which is why they were imprisoned. (i) offer to prove this, and since the transgression was in contempt of the king, they seek judgement that (ii) should answer in the present court.

Since the king is a party to the plea, it is decided that (ii) should answer in the present court, saving their liberties as far as rightful.

(ii) plead innocent, and place themselves on the county saving their liberties as far as rightful; (i) likewise.

A jury comes *coram rege*, 13th November; (ii) are essoined; adjourned to 27th January, 1294.

On which day the jurors say (ii) imprisoned (i) against the king's peace because they were returning the writ to deliver the abbot's chattels.

Judgement: (i)'s damages assessed by jurors, and at the justices' discretion, at 5 marks against (ii); liberty of Dunwich to be taken into the king's hands.

fo 77r B. Writ of fieri facias ordering recovery of 5 marks from (ii) if they are found, and seizure of liberty of Dunwich into king's hands. Sheriff to have writ at Westminster, 2nd February, 1294.

Note: 111a printed, G. O. Sayles, *Select Cases in the Court of King's Bench, Edward I* (Selden Soc. lvii, 1938), ii. no. 59, from Coram Rege no. 137.
[1] Coram Rege, £40
[2] Henceforward verbatim copy of Coram Rege roll; hitherto, summary only.

112. (i) The abbot of Leiston (ii) Michael son of John of Dunwich and others[1], concerning unjust distraint. 1293 and after.

A. Pleading at Westminster before J. de Metinham and associates, justices de banco, *7th June 1293.*[2]

ff 77r–78v (ii) attached to answer (i) on the following plea: whereas (i) neither holds nor claims to hold of (ii) and owes no service to (ii), (ii) with Andrew Terry and others[3] distrained by force and arms, at Leiston on 19th October 1292, (i)'s goods and chattels, i.e. anchors, ropes, sails, and rudders, whence (i)'s damages are £100. (i) produces suit.

The bailiffs of Dunwich come and claim that (ii) should not answer in the present court, producing a charter of Henry III conceding that burgesses of Dunwich need not stand to right outside their town; and they claim their own court. The charter was read to the king's council, which decided that the burgesses should not have their own court since the crime was committed outside their liberty.

(ii) deny force and tort, saying that on the aforesaid day certain men of (i) came with ships laden with merchandise and other things into Minsmere where the bailiffs of Dunwich had taken toll time out of mind from each ship landing; (ii) demanded toll on the contents, and when this was refused, reasonably and lawfully distrained upon them.

(i) denies the justice of the distraint; Minsmere lies between Westleton and Leiston, and while the bailiffs are entitled to toll on the Westleton side, they never have been so entitled on the Leiston side, which is within the abbot's manor of Leiston where, when the tide comes in, the ships of (i) and others often land. (i) seeks a jury.

(ii) say that when the liberty of Dunwich was in royal hands toll was taken on both sides of Minsmere, as it was when the burgesses and their ancestors held the town at farm; and they place themselves on the country; (i) likewise.[2]

Sheriff ordered to assemble a jury at Westminster on 30th September, on which day (ii) are essoined; adjourned to 10th May 1294; on which day a jury is lacking for want of knights and other jurors; adjourned to 13th October; on which day Michael has letters of protection, as those named in the writ are in royal service. The king orders the judges to be superseded in the plea, and the justices order (i) to await the end of the war.

fo 78v   B. Writ of venire facias ordering sheriff of Suffolk to bring (i) to the exchequer at Westminster on the morrow of Trinity Sunday to explain why, since all tolls in Minsmere belong to the king and ought to be collected by his bailiffs of Dunwich, (i) has appropriated such tolls to himself and his church, not allowing the bailiffs to collect them, in contempt of the king, as the bailiffs say.

On which day the abbot did not appear, and the following writ was sent:

fo 78v–79r   C. Writ ordering sheriff of Suffolk to distrain lands and chattels of Nicholas, abbot of Leiston, until further notice; and to bring him to the exchequer at Westminster on 27th January, to explain why, etc. as in B.

122

fo 79r   D. (i) attached to answer the king on the above offence.

Michael son of John of Dunwich, pleading for the king and the men of Dunwich, says that toll on all merchandise coming by sea into the king's port of Minsmere belongs to the king and should be collected by the bailiffs of Dunwich, but has been appropriated by (i); and that ships used to come into the port with merchandise and stay until the merchandise was sold and the toll paid; but that (i) has widened and deepened a certain channel (*trenchea*) from Leiston to the port, such that ships are received there and toll taken. He alleges (i)'s bailiffs have taken 20s toll from the ships of Stephen le Frere, 1 mark from the ship of John le Wyte, 1 mark from that of Denis, 20s from that of Walter Gyn, and £20 from other ships in contempt of the king and to the impoverishment of Dunwich, and claims damages of £1,000. He offers to prove this.

(i) denies force and tort, and says that Minsmere is not a royal port, but an opening made by (i)'s men in the ground of Leiston manor, that it lies a league away from the boundary of Dunwich, being in the body of the county, not in the town's liberty, and not belonging to the farm of the town. (i) admits that an ancient channel extends from Minsmere into his manor of Leiston, but denies ever widening or enlarging it; and although ships stay there, he has never taken toll, but says that those who have an easement on his ground and damage the grass pay him for that; he says he has never attracted ships there to damage the king, and asks for an inquest.

Michael says the king's bailiffs used to take toll from ships in Minsmere time out of mind until the abbot stopped them, and also asks for an inquest.

The sheriff to summon a jury for 27th January; the jury does not come; adjourned until the morrow of the Sunday after Easter; again the jury does not come; adjourned until the quindene of Trinity.

On which day a jury comes, Robert de Burneyle and others, who say on oath that Minsmere is a river which runs between (i)'s land and the vill of Westleton, which is of the honour of Eye, and then flows to the sea, and is one league distant from the boundary of Dunwich; they say that from the time of the abbey's foundation there has been a channel from the abbey to Minsmere. Of old the lords of Westleton used to take toll from ships which anchored off Westleton; there was contention between the men of Dunwich and the men of Westleton, the former taking toll from the latter coming to Dunwich with their merchandise, and they finally agreed that the men of Dunwich should take toll where the lords of Westleton used to, that is on the Westleton side, and that the men of Westleton should be free of toll in Dunwich: this was when they first took toll in Minsmere. The jury say that (i) takes no toll in Minsmere or in the channel, but it sometimes happens that in bad weather ships sheltering in the channel break its banks, and fishermen throw their nets on the grass to dry, and trample (i)'s pasture: (i) in the usual way takes compensation, as his predecessors have since the abbey's foundation, by mutual agreement. They say that the men of Dunwich take toll on the Westleton side; as for widening and deepening the channel, they say (i) is perfectly entitled to do so as it is on his land. They say (i) does not impede the men of Dunwich from taking toll on the Westleton side. Asked how long the men of Dunwich had taken this toll and how much it was worth, they said, for thirty years, and 10s yearly. Asked why (i) had enlarged the channel, they said he had merely cleared it of sand washed into it by the sea.

123

Judgement: (i) acquitted; and the men of Dunwich had been taking toll without warrant.

[1] De Banco Roll adds John le Folur, Robert Sparewe, Henry Ringulf, Thomas Dionis', John Ousyng, John de Clyf, Robert Joce, Robert Bullok, Alexander Joce, William Bedale, Peter son of John, Andrew Austyn, Geoffrey Sort, Adam le Clerk, Henry le Ray, Jocelin Perceval.
[2] ....[2] Transcript of De Banco Roll no. 101 (Trinity Edward I), m. 90. Cartulary adds, 'roll 90c'.
[3] Roll adds John Joce, Geoffrey Fygat.

113. (i) The king and Thomas Wilpyn, bailiff of Dunwich   (ii) Nicholas, abbot of Leiston, Ric' de Ellingham, Walter de Glanveyle, Roger de Bocking, Adam del Chirche, John de Ryk', John Curteys and John Sparke. No date (in or after 1294).

fo 80v–81v   A. Writ of venire facias ordering sheriff of Suffolk to bring to the exchequer at Westminster on the quindene of Trinity, (ii) and Robert de Ellingham, John de Eye, Seman de Elmswell, Walter de Kyndale, John Geffrey, Walter Hunde, Denis Sutere, Robert Syke, Seman Kempe, Roger Sparke, Thomas Brodheye, William son of Stephen and Adam Skyl, to show why, when Thomas Wilpyn, as bailiff of Dunwich, siezed certain goods, chattels and merchandise of the abbot by way of toll and custom and put them in a sure place in the town of Dunwich, they attacked him with force and arms, beat, wounded and ill-treated him, carrying off the said goods and chattels, and performing other enormities in contempt of the king, to the damage of the said Thomas, and in breach of the peace.

fo 81r–v   B. Pleading resulting from the previous writ.
(ii) attached to answer (i) on a plea of trespass. Thomas, pleading for the king and himself, said that when on 28th October 1293 he arrested in the port of Minsmere a certain ship of Stephen le Frere containing goods to the value of £20 in order to take toll and placed them within the liberty of Dunwich, the abbot and others, together with others unknown, insulted, beat, wounded and ill-treated him, and the next night took the ship with the goods out of the liberty of Dunwich and into the abbot's liberty along a certain channel leading from Minsmere to Leiston abbey, and continue to detain the said ship, in contempt of the king, to the damage of the said Thomas of £20. He offers to prove this.

   (ii) deny force and tort, deny the offence and ask for an inquest; Thomas likewise.
   The sheriff is ordered to summon a jury three weeks after Easter.

114. Inquisition *ad quod damnum*, 1345.

A. Writ to John Howard, escheator in Norfolk and Suffolk, 1st February 1345. (i) Margery, widow of (ii) Theobald de Leyston (iii) Rose and William de Schotesham (iv) Margery, wife of John Bokel of Friston, and Joan, wife of Richard Bokel, neices and heiresses of (ii) (v) Richard de Burgstede, parson of Framlingham, William Scarlet, parson of Gunton, John Gerard, chaplain, and John Frounceys of Shadingfield (vi) John Blame.

The manor of Wade Hall with appurtenances and 125 acres of land, 70 acres of heath, 10 acres of marsh, 20s rent with appurtenances in Leiston, Aldringham, Theberton, Knodishall, Buxlow, Friston, Kelsale, (Ched)iston[1], Fordley, and Yoxford, was demised by (ii) to (iii) such that (i) held of (iii); (iii) demised it to (iv), such that (i) held it of (iv); (iv) assigned it to (v), such that (i) now holds of (v).

The escheator is to enquire to whose damage it would be and how much, if (v) concede the properties to the abbot and convent of Leiston and to (vi), who wishes to remit to the abbot and convent 6s 2d rent in Knodishall and Buxlow, such that after the death of (i) the properties shall revert to the abbot and convent; in part satisfaction of £20 in lands and rent which the abbot and convent have permission to acquire, unless held in chief of the king.

The escheator is to enquire into how the said property is held, by what service, and how much they are worth; the number and identity of any lords lying between the king and (v); how much would be left to (v) after this concession; where, how much, from whom and for what service (v) hold, and whether (v) would still be able to perform services due, in suit of court, view of frankpledge, aids, tallages and other burdens, and whether (v) and their descendants would still be able to serve on juries as their ancestors did, without burdening the country any more than usual.

The result is to be returned to the chancery with the writ.

fo 82v–83v B. Inquisition taken at Leiston, 26th May 1345, before John Howard, escheator in Norfolk and Suffolk, by oath of Henry Attebregge, Martin Love, Thomas le Poer, Richard de Denham, Roger de Eldirhegg, John Umfrey, Peter Cosyn, Richard de Meriel, Simon le Coliour, William Margrete, Robert de Hoxne and Richard Austyn, who say it is to no one's disadvantage if (v) concedes the above properties to the abbot and convent of Leiston.

The above manor is held as one sixth of a knight's fee and for 15s 1d yearly, and the lands and rent in socage for 12s 2d yearly. The manor is worth 56s 4d yearly, viz. the capital messuage 6d; 60 acres of arable 25s, at 5d per acre; 60 acres of heath 7s 6d, at 1½d per acre; 2 acres of meadow 2s; assised rents 15s 2d; customary services 4s 2d; perquisites of the court, 2s; rent due from the manor, 15s 1d; and thus the true value of the manor is 41s 3d.

The above lands are worth 26s 2d yearly, viz. 125 acres of land 16s 3d,[1] at 1½d per acre and no more, as the land is in the common field and so sandy that it can only be sown to any profit twice in ten years; 12 acres of pasture 4s; 70 acres of heath 2s 11d, at ½d per acre and no more, as it is common; the marsh 3s and no more, as it is under the sea from time to time. Rents due from the land, 12s 2d; and thus the true value is 14s.

125

The rent in Knodishall and Buxlow is held of John de Wimundeville[2] in free socage by fealty. The abbot holds in free, pure and perpetual alms of the heirs of Rannulf de Glanville: thus the abbot, the heirs of Rannulf, and John Kyriel are between the king and (v); and John de Wumundeville,[2] John de Braham and the earl of Suffolk, as lord of the honour of Eye, are between the king and (vi).

Richard de Burstede and John Gerard have no other lands or tenements as they are clerks and have no lay fee; John Fraunceys has 100s land and rent in Shadingfield, and William Scarlet 20s land in Heveningham held of Edward de Mountagu and others, by divers services; John Blome has 20s land and rent in Friston held of John de Wimundeville[2] and other lords by divers services. These holdings are sufficient to acquit the service of both the above manor and properties, and of the lands (v) retain.

The jurors have added their seals.

[1] recte, 15s 7½d?
[2] reading uncertain

Note: licence given to acquire the above land in mortmain, 12th July 1345 (CPR 1343–5, 529).
See Introduction, 26–7.

115. B. L. Harley charter 49 A 6. 30th June 1290. At London. (i) Nicholas de Cryel, miles (ii) dominus Gydo Ferre junior.

Grant of the manor of Benhall, with the advowsons of the priories of Butley and Leiston and all other appurtenances.
To hold to (ii), his heirs and assigns, by heredity and in fee of the chief lords of the fee by the service due (unspecified).
Warranty clause.
Witnessed by, dominis Johanne de Sancto Johanne, Rogero filio Petri filii Osberti, Adam' de Creting', Rogero de Soterle, Petro de Melles militibus, Johanne de Metingham, Johanne de Berewyk, Hugone de Cressingham, Willelmo de Carleton, Johanne Bacoun et aliis.

Size: 22.5 × 17.9 cm.
Seal: round, 2.2 cm; black wax mended with red/orange wax; on tag.
    Legend: S NICHOLAI DE CRIEL
    Device: lion passant.
Note: inspeximus and confirmation, 1294, CPR 1292–1301, 78.

116. B.L. Additional charter 10294. 1260–75. (i) Robert de Monte Alto (ii) Abbot Gregory and the convent of Leiston, their successors, and the church of Leiston.

Confirmation of all lands, tenements, and appurtenances held by (ii) of the fee or lordship (dominatio) of (i) in Pettaugh (Pethaye), Helmingham, Framsden, Cretingham, Stanham, Winston and Coddenham, or other vills, held of Roger de Colevile or acquired from any other, and release of all rights of (i) and his heirs to (ii) in the aforesaid lands, tenements and appurtenances. To hold to (ii) in pure and perpetual alms free of all secular service for ever. Promise not to distrain, by (i) for himself and his heirs.

Witnessed by, *domino* Willelmo de Weylaund, *domino* Thoma fratre eius, *domino* Roberto de Valeyns, *domino* Johanne de Bocking, *domino* Roberto de Wynestune, Johanne de Uluestune, Yvone de Kenetune, Willelmo de Wynestune, Johanne le Poer et aliis.

Endorsement: contemporary.
Size: 26.6 × 11.4 cm.
Seal: oval, 2.0 × 2.3 cm; dark blue/green wax; on tag.
     Legend: +SIGILLUM ROBERTI
     Device: a gem – head facing right?
Date: the Montalt family, hereditary seneschals of Chester, were tenants on the Chester lands in Suffolk. There were two later 13th century Roberts: the father, who succeeded c 1260 and died 1275 (Copinger, vii. 141–2; *C Inq PM* ii. no. 128); and his second son, who succeeded his brother Roger in 1296, died 1329 (*C Inq PM* iii. no. 408; vii. no. 471). If the Thomas de Weyland who witnesses was the prominent royal justice disgraced in 1289, the father is the more likely.

117. Bodleian Library, Suffolk charter 222. 10th July 1367, at Leiston. (i) Abbot John and the convent of Leiston (ii) Thomas (Percy), bishop of Norwich, and the cathedral church of Norwich.

(i) will submit to the decision of (ii) concerning an indemnification of (ii) and of the archdeacon of Suffolk for loss of first fruits and other damages, consequent on the appropriation of the church of Corton to (i); and (ii) may compel (i) to do so notwithstanding their privileges.

(i) renounce all legal action, not intending thereby to derogate from their privileges.

Endorsement: contemporary.
Size: c 31 × 13 cm.
Sealing: slit for tag.

118. Bodleian Library, Suffolk charter 221. 1st and 2nd May 1380. Henry (Despenser), bishop of Norwich, appropriates the church of Theberton to Leiston abbey.

The monastery of Leiston having been destroyed by inundation of the sea and its goods largely wasted, a new monastery was constructed on papal authority in a more suitable place, but except for the church was subsequently destroyed by fire. As a result the convent is burdened with debt and no longer able to offer hospitality to the poor, and, being near a public road, to travellers. The abbot and convent, by brother John of Darsham the abbot's proctor, have therefore requested the appropriation of Theberton church, which is in their patronage. The bishop has caused diligent enquiry to be made, and, having obtained the counsel and consent of the prior and convent of Norwich and of the archdeacon of Suffolk, out of his special devotion to the Virgin Mary, appropriates the said church to Leiston abbey. On the death, retirement or removal of brother Robert of Darsham, the present rector, the abbot and convent shall be able to enter upon the said church, by this authority as well as by that of pope Celestine's privilege, and dispose of its revenues as they think fit. Robert meanwhile is to continue to pay an annual pension of 20s on St Margaret's day to the abbey. In future the church is to be served not by a perpetual vicar, but by a secular priest deputed for a term of years without interference by the bishop or his successors as long as hospitality, first fruits and other dues from the church are paid: at the next vacancy the due tax is to be paid within a year, and thereafter an annual pension of 40s payable in equal portions at the Easter and Michaelmas synods, plus 4s at each synod at the high altar of the cathedral, plus 10s to the archdeacon of Suffolk at the next Ipswich synod after each vacancy of Leiston abbey. This is to be observed on pain of ecclesiastical censure and a fine of 20s to the cathedral, the right of visitation and other episcopal customs being reserved to the bishop and his successors. Sealed by the bishop and chapter of Norwich, at Norwich, 1st May 1380.

Prior Nicholas and the convent of Norwich add their ratification and confirmation, in the chapter house at Norwich, 2nd May 1380.

Endorsement: contemporary, including vj^{xx} ix.
Size: c 50 × 36.2 cm – probably truncated as no sign of sealing.

119. Royal letters patent of Richard II. 25th August 1388.

The abbey of Leiston, having been founded by Rannulf de Glanville, whose gifts were confirmed in divers charters of Henry II, the advowson was granted to Michael de la Pole, formerly earl of Suffolk, by whose forfeiture it is now in royal hands; wherefore the manor of Leiston and all the monastery's possessions are confirmed to the canons in perpetuity, together with the freedom to elect an abbot without royal licence or that of any other patron, the right to administer the temporalities of the house during a vacancy without the intrusion of any royal official or the official of any other patron, and the freedom from granting corrodies or pensions at the request or command of the king or of any other patron.

Printed: Monasticon vi(ii). 880; Suckling ii. 434–5.
Enrolled: CPR 1385–9, 510.

BUTLEY PRIORY CHARTERS

120. Rannulf de Glanville has endowed Butley priory. Before Jan. 1174.
Cambridge, Corpus Christi College, MS 111, no. 118, p 260.

Sciant tam presentes quam posteri quod ego Ranulphus de Glanvilla dedi et
concessi et praesenti carta confirmavi deo et Sanctae Mariae de Buteleia, et
canonicis regularibus quos ibidem constitui quique in perpetuum substi-
tuendi sunt regulariter deo servituri, ecclesiam de Buteleia, et ecclesiam de
Capella, et ecclesiam de Baudresheia, et ecclesiam de Benhalleia, et ecclesiam
de Fareham, et ecclesiam de Wantesdenia, et quartam partem ecclesiae de
Clemham, quam Robertus presbyter tenuit cum universis ad easdem
ecclesias pertinentibus, quantum est meum concedere et haeredum et
successorum meorum et totam terram de Reileia,[1] et totam terram quae fuit
Rogeri Fileoli[2] in Buteleia, et terram quae fuit Ernaldi presbyteri in Buteleia,
tenendas in liberam, puram et perpetuam elemosynam ad sustentandos
eosdem canonicos imperpetuum, pro salute mea et uxoris meae et natorum
meorum, et pro animabus patrum et matrum nostrorum, et dominorum et
amicorum meorum, haeredum et successorum, parentum et minorum, et
omnium fidelium viventum seu defunctorum. Hanc autem donationem feci in
praesentia domini Willielmi Norwicensis episcopi, et sub eius testimonio,
praesente uxore mea et consentiente et confirmante; et subscriptis hiis
testibus, Willielmo archidiacono, magistro Stephano, magistro Rogero
scriptore episcopi, Hamiddo, magistro Stangrimo, magistro Nicholao,
magistro Roberto de Wacstunesham, Osberto clerico de Baldreseie, Roberto
de Waluines[3], Radulpho de Valuines[3], Osberto de Glanvil, Gilberto de
Colevile, Gerardo de Glanvile, Rein' de Wacst'[4], Willielmo de Sternefeld,
Willielmo de Hereford, Roberto filio Rocelni, Ranulfo filio Nigelli, Ermeg'
filio Osberti, Roberto filio Willielmi, Willielmo filio Gilberti, Galfrido de
Muriols, Ricardo de Riebos, Ranulfo de Baudreseie, Herveo de Glanvile,
Savari de Valeines et plures multi.

[1] Rent-roll (see Introduction, 1) 'Relera'
[2] ibid., 'Rogeri filii Toly'
[3] Dugdale reads 'Walmues'; 'Valuines' etc. = Valeines – Robert de Valeines being
the brother of Rannulf's wife Bertha on whose marriage-portion the monastery
was founded (Intro., p 1).
[4] Dugdale reads 'Rem' de Wacst'; Reiner of Waxham ('Wacstunesham') was Rannulf
de Glanville's steward.

Printed: Monasticon, vi(i). 379.
Date: William, bishop of Norwich.
Note: the MS is a sixteenth century anthology of monastic foundation charters and
other miscellanea: see M. R. James, *A Descriptive Catalogue of the Manuscripts in the
Library of Corpus Christi College, Cambridge*, Cambridge 1912, i. 245. The rent roll
includes a summary; the MS copy seems slightly corrupt in places.

121. Henry II, charter of Liberties. December 1184–May 1185. Public Record Office, Cartae Antiquae Roll no. 21, m. 1.

Rubric: Carta Canonicorum de Butteleya.

Henricus dei gratia Rex Anglorum et Dux Normannorum et Aquitanorum et Comes Andegavorum, Archiepiscopis, Episcopis, Comitibus, Baronibus, Iustic', Vicecomitibus, Ministris, et omnibus fidelibus suis francis et anglis, Salutem. Sciatis me concessisse et presenti carta mea confirmasse deo et ecclesie sancte Marie de Butteleya et canonicis ibidem deo servientibus omnes donationes terrarum et hominum et elemosinarum que eis ration-abiliter facte sunt in ecclesiis et omnibus aliis rebus et possessionibus. Quare volo et firmiter precipio quod predicti canonici omnes terras et possessiones et elemosinas suas habeant et teneant cum socha et sacha et thol et theam et infangenetheof et cum omnibus aliis libertatibus et liberis consuetudinibus et dem(andis), in bosco et plano et pratis et pascuis, in aquis et molendinis, in viis et semitis, in stagnis et vivariis et mariscis et piscariis et grangiis et virgultis, infra burgum et extra et in omnibus locis et in omnibus rebus solutas (liberas et) quietas (de) sectis schyr et hundr', et placitis et querelis et de pecunia danda pro forisfacturo de murdro et de wapentac et scutagio et geldis et denegeld et hidag' et assisis et de operationibus castellorum et parcorum et pontium et calcearum (et de ferdwita) et de hengewite et de flemenefrenthe et de hamsocha et de warpeni et de averpeni et de blodwit et de fichtwit et de leirwita et de hundr(ed)peni et de ledingp(eni) nisi in introitu et sint quieti de omni theloneo et (.....)[1] lestagio et stallagio et de omni seculari servitio et opere servili et exactione et omnibus aliis occasionibus et consuetudinibus secularibus excepta sola iustitia mortis et membrorum. Hec omnia eis concessi in perpetuam elemosinam pro dei amore et pro (salute anime) mee et omnium antecessorum et successorum meorum. Testibus Baldewino Cantuariensi electo Wigorniensi episcopo, Johanne Norwicensi, Galfrido Eliensi, Hugone Dunelmensi, Reginaldo Bathoniensi, S' Cyces-trensi Episcopis, Herberto Cantuariensi Archidiacono, Godefrido de (Luci) Richemond' Archidiacono, Huberto Walteri, Hamelino Comite de Warenn, Willelmo Comite de Sussex, Comite Alberico, Ricardo Comite de Clara, Bernardo de Sancto Walerico, Waltero filio Roberti, apud Westmonasterium.

[1] MS illegible

Note: the MS is damaged, and the bracketed words are supplied from no. 25, which is almost identical.
See Introduction, 33.

122. Richard I, confirmation charter. 1st August 1190. Public Record Office, Cartae Antiquae Roll no. 21, m. 1.

Rubric: Carta Canonicorum de Butteleya.

Ricardus dei gratia Rex Anglie, Dux Normannie et Aquitanie, Comes Andegavie, Archiepiscopis, Episcopis, Abbatibus, Comitibus, Baronibus, Iustic', Vicecomitibus, Ministris, et omnibus baillivis et fidelibus suis totius Anglie, francis et anglis presentibus et futuris, Salutem. Sciatis nos (ad

132

petitionem) fidelis nostri Rannulfi de Glanvill concessisse et presenti carta confirmasse omnes donationes quas Henricus Rex Anglie pater noster et ipse Rannulfus de Glanvill' et alii donatores et fundatores fecerunt deo et ecclesie constructe in honore beate Marie apud Buttele (et cano)nicis ibidem deo servientibus in ecclesiis et tenementis et in omnibus aliis elemosinis in puram et perpetuam elemosinam sicut carte Henrici Regis Anglie patris nostri et aliorum donatorum testantur. Quare volumus et firmiter precipimus quod predicti canonici (et eorum homines) omnes possessiones et elemosinas suas habeant et teneant cum socha et sacha et thol et theam et infangenetheof in bosco et plano et pratis et pascuis, in aquis et molendinis, in viis et semitis, in stagnis et vivariis (et mariscis et piscariis, et grangiis et virgultis, infra) burgum et extra et in omnibus rebus et in omnibus locis solutas, liberas et quietas de sectis schyrarum et hundr(edorum) et de placitis forest' et querelis et de pecunia danda pro forisfacturo de murdro, et de (wapentachio et scutagio ......et de operationibus) castellorum et parcorum et pontium et calcearum et de ferdwita et de leirwita et de hundredepeni et de tiedeinpeni nisi in introitu et de hengenewita et de flemenefrenthe et de hamsoca et de (warpeni......)wita et sint ipsi et homines sui quieti per totam terram nostram de omni theloneo et de omnibus rebus quas ipsi canonici vel homines sui poterunt assecurare quod emant vel vendant ad proprios usus canonicorum ipsorum vel hominum (suorum..... de pont)agio et lestagio et stallagio et de omni seculari servitio et opere servili et exactione et omnibus aliis occasioni-bus et consuetudinibus secularibus et omnibus aliis quietantiis et libertatibus quas Henricus pater noster eis fecit integra (.........)perpetuam elemosinam pro dei amore et salute anime nostre et animi domini Regis Henrici patris nostri et omnium antecessorum et successorum nostrorum. Hiis testibus, Baldewino Cantuariensi Archiepiscopo, Warino filio Henrici filio Geroldi, Bertramno de Verdun.......[1]hidi(aconi.) Datum apud Marsiliam primo die Augusti per manum Willelmi filii Ricardi regni nostri anno primo.

[1] Landon adds Gilbert Pipard

Note: Landon, L. *The itinerary of King Richard I*, PR Soc, NS xiii, 1935, no. 335. Bracketed words supplied from no. 23, which is very similar. See Introduction, 34.

DEBENHAM

123. Bodleian Library, Suffolk charter 193. 1st and 4th June 1361. (i) Prior and convent of Ely, appropriators of Winston church (ii) Prior and convent of Butley, appropriators of Debenham church.

Cyrograph.
For a time beyond the memory of man (i) and (ii) have each been receiving garb tithes and tithe of peas from within the limits of the other's parish, whence dissension has arisen between their respective collectors, who have demanded, and many times carried off, tithes which are not due to them;

wherefore (ii) agree that (i) shall have all such tithes accruing to the south of the following boundary:

from the eastern bank of a certain water anciently called Shepwaysh to the eastern end of a road called Kolersweye where a cross is sited, tending then to the west across the road, along the processional way of Debenham to the head of the boundary on the eastern end of the field called Bromistoneshegg, which boundary turns north to the southern end of the piece of land belonging to Adam le Dextere of Debenham called Hungrisdonne; thence along the said end of the same piece westwards by the said processional way to the southern end of the boundary between Bromistoneshegg on the south side and the field called Hungerdonne on the other; thence northwards to the southern end of the piece, formerly of Warin Chapman of Debenham, called Wynstonefeeld; from the said southern end westwards to the boundary between, on the east, the land formerly of Thomas Spytelman called Bromistoneshegg, from which (i) takes tithe, and on the other the land formerly of John de Hoxn' from which (ii) takes tithe; which boundary extends far to the south, to the northern end of a piece called Kurlepetacre, turning back by the boundary lying to the west of the said piece formerly of John de Hoxn' northwards to the southern end of a piece of land of the said Adam Dextere; thence westwards across the tops of two pieces of land until the southern end of a close anciently called Bromiessedge, turning away by the boundary to the west of the said close a long way to the north as far as the eastern end of another boundary, between Adam Dextere's land to the north and the villein land of (i) called Yulueredingg on the other side; from the said eastern end westwards to the western cart-track (*carrierio*) of a lake anciently called Goldmereshay, turning off the track by a baulk (*sulcus*) extending through the middle of the land of Mabille Child of Debenham northwards to the east end of the boundary at Katenhowe between a piece of the said Mabille's land on the south and the land of the said Adam and William Ingre on the other side, which boundary extends a long way westwards to a meadow called Hayesmedwe.

Beyond this meadow (i) shall have tithe from one piece of land only, called Manshort and containing two acres, and one small piece in (i)'s wood, of old called Keedyng, by Walter Towgh's close abutting onto the said meadow.

There are excepted six pieces of (ii)'s demesne lying on the Winston side of this boundary, which are not and never used to be tithed:

(1) between land of William Hert to east, and Roger Baldry's to the other, the north end abutting on a meadow called Estmedwe,

(2) to the southern end of (1) and of a piece of Adam Dextere's land, with (i)'s land on both sides,

(3) lies in the same *quarentena* in the field called Bluedonne, with land formerly William Ingre's to east and the lands of Sayer Barkere and John Lemman to south, abutting on Estmedwe to north,

(4) lies in the same place, abutting on (3) to south and on Kolerweye to north,

(5) lies in the same place between the land of Stephen de Northhagh to north ....[1], abutting as (4),

(6) lies in the same field, with land of William Hert to west, and that which Henry Towgh.....[1] and the north end abuts on Kolerweye.

Also excepted are three pieces of land of the dowry of the church of Winston, belonging to the vicar, lying in Debenham, which are not and never used to be tithed:

(1) in the field called Hungresdonne between land of Thomas le Whyte held by (i)'s serfs to west.....[1]

(2) lies east and west by the headlands (*per capita*) next to Debenhambrock on the north,

(3) at Gooldeshay, between land of Adam Dextere to west, and William Hert's on the other, northern end abutting on Gooldeshaymedwe.

Sealing clause. Given at Ely in the chapter house, 1st June, and at Butley in the chapter house, 4th June, 1361.

[1] MS damaged

Size: c 46.5 × c 29.5 cm: damaged in parts, probably truncated.

DENNINGTON

124. Gerard son of Benedict of Dennington has granted two men, their tenements, homage and service. Before 1230.
BL Harley charter 49 F 13.

Sciant presentes et futuri quod ego Gerardus filius Benedicti de Dinniueton' concessi, dedi, et hac carta mea confirmavi deo et ecclesie sancte Marie de Buttel' et canonicis ibidem deo servientibus et in perpetuum servituris pro salute anime mee et Marger' et Yde uxorum mearum et omnium antecessorum et successorum meorum in liberam, puram, et perpetuam elemosinam homagia duorum hominum meorum scilicet Ricardi Coc, et Jordani filii Osberti de Dinniueton' cum tenementis eorum que de me tenuerunt, et servitiis que mihi fecerunt, scilicet duobus solidis per annum, quorum unus videlicet Ricardus Coc eis singulis annis tredecim denarios persolvet, et alius scilicet Jordanus undecim denarios ad quatuor terminos, scilicet ad Nativitatem sancti Johannis Baptisti Ricardus tres denarios, et Jordanus duos denarios et obolum, et ad festum sancti Michaelis Ricardus tres denarios et Jordanus duos denarios et obolum, et ad festum sancti Andree Ricardus tres denarios et Jordanus duos denarios et obolum, et ad Pasch' Ricardus quatuor denarios, et Jordanus tres denarios et obolum similiter et heredes eorum post eos imperpetuum. Volo etiam et firmiter concedo quod predicti duo homines et heredes eorum per tenementa sua prefatis canonicis sint iusticiabiles, et faciant eis quicquid mihi vel heredibus meis facere debuerunt, preter sex denarios tantum quos dominus prefate ville qui pro tempore fuerit, per manum meam et heredum meorum post me singulis annis debet percipere. Et ego et heredes mei warantizabimus prenominatis canonicis imperpetuum prefatos homines et heredes illorum cum illorum servitiis et tenementis contra omnes homines. Hiis testibus, Henrico parcario, Willelmo filio Ricardi, Petro filio Huberti, et Huberto filio eius, Ricardo filio Roberti, et Rannulfo fratre eius, Willelmo de Sancto Edmundo, Johanne filio Gerardi, Gaufrido filio Huberti, Gaufrido filio Gileberti, et Roberto fratre eius,

Matheo parvo, et Waltero fratre eius, Rogero de Holesl', Radulfo de Ketleberg', Godefrido de Mendham, Johanne de Mendham, Gileberto Bordemal, Rogero de Fleg', Willelmo de Sutton'.

Endorsement: (contemporary) Gerard' fil' Benedicti de Dinnieueton' de duobus solidis per annum.
Size: 19 × 6.3 cm.
Seal: vesica; 3.9 × 4.9 cm; very dark green wax; on tag.
    Legend: +SIGIL' GERARD FIL'I BENETI D DENIN
    Device: an 'eagle' displayed.
Date: Henry parcarius.

125. Gerard son of Benedict of Dennington has granted 11½ acres in Dennington, with his body for burial. Before 1230.
BL Harley charter 49 F 14.

Sciant presentes et futuri quod ego Gerardus filius Benedicti de Dinnieueton' concessi dedi et presenti carta mea confirmavi deo et ecclesie sancte Marie de Buttel' et canonicis ibidem deo servientibus et in perpetuum servituris pro salute anime mee et animarum Margar' et Ide uxorum mearum et omnium antecessorum et successorum meorum in liberam, puram et perpetuam elemosinam quandam partem terre mee cum corpore meo quod bone devotionis intuitu apud prefatam ecclesiam tradidi sepeliendum, scilicet undecim acras terre et dimidiam in Dinnieueton', quarum quatuor sunt infra curiam meam cum domibus et omnibus aliis rebus que infra predictam curiam continentur, et due iacent ad Northwall', et una et dimidia ad Luuerunesbusc, et una ante portam meam, et dimidia ante portam Crasc, et dimidia ad Halihoc, et una acra nemoris iuxta predictam curiam, et una acra prati ad Northwall' cum omnibus ad prenominatas terras pertinentibus, habendas et tenendas in perpetuum liberas et solutas ab omni seculari servitio et demanda. Et ego et heredes mei warantizabimus eis has terras predictas imperpetuum contra omnes homines, et adquietabimus eas de omnibus rebus sicut liberam puram et perpetuam elemosinam. Ut autem hec concessio et donatio mea perpetuam optineat firmitatem, eam presenti scripto et sigilli mei appositione roboravi. Hiis testibus, Henrico Parcario, Willelmo filio Ricardi, Petro filio Huberti, et Huberto filio eius, Ric' filio Roberti, et Rannulfo fratre eius, Willelmo de Sancto Edmundo, Johanne filio Gerardi, Gaufrido filio Huberti, Gaufrido filio Gileberti, et Roberto fratre eius, Matheo parvo, et Waltero fratre eius, Rogero de Holesl', Radulfo de Ketlebcrg, Godefrido de Mendham, Johanne de Mendham, Gileberto Bordemal', Rogero de Fleg', Willelmo de Sutton'.

Endorsement: (contemporary) Gerard' fil' Benedicti de xi acris terre et dimidia.
               (14th century) v.
Size: 18.7 × 8.5 cm.
Seal: as no. 124. Repaired with red/orange wax.backing.
Date: as no. 124.

126. Richard son of Henry son of Benedict of Dennington has confirmed no. 125. Early thirteenth century, poss. 1229–c 1235. BL Harley charter 49 F 15.

Sciant presentes et futuri quod ego Ricardus filius Henrici filii Benedicti de Dinieuetun' nepos et heres Gerardi parcarii concessi et presenti carta mea confirmavi deo et ecclesie sancte Marie de Buttel' et canonicis ibidem deo servientibus et in perpetuum servituris undecim acras terre et dimidiam in Dinieuetun', quas prefatus Gerardus patruus meus eis in liberam puram et perpetuam elemosinam dedit et carta sua confirmavit, quarum quatuor sunt infra curiam que fuit prefati Gerardi cum domibus et omnibus aliis rebus que infra prefatam curiam continentur, et due iacent ad North Walle, et una et dimidia ad Luuerunesbusc, et una ante portam predicti Gerardi, et dimidia ante portam Crasc, et dimidia ad Haliohc, et una acra nemoris iuxta predictam curiam, et una acra prati ad Northwalle, cum omnibus ad prenominatas terras pertinentibus, habendas et tenendas imperpetuum liberas et solutas ab omni seculari servitio et demanda. Et ego et heredes mei warantizabimus eis has terras predictas cum omnibus earum pertinentiis in perpetuum contra omnes homines, et adquietabimus eas de omnibus rebus et exactionibus sicut liberam puram et perpetuam elemosinam, et ad hoc firmiter observandum fidem pro me et pro heredibus meis corporaliter prestiti et juravi. Ut autem hec concessio mea et confirmatio processu temporis nemini possit venire in dubium, hanc cartam sigillo meo signatam dictis canonicis reliqui in testimonium. Hiis testibus, Huberto Gernegan tunc temporis senescallo Ele, Heiberto de Alencun, Alano de Wiresdal', Ricardo de Kalestun', Adam de Bedingfeld', Huberto fratre eius, Sewal' de Neutun', Willelmo Bule, Roberto Parcario, et Henrico fratre eius, Rannulfo Godefr', Henrico filio Julian', et Willelmo filio eius, Willelmo de Bradeker'.

Endorsement: (contemporary) Confirmatio Ricardi filii Henrici filii Benedicti de Dinieueton de xi acris terre et dimidia in Dinieueton ex dono Gerardi parcarii.
Size: 16.2 × 9.2 cm.
Seal: vesica; 4 × 2.9 cm.; very dark green wax; on tag.
    Legend: +SIGILL' RICARDI FIL' HENRICI
    Device: a symmetrical scroll tendril.
Date: Gernegan seneschal of Eye.
Notes: Sewal de Newton occurs in 1210 and 1222 (*PR 12 John*, 30; *CRR* x. 270).
William Bule occurs in 1220 (*CRR* viii. 337; ix. 51, 214).

127. Godfrey de Waiva has confirmed no. 125. Probably before 1230. BL Harley charter 57 F 25.

Omnibus ad quos presens scriptum pervenerit, Godefridus de Waiua Salutem. Sciatis me bone devotionis intuitu, causa dei et pro salute anime mee concessisse et hac carta mea confirmasse donationem quam Gerardus filius Benedicti de Dinnieueton' fecit deo et ecclesie sancte Marie de Buttel' et

137

canonicis ibidem deo servientibus et in perpetuum servituris de quadam parte terre sue quam cum corpore suo quod ad prefatam ecclesiam tradidit sepeliendum, in liberam, puram et perpetuam elemosinam dedit et carta sua confirmavit, scilicet de undecim acris terre et dimidia in Dinnieueton', quarum quatuor sunt infra curiam que fuit predicti Gerardi cum domibus et omnibus aliis rebus que infra prefatam curiam continentur, et due iacent ad Northwall' et una et dimidia ad Luuerunesbusc, et una ante portam prenominati Gerardi, et dimidia ante portam Crasc, et dimidia ad Halihoc et una acra nemoris iuxta predictam curiam, et una acra prati ad Northwall' cum omnibus ad prenominatas terras pertinentibus habendas et tenendas in perpetuum liberas et solutas ab omni seculari servitio et demanda. Quare volo et firmiter concedo quod pretaxati canonici habeant et teneant has prenominatas terras cum omnibus que ad eas pertinent in perpetuum bene et in pace, libere et quiete et honorifice sicut liberam, puram et perpetuam elemosinam. Ut autem hec mea concessio et confirmatio processu temporis nulli veniat in dubium, hoc scriptum sigillo meo signatum dictis canonicis reliqui in testimonium. Hiis testibus, Henrico parcario, Willelmo filio Ricardi, Petro filio Huberti et Huberto filio eius, Ricardo filio Roberti et Rannulfo fratre eius, Willelmo Russel', Willelmo de Sancto Edmundo, Johanne filio Gerardi, Gaufrido filio Huberti, Gaufrido filio Gilleberti et Roberto fratre eius, Matheo parvo et Waltero fratre eius, Rogero de Holesl', Radulfo de Ketleberg, Godefrido de Mendham', Johanne de Mendham', Gilleberto Bordemal', Rogero de Fleg, Willelmo de Sutton' et aliis.

Endorsement: (contemporary) Confirmatio Godefridi de Waure de xi acris terre et dimidia in Dinnieueton'.
Size: 17.6 × 9.5 cm.
Seal: vesica, 2.6 × 3.4 cm; dark honey-coloured wax; on tag.
    Legend: +SIGILL' GODFREI DE WAVERE
    Device: antique gem, 1 × 1.3 cm, naked youth.
Counterseal: oval, 1.9 × 2.4 cm.
    Legend: +FRANGE LEGE
    Device: antique gem, 1.2 × 0.8 cm; head of Jupiter, facing right.
Date: seems to have been given on the same occasion as nos. 124 and 125.
Notes: for Godfrey de Wavere, see no. 18 n.
Peter son of Hubert held land in Weybread, Instead and Colton in 1209 (Dodwell, *Fines* ii. nos. 185, 190, 198, 497).
William de St Edmund held land in Wetherden in 1234 (*Exc e R Fin* i. 225). He was a royal messenger to Rome in 1239–40 (*C Lib R* i. 438).

128. William son of Reginald of Beccles has undertaken to pay Butley 8s yearly for land in Dennington. 1224–c 1236.
BL Harley charter 45 G 64.

Omnibus Christi fidelibus ad quos presens scriptum pervenerit, Willelmus filius Reginaldi de Becls' Salutem. Noverit universitas vestra quod ego teneor solvere karissimis dominis meis priori et conventui de Buttel' singulis annis octo solidos ad quatuor termos, pro terra quam teneo de eis in villa de Dingneveton', scilicet duos solidos ad festum sancti Micahelis, et duos solidos ad festum sancti Andree apostoli, et duos solidos ad Pasch' et ad nativitatem sancti Johannis Baptisti, duos solidos. Et in huius rei testimonium, presens scriptum sigillo meo munitum, eis confeci. Hiis testibus, Ricardo Aguillun' tunc Constabulario Orford', Godefrido de Wavere, Reginaldo de Kaketon', Waltero fratre suo, Ric' Erchebaut', Alano de Blu(m)vill', Johanne de Horkele, Johanne de Mendham', Willelmo Hostellario, Dionisio de Cotton.

Endorsement: (contemporary) Carta Willelmi de Becl' super redditu viij solidis per annum pro terra de Dinieu'.
Size: 12 × 6.8 cm.
Seal: round, 2.1 cm; buff-coloured wax; on tag.
    Legend: +SIG' SECRETI
    Device: a hand holding a sceptre or staff.
Date: Richard Aguillun, Constable of Orford in 1224 (*R Litt Claus* ii. 7), was still in 1230 (*Memoranda Roll 14 Henry III*, 26), had ceased to be before 1236 (*CPR*, iii. 143).

WANTISDEN AND BUTLEY

129. William Oudyn and Alice his wife quit-claim for 2 marks lands of John de Capel, Alice's father, in Wantisden and Butley over which they sued the canons by mort d'ancestor. 1229–54.
BL Harley charter 54 E 28.

Pateat universis per presentes quod nos Willelmus Oudyn de Weybrede et Alic' filia et heres Johannis de Capele uxor mea remisimus et omnino quietum clamavimus de nobis et heredibus nostris in perpetuum deo et ecclesie sancte Marie de Buttele et canonicis ibidem deo servientibus et in perpetuum servituris omnes terras et tenementa cum omnibus suis pertinentiis que aliquando fuerunt Johannis de Capele in quibus misimus clamium per breve domini Regis de morte antecessoris penes antedictos canonicos in villis de Wantesden et de Buttele, ita quod neque nos neque heredes nostri seu quicumque aliis nomine nostro aliquid iuris vel clamii in predictis terris et tenementis cum omnibus suis pertinentiis decetero poterimus exigere, vendicare, vel habere. Insuper ad maiorem huius rei securitatem faciendam fide media et per sacramentum tactis sacrosanctis Ewangeliis nos obligavimus quod dictam ecclesiam et dictos canonicos super predictis terris et tenementis et eorum pertinentiis laboribus et expensis aliquo tempore minime inquietabimus seu fatigabimus, seu inquietari vel fatigari procurabimus. Pro hac autem remissione et quieta clamantia dederunt nobis predicti canonici duas marcas argenti. Hiis testibus, Ivone de Keneton', Johanne de Kettleberg', Rogero le Esturmy militibus, Ricardo de Avilers, Hamone de Vkenhille, Johanne de Kaceton', Rogero Clerbaud, Roberto Meer, Willelmo le Veel, Willelmo Edrich, Rogero Cunin et multis aliis.

Endorsement: (contemporary) Quieta clamatio Willelmi Oudyn et Alicie uxoris sue super omnibus terris et tenementis in villis de Wantesden et Weybrede que aliquando fuerunt Johannis de Capele. (14th century) xxvi.
Size: 23.2 × 9.1 cm.

Seals: William Oudyn: round, 2.1 cm; very dark green wax, repaired with red/
orange wax backing; on tag.
Legend: +S.....OUDYN
Device: lion passant.
Alice Oudyn: round, 1.9 cm, colour and attachment as above.
Legend: +S' ALIC' OUDIN
Device: a squirrel (?)
These two seals are clearly by the same artist.
Date: Roger le Esturmy succeeded his father, and was succeeded by his son William
(*Exc e R Fin* i. 181; ii. 182).

WEYBREAD

**130. Termination by Geoffrey Archdeacon of Suffolk and Egelinus Prior
of Snape, delegates of Hubert Archbishop of Canterbury, after an appeal
to the Court of Audience, of a case between Butley and Mendham Priories
over 1 acre and 3 roods belonging to Weybread church. 1193–1205.
BL Harley charter 43 I 18.**

Universis sancte matris ecclesie filiis, G. Archidiaconus Suffolch', et E. Prior
de Snap' Salutem. Mandatum domini Cantuariensis in hec verba suscepimus.

Hubertus dei gratia Cantuariensis Archiepiscopus totius Anglie primas,
dilectis filiis in Christo G. Archidiacono Suffolch' et Priori de Snap' Salutem
et benedictionem. Significaverunt nobis dilecti filii Prior et canonici de
Buttel' quod cum inter ipsos ex una parte et Priorem et monachos de Herst
super quadam terra controversia moveretur, ad promptiorem litis decisionem
ex utraque parte in arbitros est compromissum, fidesque hinc inde prestita,
quod arbitrium servaretur. Cumque arbitri de communi consensu electi
arbitrati fuissent, predicti Prior et monachi de Herst fidei religione con-
tempta, arbitrio stare recusaverunt, propter quod pars adversa sentiens se
iniuste gravari, ad nostram audientiam appellavit, et quia nobis non constat
de premissis, discretioni vestre mandamus quatinus si de appellatione ad nos
rite interposita vobis constiterit, causam audiatis, et eam fine canonico
decidatis, provisuri quod dicti Prior et monachi de Herst ad observationem
fidei sicut iustum fuerit per censuram ecclesiasticam a vobis compellantur.

Huius igitur auctoritate mandati, partibus a nobis canonice convocatis et in
presentia nostra constitutis, causa que vertebatur inter predictos canonicos de
Buttel' et monacos de Herst super una acra terre et tribus rodis pertinentibus
de iure ad ecclesiam de Weiebred' cum earum decimis in loco qui dicitur
Hareland sub hac forma amicabili compositione coram nobis et viris discretis
nobiscum assidentibus in ecclesia de Thebertun' sopita est. Prior enim et
monachi de Herst ius quod dicebant se habere in predictis terris et earum
decimis in manus nostras sponte resignaverunt, et prestita ab eis cautione
iuratoria fideliter affirmaverunt, quod decetero non traherent in causam
Priorem et canonicos de Buttel' super predictis terris neque earum decimis,
neque aliquam molestiam vel gravamen eis inferent. Prior vero et canonici de
Buttel' concesserunt predictis Priori et monachis de Herst tres prefatas rodas

terre reddendo inde annuatim ad assumptionem beate Marie virginis ecclesie de Weiebred' unum denarium, et predictam acram terre in predicto loco versus orientem, libere et quiete retinuerunt in manu sua cum decimis tam ipsius acre, quam predictarum trium rodarum. Et ad maiorem huius compositionis securitatem et confirmationem, predicti Priores capitulorum suorum sigilla huic scripto coram nobis apposuerunt. Et ut hec compositio inter Priorem et canonicos de Buttel', et Priorem et monacos de Herst coram nobis facta in perpetuum rata et inconcussa habeatur, et ne alicuius malignitate in posterum concuti possit aut evelli, eam perpetuo observandam utraque pars prestita iuratoria cautione affirmavit, et eam auctoritate qua in causa fungimur, tam scripti nostri munimine quam sigillorum nostrorum appositione corroboravimus. Testibus L(aurentio) Abbate de Sibeton', P(hilippo) Abbate de Leeston', S(imone) Decano de Hoxn', R. capellano de Mendham, R. tunc temporis capellano de Weiebred', Warino de Colevill' capellano, Magistro T(homa) de Beverlac', Magistro Johanne de Hunt-ingef(eld), Waltero Malet, David' de Thikebrom, Ric(ardo) de Mendham' clerico, Gaufrido de Wineston', Adam Sille.

Endorsement: (contemporary) Transactio inter nos et monacos de Herst super quadam terra.
Size: 19.7 × 17.8 cm.
Seals: left, Geoffrey Archdeacon of Suffolk:
  vesica, 3 × 4.6 cm; bright green wax; on tag.
  Legend: .....G...HIDI S....LC
  Device: standing figure holding book and staff.

  centre, Egelinus Prior of Snape:
  vesica, 3.6 × 2.2 cm; mid to pale honey-coloured wax; on tag.
  Legend: +SIGILLUM PRIORI DE SNAPE
  Device: standing ecclesiastic clasping book.

  right, Prior of Mendham:
  vesica, 3.8 × 5.4 cm, damaged; white wax varnished brown; on tag.
  Legend: (SI)GILL...HERS...
  Device: Virgin and child seated, image reversed.
  Counterseal: Legend: +S....
          Device: antique gem (?), standing figure.
Date: Archbishop Hubert.
See Introduction, 36.

131. Final *actum* **(1205/6) by papal judges-delegate, on mandate of Innocent III (13th July 1205), in suit concerning alienation of land belonging to the church of Weybread.**
BL Harley charters 44 I 25 ('A') and 26 ('B').

Universis sancte matris ecclesie filiis L(aurentius) Abbas de Sybetun' et E(gelinus) Prior de Snap' et Willelmus Decanus de Donewico Salutem in Christo. Mandatum domini Pape in hec verba suscepimus.
  Innocentius Episcopus Servus Servorum Dei, dilectis filiis Abbati de Sibetun', Priori de Snap', et Decano de Donewyco Norwicensis diocesis Salutem et Apostolicam Benedictionem. Exhibita nobis dilectorum filiorum Prioris et conventus de Buttel' petitio continebat quod A. clericus de

Weiebrade Norwicensis diocesis quasdam possessiones ad eorum ecclesiam de Weibrade rationabiliter pertinentes G. laico et quibusdam aliis eiusdem diocesis ipsorum consensu irrequisito concessit in grave ipsius ecclesie detrimentum. Quocirca discretioni vestre per apostolica scripta mandamus, quatinus vocatis qui propter hoc fuerint evocandi, audiatis causam, et appellatione remota fine debito terminetis, et faciatis quod iudicaveritis per censuram ecclesiasticam firmiter observari. Testes autem qui fuerint nominati, si se gratia, odio vel timore subtraxerint, per censuram eandem cessante appellatione cogatis veritati testimonium perhibere. Nullis litteris veritati et iustitie preiudicantibus a sede apostolica impetratis; quod si non omnes hiis exequendis potueritis interesse, duo vestrum ea nichilominus exequantur. Datum Rome apud Sanctum Petrum Non' Ianuarii pontificatus nostri anno septimo.

Huius auctoritate mandati partibus a nobis canonice convocatis, et in presentia nostra constitutis, causa que vertebatur inter eas super quadam terra in Weiebrad' de iure pertinente ad ecclesiam de Weiebrad' adhibitis nobiscum viris discretis et iuris peritis in ecclesia de Crattefeld' anno primo quo Hubertus Walteri Cantuariensis Archiepiscopus infata concessit, amicabili compositione in hunc modum sopita est. G. enim tanur de Fresingefeld toti terre pertinenti ad ecclesiam de Weiebrade quam dicebat se tunc temporis possidere, sponte renuntiavit, et eam in manus nostras resignavit, et tactis sacrosanctis coram nobis fideliter affirmavit, quod de cetero nunquam Priori et canonicis de Buttel' aliquam molestiam super ea inferret vel gravamen, neque super predicta terra eos in causam traheret. Predicti vero Prior et conventus de Buttel' intuitu pietatis prefato G. unam acram terre et dimidiam de remotiori terra quam habent versus Wiresdal' et heredibus suis inperpetuum tenendam de eis concesserunt, reddendo annuatim sex denarios ad duos terminos, scilicet ad Pascha tres denarios et ad festum sancti Michaelis, iiid. Et ut hec compositio inter predictos Priorem et conventum et sepedictum G. de Fresingefeld' coram nobis facta rata et inconcussa in perpetuum habeatur, auctoritate domini Pape qua in hac causa fungimur, eam perpetuo observandam et sigillorum nostrorum appositione corroboramus. Testibus G. Archidiacono Sutf', Simone Decano de Hox', Willelmo Decano de Redehal', Magistro Thoma de Beverlaco, Warino capellano predicti Archidiaconi, Alexandro capellano de Buttel', Parchemino coco, Thoma filio Albrici, Osberto de Esfeld', Warino de Framesden'.

Endorsement: A (contemporary) Transactio ('cyrographum' cancelled, in A only) de terra de Weybred'. (14th century) xxxi.
B, as A; also, (15th century ?) .... de Fresingefeld...vi d.
Size: A, 25.2 × 15.1 cm; B, 25.7 × 14.4 cm.
Seals: left, abbot of Sibton:
    vesica, 2.4 × 3.6 cm; dark fawn wax; on tag. Birch, no. 4020.
    Legend: SIGILL' ABB...DE SIBET..
    Device: a hand holding pastoral staff, an estoile below the wrist.

    centre, prior of Snape – as no. 130. Dark, parchment-coloured wax;
        A only, repaired with red/orange wax backing.

    right, William, rural dean of Dunwich:
    oval, 2.2 × 2.4 cm; dark fawn wax; on tag.
    Legend: +SIGILL' WILLI' DEC DE DONOWIC
    Device: a gem, standing figure.
Date: archbishop Hubert died 13th July 1205.

132. Robert Maloisel of Weybread has granted 5 acres meadow of his demesne in Weybread, for 8d yearly, 1d scutage when required, and 7 marks entry fine. Before 1214?
BL Harley charter 53 C 45.

Omnibus Christi fidelibus ad quos presens carta pervenerit, Robertus Mal Oisel de Weibred' Salutem. Sciatis me concessisse et dedisse et presenti carta mea confirmasse Priori et conventui ecclesie sancte Marie de Buttel' quinque acras prati de dominio meo in villa de Weibred' iuxta Assemedwe, scilicet in latitudine et in longitudine quantum pertinet ad quinque acras per perticam sexdecim pedum, et siquid superfuerit in longitudine predicti prati, a filo ripe usque ad vetus fossatum apud meridiem, cum omnîbus aisiamentis ad illud pratum pertinentibus tenendas de me et de heredibus meis in perpetuum libere et quiete et honorifice per servitium octo denariorum mihi et heredibus meis singulis annis ad festum sancti Michaelis solvendorum. Et ad servitium domini Regis scilicet ad scutagium quando evenerit, tantum i. denarium pro omni alio servitio et exactione. Pro hac autem concessione et donatione et carte mee confirmatione dederunt mihi predicti canonici de Buttel' septem marcas argenti in gersumam. Et ut hec mea concessio et donatio et carte mee confirmatio rata et firma et inconcussa in perpetuum permaneat, eam presentis scripti testimonio et sigilli mei appositione ˉcorroboravi. Hiis testibus, Herveio de Baudreseia, Henrico parcario de Sterston', Rogero Barat', Gilleberto Bordemal', Rannulfo filio Stephani de Culesl', Stephano filio Willelmi de Culesl', Roberto filio Ric' de Oreford', Huberto marescallo, Radulfo de Sancto Edmundo marescallo, David' de Thikebrom et Alano filio eius, Willelmo filio Oselac, et Roberto filio eius et multis aliis.

Endorsement: (contemporary) Carta Roberti Maloisel de v. acris prati
                (14th century) xiii Weybrede.
Size: 17 × 13.1 cm.
Seal: round, 4.6 cm; dark green wax; on tag.
      Legend: +'SIGILLUM RODBERTI MALOISEL
      Device: a bird (duck ?). Presumably a rebus.

133. Robert Maloisel has received 7 marks entry fine from Butley priory for 5 acres of meadow in Weybread: if the meadow cannot be warranted, the money is to be repaid within 15 days. Before 1213.
B.L. Cotton charter v 64.

Universis sancte matris ecclesie filiis ad quos presens scriptum pervenerit, Robertus Maloisel de Weibred' Salutem. Sciatis quod dominus W(illelmus) Prior et conventus ecclesie sancte Marie de Buttel' dederunt mihi in gersumam septem marcas argenti pro quinque acris prati in Weibred' scilicet iuxta Assemedwe tenendis de me et de heredibus meis per annuum servitium octo denariorum et unius nummi ad servitium domini Regis. Et si ita contingat quod ego et heredes mei prefatis canonicis prenominatas quinque acras prati warantizare non poterimus, predictas septem marcas argenti quas mihi dederunt in gersumam infra quindecim dies postquam de predicto prato

143

dissaisati fuerint, eis integre et plenarie persolvemus. Et ad hoc firmiter tenendum, tactis sacrosanctis evangeliis pro me et pro heredibus meis iuravi, et fidem corporaliter prestiti, et in huius rei testimonium huic scripto sigillum meum apposui. Hiis testibus, Herveo de Baudreseia, Henrico parcario de Sterston', Rogero Barat, Gilleberto Bordemal', Rannulfo filio Stephani de Culesl', Stephano filio Willelmi de Culesl', Roberto filio Ric' de Oreford', Huberto marescallo, Radulfo marescallo de Sancto Edmundo.

Endorsement: (contemporary) Carta Roberti Maloisel de . . . gersuma vii. marc'. (14th century) xiii Weybrede.
Size: 16.5 × 9.8 cm.
Seal: as no. 132.
Note: it is likely that this charter was given on the same occasion as no. 132 – not only are the witnesses common, but the script and sealing-wax are identical. Prior William had been succeeded by 1213.

134. Robert Maloisel grants the homage and tenement (described) of a man in Weybread, and the rest of his meadow, for 4d yearly and 1d per £1 scutage, for a 7 mark entry-fine. 1189–1221.
BL Cotton charter xxvii 17.

Robertus Mal Oisel de Weiebred', omnibus amicis et hominibus suis et omnibus hominibus presentibus et futuris, Salutem. Sciatis me dedisse et concessisse et presenti carta mea confirmasse Priori et conventui ecclesie beate Marie de Buttel' homagium Rogeri filii Warini filii Bonde de Aldeberg' cum toto tenemento quod de me tenuit in Weiebred' sine aliquo retinemento mihi vel heredibus meis, scilicet duas acras et dimidiam terre arabilis cum pertinentiis, scilicet totum essartum de bosco Thurstani cum masuagio, et duas acras et dimidiam de prato in Essemedwe iuxta pratum canonicorum de Buttel' versus orientem unde mihi solebat reddere decem et octo denarios censuales per annum pro omni servitio, salvo servitio domini Regis scilicet ad scutagium viginti solidorum quando evenerit, duobus denarios, et preterea totum residuum prati mei in predicto Essemedwe tenendum de me et de heredibus meis imperpetuum per annuum servitium quattuor denariorum censualium mihi et heredibus meis singulis annis ad terminum Pasche pro omni servitio solvendorum salvo servitio domini Regis scilicet uno denario tantum. Pro hac autem donatione et carte mee confirmatione dederunt mihi prefati Prior et conventus de Buttel' septem marcas argenti in gersumam. Hiis testibus, Domino Rogero Bigot Comite Norf', Waltero de Raveningham, Henrico de Boyton, David de Thikebrom, Adam Noloth, Willelmo de Thikebrom et Roberto filio eius, Roberto filio (Or)ding, Ricardo de Mendham, Rannulfo filio Stephani de Culesl', Huberto marescallo, Radulfo de Sancto Edmundo marescallo, Stephano filio Willelmi de Culesl', Roberto filio Ricardi.

Endorsement: (contemporary) Carta Roberti Maloisel de homagio Rogeri filii Warini.
(14th century) Weybrede xvi (on tag).
Seal: as no. 132.
Date: Roger Bigod received the earldom after Richard I's coronation (*Complete Peerage* ix. 587).

144

Notes: Walter de Raveningham occurs in 1207 (*CRR* v. 104) and was vouched as a witness of a charter of the earl in 1208 (ibid., 272). *Henry de Boyton* occurs in 1220 (*CRR* viii. 291).

135. Alexander, son and heir of Robert Maloisel, has granted part of his land in Weybread. Mid-thirteenth century.
BL Cotton charter xxvii 18.

Notum sit universis presens scriptum inspecturis vel audituris, quod ego Alexander Maloisel filius et heres Roberti Maloisel intuitu caritatis divine et pro salute anime mee et antecessorum meorum et successorum meorum, concessi et dedi et hac presenti carta mea confirmavi deo et beate Marie de Buttll' et Priori et canonicis ibidem deo et beate Marie servientibus in puram et perpetuam elemosinam, unam partem terre mee in villa de Weybrad', scilicet totam illam partem terre que iacet inter terram Johannis filii Rogeri capellani ex parte occidentali, et terram Roberti Cubald ex parte orientali, habendam et tenendam illis et eorum successoribus in perpetuum. Et ut hec mea concessio et donatio firma et stabilis in perpetuum permaneat nec ab aliquo possit infringi presens scriptum sigilli mei appositione corroborare dignum duxi. Hiis testibus, Alano de Wytheresdal', Al' de Semere, Gerardo Noloht, Willelmo de Thikebrom, Alexandro March', Alano filio Godefrei, Willelmo filio suo, Wlfrico Herolf, Roberto filio suo, Al' Herol et aliis multis.

Endorsement: (contemporary) Carta Alexandri Maloisel super una pecia terre in Weybred'. (14th century) xv.
Size: 13.3 × 9 cm.
Seal: roughly round, 3.1 × 3.6 cm; white wax with mid-honey-coloured varnish; on tag.
    Legend: +SIG' ALEXANDRI MALOISEL
    Device: a bird with wing raised. Presumably a rebus.
Date: presumably after the death of Robert Maloisel; for *Alan de Witherdale* see no. 140.

136. BL Harley charter 51 C 35. Mid-thirteenth century. (i) Geoffrey Harolf of Weybread (ii) the church and canons of Butley.

Release by (i) for himself and his heirs to (ii) of all rights and claims in a 'piece' of land in Weybread, lying between the canons' wood to north and the land of (i) to south as the boundary divides it. For this (ii) have given (i) half a mark.
Witnessed by, Johanne de Capeles, Johanne de Attleburg', Willelmo de Norwyco, Roberto de Laceles, Willelmo Oudyn, Ricardo Noloz, Nicholao de Tybeham, Johanne de Kent et aliis.

Size: 17.1 × 8.9 cm.
Seal: fragment 1 × 0.6 cm; dark brown wax; on tag; repaired with red/orange wax.
Date: John de Capel and William Oudyn appear in no. 129. The others are quite obscure.

137. BL Harley charter 51 G 49. In or before 1271. (i) Robert Hovel, *miles* **(ii) the prior and canons of Butley.**

Grant in free, pure and perpetual alms to (ii) of all the tenement which Walter Cubald son of Robert Cubald once held of (i)'s fee in Weybread.
Warranty clause.
In return (i) and Alienor his wife have been received into confratenity. Witnessed by, domino Willelmo de Medefeld milite, Ricardo le Vel et Willelmo filio suo, Valentino de Schotford', Alexandro de Chebehal', Willelmo de Thykebrom, Willelmo de Blanchevill', Roberto Charneleyn, Reginaldo de Creting', Thoma Houdyn, Reginaldo le Tanur, Thoma Bolle, Alano Marthoys, Galfrido Herlof, Seman' Spirhard, Huberto Fletheshehe, Thoma Weribaud et aliis.

Size: 23 × 11.7 cm.
Tag for seal.
Date: mentioned in no. 141.

138. Reginald Thanur son of William Barbere of Weybread has exchanged 2 acres in one piece for 4 pieces of Butley's land in Weybread. Before 1262.
BL Harley charter 45 F 60.

Sciant presentes et futuri quod ego Reginaldus filius Willelmi Barbere de Weybrad concessi, dedi et presenti carta confirmavi pro me et heredibus meis in perpetuum excambium, Priori et conventui de Buttel' unam peciam terre duarum acrarum in villa de Weybrade, iacentem in crufto Ascilie et albutantem ex parte orientali super terram meam, et ex parte occidentali, australi et boriali, super terram Alicie March, pro quatuor peciis terre predictorum Prioris et conventus in predicta villa, quarum una pecia iacet inter terram Willelmi de Thikebrom ex parte occidentali et terram meam ex parte orientali, et alia pecia inter terras dicti Willelmi, tercia pecia iacet inter terram Roberti Spirhard ex parte occidentali, et terram Willelmi predicti ex parte orientali, et quarta pecia iacet iuxta cruftum Roberti Tastepin ex parte orientali, et ex parte australi iuxta terram Edrici de Strate et Roberti Spirhard. Et ego Reginaldus et heredes mei warentizabimus acquietabimus et defendemus dictis priori et conventui predictam peciam terre per predictum escambium contra omnes homines imperpetuum. In huius rei testimonium huic scripto sigillum meum apposui. Testibus, domino Alano de Wyderesdal', Willelmo filio suo, Rogero de Scotford, Thoma fratre eius, Waltero de Eshom, Willelmo et Rogero filiis suis, Thoma de Walsok', Gregorio de Hoyland, Johanne de la Dune, Matheo de Walpol et aliis.

Endorsement: (contemporary) Carta Reginaldi filii Willelmi Barbere de Weyebred.
(14th century) xv.
Size: 16.2 × 7.3 cm.
Seal: round, 2.9 cm; honey-coloured wax; on tag.
Legend: +SIGILL, REG, THANUR
Device: four parallel horizontal projections above a straight-sided bowl – rebus?
Date: Alan de Witherdale (see no. 140).

139. Walter de Hesham son of Robert de Stonhawe exchanges all his land of the Maloisel fee in Weybread, for 12 pieces of Butley's land (described) in Weybread. 7th January 1240.
BL Harley charter 51 E 40.

Sciant presentes et futuri quod ego Walterus de Hesham filius Roberti de Stonhawe concessi, dedi, et presenti carta mea confirmavi pro me et heredibus meis, Priori et conventui de Buttel' in perpetuum escambium totam terram quam habui de feodo Maloysel in villa de Weybrade que vocatur Ayleucstoft, et iacet inter viam que tendit versus Sotford' et terram Prioris de Mendham, pro duodecim peciis terre dictorum Prioris et conventus de Buttel' in parochia de Weybrade, quarum undecim iacent in campis de Hesham, scilicet una pecia que iacet inter terram que fuit Alwini, et terram Symonis Penne, et tota illa pecia que iacet inter liberam terram ecclesie de Hesham et terram Ric' Huleman, et tercia pecia que iacet inter terram Thum' Sarpe et terram meam, et quarta pecia que iacet inter terram Mathei Capellani, et terram Willelmi Merum, et quinta pecia que iacet inter terras predicti Mathei ex utraque parte, et sexta pecia que iacet inter terram Johannis del Hak et terram dicti Willelmi Merum, et una selio que iacet ad capita eiusdem terre versus occidentem, et octava pecia que iacet inter terram predicti Mathei et terram Roberti Wathelof, et tres particule que iacent super collem de Horspol', et duodecima pecia que iacet in campis de Weybrade inter pratum Gerardi Nolod' et terram meam, habendam et tenendam in perpetuum escambium. Et ego et heredes mei adquietabimus singulis annis versus Priorem de Herst' pro dicta terra de duodecim denariis ad duos terminos, scilicet ad festum sancti Andree sex denarios, et ad Pascha sex denarios, et de scutagio scilicet ad viginti solidos, duos denarios, et ad plus plus, et ad minus minus, et de auxilio vicecomitis unum denarium, ita quod pro defectu nostre adquietationis et defensionis dicti Prior et conventus nullam lesionem vel iacturam incurrent. Et ego Walterus et heredes mei warantizabimus totam predictam terram dictis Priori et conventui per predictum escambium contra omnes gentes in perpetuum. Et ut istud escambium firmum et stabile in perpetuum perseveret, presens scriptum sigilli mei inpressione roboravi. Actum apud Buttel' in crastino Epiphanie, consecrationis Willelmi de Rahelem Episcopi Norwicensis anno primo. Hiis testibus, domino Osberto de Baudreseia, Roberto persona de Anhus, Willelmo filio Ade de Cambes, Johanne de Horkel', Matheo de Walepol, Johanne de Linstede, Nicholao de Bramford', Johanne de Stradebroch, Alexandro le Marocis, Alano Godefrei, Willelmo filio eiusdem, Waltero Eysevilen, Waltero Cubaud, Thoma Scarp, Johanne del Hawe, et aliis.

Endorsement: (contemporary) Carta Walteri de Esham super quodam escambio in
             villa de Weybred.
             (14th century) xviii.
Size: 21.2 × 13.1 cm.
Seal: vesica, 2.6 × 3.9 cm; white wax with mid-brown varnish; on tag.
             Legend: ......ALTERI FILI'....
             Device: a form resembling capital T with drooping crossbar.

140. Alan de Witherdale has exchanged with Butley Priory 1 1/13 acres in Weybread. Early thirteenth century.
BL Harley charter 58 D 24.

Sciant presentes et futuri quod ego Alanus de Wytheresdal' filius Willelmi de Wytheresdal' concessi, dedi et presenti carta confirmavi deo et ecclesie sáncte Marie de Buttel', et canonicis ibidem deo servientibus unam acram terre mee et terciam decimam parte unius acre terre in villa de Weybrede iacentes in tuftis ad exitum ianue sue in eadem villa iuxta pasturam meam versus orientem ex úna parte que vocatur Calvescroft, et ex altera parte iuxta viam dictorum Prioris et conventus versus occidentem, et unum capud abutat super viam que est ad ianuam dictorum Prioris et conventus versus austrum, et aliud capud super le Stanstrete versus aquilonem in perpetuas escambias pro una acra libere terre sue in eadem villa et tertiadecima parte unius acre terre in crufto suo que vocatur Churchecroft, unde unum capud se extendit versus austrum super cimiterium, et super viam eorum que ducit versus ecclesiam eorum, et aliud capud super terram meam versus aquilonem. Habendas et tenendas de me et heredibus meis libere et quiete, integre et plenarie, pro omnibus rebus consuetudinibus et demandis pro predictis escambiis in perpetuum. Et ego Alanus et heredes mei warantizabimus predictis Priori et conventui predictam terram per predictas escambias contra omnes homines in perpetuum, et tam contra iudeos quam christianos de omnibus rebus adquietabimus et defendemus. In cuius rei testimonium presenti scripto sigillum meum apposui. Hiis testibus, Alano de Mouney, Ricardo de Caam, Radulfo Treily, Adam de Mendham, Hugone Buurt, Willelmo le Dene, Gerardo Nolod, Willelmo Thikebrom, Alexandro le March', Alano Godefr', Willelmo Oudin, Waltero clerico et aliis.

Endorsement: (contemporary) Carta Alani de Witherisdal'.
             (14th century) xxii.
             (15th century ?) . . . terra in Weyb . . .
Size: 20 × 13 cm.
Slit for seal tag.
Date: see below, and Introduction, 11 for Richard de Caen.
Notes: Alan de Witherdale came of age between 1201 and 1209 (*R Obl et Fin* 137; *PR 3 John* 139; *9 John* 169; *CRR* i. 174, 208; Dodwell, *Fines* ii. no. 530), and was dead by 1262 (*Exc e R Fin* ii. 369).
Adam de Mendham, son of Robert, came of age between 1208 and 1217 (*CRR* v. 166; *R Litt Pat* i. 334). *Alan de Mounnay* was on a jury in 1225 (*CRR* xii. no. 1023).

141. BL Harley charter 49 A 51. 10th June 1271, at Weybread.
(i) Valentine Cubald of Weybread   (ii) the Prior and convent of Butley.

Release by (i) for himself and his heirs to (ii) of all rights and claims in the lands and tenements in Weybread once held by Walter Cubald of the demesne of Robert Hovel.
Witnessed by, dominis Roberto Hovel, Roberto Cokerel, Ricardo de Enges

clerico, Willelmo Sckebrom, Thoma Houdyn, Ricardo le Vel, Willelmo filio suo, Walentino de Schotford, Willelmo de Blaunchevyle et aliis.

Size: 19 × 4.5 cm.
Seal: vesica, 2.8 × 5.1 cm; darkish brown wax; on tongue; tying tag.
    Legend: +SIG' VALENT' C..BALD
    Device: three upright prongs diverging slightly at top, the side ones separated
        from the central by a large dot.
Note: a confirmation of no. 133.

142. BL Harley charter 55 G 45. 16th July 1270, at Butley. (i) Nicholas de Schelton   (ii) the Prior and convent of Butley.

Confirmation of all the tenement held by (ii) of the gift of Robert and Alexander Maloisel, their predecessors and anyone else in Weybread, in return for 10*s*.
To hold to (ii) and their successors in pure and perpetual alms.
Warranty clause.
Witnessed by, dominis Ricardo de Brahuse, Willelmo Burt, Willelmo de Medefeld militibus, Ricardo de Henges, Semanno de Reding, Ricardo le Vel, Julianne de Brom, Willelmo Thykebrom', Thoma Houdyn et Reginaldo de Creting et aliis.

Endorsement: 15th century.
Size: 21.9 × 11.3 cm.
Tag for seal.

143. BL Harley charter 44 B 41. 1st November 1312. (i) Prior and convent of Butley   (ii) John Cubaud of Weybread.

Cyrograph.

Perpetual lease to (ii) of a piece of land containing sixty roods lying in Weybread between the land of John Alkoc to north, a greenway called Waringsgate to east, abutting on the messuage of (ii) and the land of (i). To hold to (ii) and his heirs for 12*d* annually, half at Michaelmas and half at Easter.
Warranty clause.
Distraint clause, on all the tenements of (ii) in Weybread.

Endorsement: contemporary including xxviii.
Size: 25.9 × 6 cm.
Seal: round, 1.5 cm; dark green wax; on tag.
    Legend: illegible.
    Device: eight-pointed star formed by two interlaced squares; centre, a pair of
        clasped hands; bottom right, three lines converging to a point.

144. BL Harley charter 44 B 42. 5th August 1315, at Weybread. (i) Prior William and the convent of Butley (ii) William son of Roger Aleyn of Weybread, and John his son.

Lease to (ii) of six pieces of land totalling two acres in Weybread: (1) between land of Alienor Charlis and that of Hugh Hovel, (2) between land of aforesaid Alienor to north and John Cleye to south, (3) between land of Agnes le Baxter to north and John Edrich to south, (4) and (5) between land of Hugh Hovel on both sides, (6) between land of John Edrich to south and John Foke to north. To hold to (ii) and the legitimate heirs of John's body, whether more or less than two acres, for 2s annually at the usual terms, Michaelmas, St Andrew, Easter and Nativity of St John Baptist, with reversion to (i) after the death of (ii) if John dies without heirs.
Warranty clause.

Endorsement: contemporary including xxix.
Size: 22.2 × 14.9 cm.
Tag for seal.

145. BL Harley charter 47 D 53. 10th April 1351, at Butley. (i) Roger de Bungeye, formerly rector of Groton (*Grotene*) (ii) the Prior and convent of Butley.

Confirmation of a piece of land estimated at four acres which (i) together with John de Hoxne acquired from William Oudyn of Weybread, lying in Weybread between the wood of (ii) to north, the land of Robert Spyrhard, chaplain, to south, the street called Clintweye to west, and the land of Henry dil Heythe to east.
To hold to (ii) and their successors of the chief lord of the fee for the service due (unspecified).
Witnessed by, Gilberto de Bek', Johanne de Capele, Petro Parmynhood, Willelmo de Glemham, Willelmo Mannyng et aliis.

Endorsement: contemporary, including xxxii.
Size: 28.4 × 9.4 cm.
Seal: vesica, 2.4 × 3.6 cm; dark green wax; on tag. Birch, no. 2817 ('Roger Prior of Butley').
    Legend: MARGARETA PIA P(RO) ME DEP(RE) CARE MARIA
    Device: beneath a double arcade seated figures of Virgin and Child (left), St Margaret (right). In the base under another arch a kneeling, praying figure. Below him a shield of arms, indecipherable.
Note: it seems Groton church was dedicated to St Margaret in the Middle Ages (N. Pevsner and E. Ratcliffe, *Suffolk* (Buildings of England Series) 2nd ed. 1974, 241).

150

WINGFIELD

146. Hervey Walter has granted all his fee in Wingfield, *Sikebro'*, (unidentified) and Instead (Weybread). 1171–86.
BL Harley charter 57 E 2.

Herveus Walter omnibus amicis et hominibus suis francis et anglis tam presentibus quam futuris Salutem. Sciatis me dedisse et concessisse et hac presenti carta mea confirmasse deo et ecclesie sancte Marie de Buth' et canonicis ibidem deo servientibus pro salute anime mee et Matildis sponse mee, et filiorum nostrorum, et pro salute anime Rannulfi de Glanvill' et Berte sponse sue et filiorum suorum et omnium antecessorum et parentum et amicorum nostrorum in liberam et puram et perpetuam elemosinam totum feodum meum in Wingefeld in humagiis et redditibus et in omnibus aliis rebus, et totum feodum in Sikebro' quod Oudin tenuit de me, et totum feodum meum in Isted quod Godefridus tenuit de me. Quare volo et concedo quod predicti canonici habeant et teneant prenominata feoda bene et in pace integre et quiete et absolute ab omni seculari servitio sicut puram et perpetuam elemosinam. Hiis testibus, Willelmo de Albervill', Willelmo de *Auberville* Valoniis, Stephano de Glamvill', Teobaldo de Valon', Roberto de Valon', Willelmo de Gla(n)vill', Petro Walter, Roberto filio Rocelin, Rannulfo de Baldr', Galfrido de Ykeling', Roberto de Blanchevill', Willelmo de Gla(n)vill clerico, et filiis meis Huberto Walter et Rogero et Hamone.

Endorsement: (contemporary) Herveus Valt' de feudo suo in Wigefel
    (14th century, on seal tag) viii.
Size: 19 × 8.9 cm.
Seal: round, 5 cm; white wax varnished red/brown; repaired with red/orange wax;
    on tag.
    Legend: +SIGIL . HERVEI W(ALTE)RI
    Device: equestrian, to right.
Printed: Monasticon vi(i). 380.
Date: foundation of Butley priory; Hubert Walter not yet Dean of York.
Note: this seems to be the only indication that Rannulf de Glanville had sons (line 6);
he was succeeded by his three daughters.

147. Gilbert de Hawkedon has granted 6d rent in Instead. Before Michaelmas 1205.
BL Harley charter 51 D 5.

Sciant presentes et futuri quod ego Gilebertus de Haukedune dedi et concessi et hac mea presenti carta confirmavi ecclesie sancte Marie de Buttele et deo ibi servientibus redditum vi d. in Histede prece et voluntate domini mei Tedbaldi Walteri in perpetuam elemosinam sine servitio faciendo, quia tamen fecit mihi dominus meus Tedbaldus quod predictum redditum predicte ecclesie in perpetuam elemosinam concessi. Hiis testibus, Hernaldo sacerdote, Osberto de Glanvile, Rogero de Kenteuelle, Petro Waltero, Johanne de Tudham, Rogero Ble(n)cio, Aumari de Bellaf'.

Endorsement: (contemporary) Gilleb' de Hauchedune in Histede.
(14th century) xxxiii.
Size: 19 × 5.2 cm.
Seal: round, 4.8 cm; white wax varnished deep brown; repaired with red/orange wax; on tag.
    Legend: . . . SIGILLUM.GILEBERTI.FILII ALV
    Device: lion passant.
Date: death of Theobald Walter.

148. Richard de Caen has granted 1 acre of land and ½ acre of meadow in Instead. Before 1212.
BL Harley charter 47 F 32.

Ricardus de Cadamo, omnibus amicis et hominibus suis francis et anglis et omnibus hominibus presentibus et futuris Salutem. Sciatis me concessisse et dedisse et presenti carta mea confirmasse deo et ecclesie sancte Marie de Buttel' et canonicis ibidem deo servientibus pro salute anime mee et pro animabus uxorum mearum Aeline et Sare et puerorum nostrorum et antecessorum et successorum nostrorum in liberam et puram et perpetuam elemosinam unam acram terre quam Willelmus Cubald tenet de feodo meo in Istede de qua inplacitavi predictos canonicos, et preterea concessi et dedi et hac carta mea confirmavi predictis canonicis in liberam et puram et perpetuam elemosinam dimidiam acram prati in Istede de propinquiore prato meo ad pontem Anhand' versus North. Si vero ex illa parte pontis illam medietatem perficere eis non potero, ex alia parte eam ipsis adimplebo, et tam predictam acram terre quam prenominatam dimidiam acram prati ego et heredes mei contra omnes homines sicut liberam et puram et perpetuam elemosinam, in perpetuum warantizabimus. Et ut hec concessio et donatio et confirmatio mea perpetuam optineat firmitatem, eam presentis scripti testimonio, et sigilli mei appositione corroboravi. Hiis testibus, domino Arn(aldo) Ruffo, Thoma de Mendham', Willelmo filio Roberti de Eya, Waltero de Cadamo filio meo et Ricardo clerico fratre eius, Luca de Gedding', Johanne Hunipot, Willelmo Blom', Rannulfo filio Stephani, Stephano filio Willelmi, Roberto filio Thome.

Endorsement: (contemporary) Carta Ricardi de Cadamo.
(Late 13th century ?) Weybred (14th century) xxxii.
Size: 19.2 × 9.5 cm.
Seal: oval, 2.7 × 2.3 cm; darkish green wax; on tag.
    Legend: +SIGILLUM RICARDI DE CAEM
    Device: gem?
Date: Ernald Ruffus – see Introduction, 10.
Notes: Thomas de Mendham occurs in 1198 (Dodwell, *Fines* i, no. 160) and 1208 (*CRR* v. 281). *John Hunipot* occurs in 1205 (Dodwell, *Fines* ii, no. 455) and 1207 (*PR 9 John*, 176).

149. Gerard de Campo of Wingfield quitclaims the land his brother Henry held of Butley in Wingfield, for 30s. Early thirteenth century. BL Harley charter 47 G 10.

Sciant presentes et futuri, quod ego Gerardus de Campo filius Wulrici de Campo de Wingefeld sponte remisi et quietum penitus clamavi Priori et conventui de Buttel' pro me et heredibus meis in perpetuum totam terram cum pertinentiis quam Henricus filius Wulrici frater meus tenuit de eis in villa de Wingefeld, et totum ius et clamium quod habui vel habere potui in predicta terra, pro triginta solidis quos mihi dederunt ad maximam promotionem meam. Et ego pro me et heredibus meis iuravi et affidavi, quod nullam questionem super predicta terra vel eius pertinentiis dictis Priori et conventui de Buttel' movebimus, nec molestiam vel gravamen aliquid per nos vel per alios eisdem inferemus. In huius rei testimonium presenti scripto sigillum meum apposui. Hiis testibus, Radulfo de Pesenhal', Osberto de Baudresey, Willelmo de Peyton', Waltero filio Osberti, Petro de Rising', Ric' filio Osberti, Rogero de Holeslee, Ric' de Ketleberge, Radulfo fratre eius, Waltero de Kaketon', Reginaldo de Kaketon', Thoma filio Reginaldi, Dionisio de Cotton'.

Endorsement: (contemporary) Carta Gerardi de Campo de Wingefeld.
(14th century) ix.
Size: 12.2 × 6.0 cm.
Seal: round, 3.8 cm; blue/green wax; on tag.
Legend: *SIGILL . . . IERARDI DE CAMPO
Device: a 'star' consisting of four corn ears at the principal points, divided by four flecks and eight smaller ones.
Notes: Richard de Ketelberge occurs in 1205 (*PR 7 John* 237) and 1226 (*R Litt Claus* ii. 105), and was the brother of Ralph (*PR 7 John* 237) who had a career as an attorney traceable from 1211 to 1225 (*CRRs* vi. 184, 213, 266; xii. nos. 696, 761). *Peter de Rising* occurs in 1229 (*CPR* ii. 295). For Ralph de Peasenhall, see Introduction, 15.

150. Gerard de Campo of Wingfield grants the land in Wingfield which he, and his brother Henry, held of Warin de Saham. Early thirteenth century. BL Harley charter 47 G 11.

Sciant presentes et futuri quod ego Gerardus de Campo filius Wulrici de Campo de Wingefeld' concessi, dedi et presenti carta confirmavi, Priori et conventui de Buttel' totam illam peciam terre quam tenui de domino Warino de Saham' in Wingefeld cum domibus et aliis pertinentiis suis, scilicet illam peciam terre quam Henricus frater meus tenuit de dicto Warino de Saham' iuxta domum que fuit Henrici fratris mei in Wingefeld', habendam et tenendam in perpetuum solvendo inde dicto Warino et heredibus suis singulis annis octo denarios ad duos termos, scilicet ad festum sancti Micahelis quatuor denarios, et ad Pasch' quatuor denarios, et ad scutagium domini Regis quando evenerit tres quadrantes tantum, pro omni servitio et exactione. In huius rei testimonium presenti scripto sigillum meum apposui.

Hiis testibus Radulfo de Pesenhal', Osberto de Baudresey, Willelmo de Peyton', Waltero filio Osberti, Petro de Rising', Ric' filio Osberti, Rogero de Holeslee, Ricardo de Ketleberge, Radulfo fratre suo, Waltero de Kaketon', Reginaldo fratre suo, Dionisio de Cotton'.

Endorsement: (contemporary) Carta Gerardi de Campo super una pecia terre in
  Vingefeld'.
  (14th century) ix.
Size: 12.5 × 6 cm.
Seal: as no. 149.

151. BL Harley charter 52 A 21. 29th December 1257. (i) Ernald son of John Hunipot of Wingfield (*Wyngefeud*) (ii) the Prior and convent of Butley.

Release by (i) for himself and his heirs to (ii) of all rights and claims in a messuage with land and appurtenances in Wingfield, over which (i) sued Hubert de Stradbroke (Stradebroc) on a writ of right, (ii) having warranted it to Hubert in the court of Eye and put themselves on the grand assize; given for 6½ marks.
Witnessed by, domino Alano de Wytheresdal, Th' de Schotford, Wally(ntino) de Schotford, Ric' le Viel, Philippo de Lingwd', Ric' de Newtun', Galfrido le Chaumbleng', Willelmo de Thikebrom', Ada Noloth, Petro de Parham, Gregorio de Multun', Johanne Oseberen, Roberto de Beccl' clerico et aliis.

Endorsement: contemporary including x.
Size: 18.6 × 8.7 cm.
Seal: round, 2.8 cm; white wax varnished pale brown; on tag.
  Legend: +SIGILL' ERNALDI HUNIPOT
  Device: lion passant; a flower beneath.
Note: for John Hunipot see no. 148n.

WINSTON

152. Cambridge Univ. Library, Ely Dean and Chapter Charters (1B) no. 192. 17th November 1365 at Ely, 25th November at Butley. (i) Prior and convent of Ely cathedral (ii) Prior and convent of Butley.

Licence to (ii) to acquire from Adam de Hautboys, parson of Cockfield, John de Pyssale, parson of Alderton, and Richard de Rendlesham, 14 acres of land and 2 acres of meadow in Winston (*Wynstones*) formerly Walter Ingreth's, held of (i)'s manor of Winston by fealty and for 16*d*, 4 capons and 2 suits of court. To hold to (ii) and their successors, with a relief of 16*d* and 4 capons after the

death, resignation, deposition, or deprivation of each prior of Butley; notwithstanding the statute of mortmain.
Distraint clause.
Each party to keep the part sealed by the other.

Endorsement: contemporary.
Size: 25 × 19.4 cm.
Seal: vesica, c 5 × c 8 cm; dark green wax; on tag.
    Legend: mutilated.
    Device: Virgin and Child under a gothic canopy; in the base, part of a head and
        praying hands (mutilated).

WOODBRIDGE

153. Prior William and the convent of Butley have granted the tithes of the mill at Woodbridge, given by Baldwin of Ufford, to the Prior and canons of Woodbridge for 1lb of cummin yearly. 1192–1213.
BL Additional charter 7494.

Universis sancte matris ecclesie filiis ad quos presens scriptum pervenerit, W. Prior et conventus de Buttel' Salutem in domino. Ad omnium volumus pervenire notitiam nos communi assensu et voluntate causa dei dedisse et concessisse et presenti carta nostra confirmasse dilectis in Christo fratribus nostris Priori et canonicis ecclesie sancte Marie de Wudebreg', quantum ad nos pertinet totam decimam quam Baldewinus de Ufford dedit nobis de molendino suo in Wudebreg', tenendam de nobis in perpetuum per annuam pensionem unius libre cimini nobis singulis annis pro omnibus aliis exactionibus ad festum sancti Georgii solvendam. Hiis testibus, domino Gaufrido Archidiacono Suffolch', Simone Decano de Hox', Petro Decano de Sutton', Heimfrido Decano de Carleford', Alexandro capellano de Buttel', Petro de Petton, Herveo de Baudres', Rannulfo filio Stephani de Culesl', Rogero filio Reginaldi de Capell', Rogero Picot, Huberto marescallo, Ada Sille, Stephano filio Willelmi de Culesl', Roberto filio Ricardi de Oreford, et pluribus aliis.

Endorsement: (contemporary) Conventus de Buttel.
               (14th century) x. molend' de Wodebr'.
Size: 17.8 × 9.8 cm.
Slit for seal tag.
Date: prior William and archdeacon Geoffrey; both last appear in 1210, and their successors first occur in 1213.

154. *Inspeximus* (11th September 1248) by Simon, prior of Norwich, of (a) grant by Walter Suffield, bishop of Norwich, of Little Worlingham church (1244–8), and (b) concession by bishop Walter Suffield (1244–8), that 18 acres in Upton, Norfolk, held of Butley by Master Hugh of Upton, half of which, by a charter of William Raleigh, bishop of Norwich, should go to the vicar of Upton after the death of M. Hugh, shall now go entire after M. Hugh's death to the prior and convent, who shall pay 5s yearly to the vicar.
Bodleian Library, Suffolk charter 190.

Omnibus hoc scriptum visuris vel audituris Symon Prior et conventus de Norwic' Salutem in domino. Noverit universitas vestra nos venerabilis patris W. de Suffeld dei gratia Norwicensis Episcopi cartas inspexisse sub hac forma.

Omnibus Christi fidelibus ad quos presens scriptum pervenerit Walterus de Suffeld dei gratia Norwicensis Episcopus Salutem in domino. Ad omnium volumus notitiam pervenire nos causa dei et religionis favore concessisse, dedisse, et presenti carta confirmasse ecclesie sancte Marie de Buttel' et canonicis ibidem deo servientibus in puram et perpetuam elemosinam et in proprios usus perpetuo possidendam ecclesiam de Parva W(er)lingh' sancti Petri cum omnibus ad eam pertinentibus salva in omnibus et per omnia reverentia et obedientia sancte Norwicensis ecclesie. Et ut hec nostra concessio, donatio et carte nostre confirmatio perpetuam optineat firmitatem eam presenti scripto sigilli nostri munimine corroboravimus. Hiis testibus, Magistro Willelmo de Horham Archidiacono Suff', Magistro R. de Insula Archidiacono Colecestr', Magistro Herveo de Fakeham, Adam de Wrthested', Willelmo de Whithewell', Thoma capellano et aliis.

Item. Omnibus Christi fidelibus ad quos presens pervenerit Walterus de Suffeld dei gratia Norwicensis Episcopus Salutem in domino. Ad universorum notitiam volumus pervenire nos cartam venerabilis patris Willelmi de Ralegh predecessoris nostri super taxatione vicarie ecclesie de Upton confectam inspexisse, ex cuius tenore perpendimus octodecim acrar' terre in villa de Upton ad dictam ecclesiam spectantium quas Magister Hugo de Upton de Priore et conventu[1] de Buttel' concessione speciali possidebit, medietatem post dicti Magistri decessum vicarii qui pro tempore fuerit accrescere debere portionem. Vero dictorum Prioris et conventus religionem, honestatem, et assiduam in obsequiis divinis devotionem necnon hospitalitatem et caritatis largitatem attendentes, dictas octodecim acras post decessum dicti Magistri Hugonis, eorumdem Prioris et conventus portioni quam habent in dicta ecclesia episcopali auctoritate intuitu caritatis totaliter assignamus, concedimus et confirmamus, ita tamen quod dicti Prior et conventus quinque solidos sterlingorum post decessum dicti Magistri vicario qui pro tempore fuerit annuatim die sancte Margarete in perpetuum persolvent. Et ut hec nostra assignatio, concessio et confirmatio perpetuam optineant firmitatem, eas presenti scripto et sigilli nostri appositione corroboravimus. Hiis testibus, Magistro Willelmo de Horham Archidiacono Suff', Magistro Roberto de Insula Archidiacono Colcestr', Magistro Herveo de Fakeham, Adam de Wrthestede, Willelmo de Whitewell, Thoma capellano et aliis. Nos autem huic concessioni et confirmationi sicut canonice facta est assensum nostrum prebentes, presens scriptum sigilli munimine corroboravimus. Datum apud Norwycum tertio idus septembris pontificatus dicti Walteri Episcopi anno quinto.

[1] MS de prioris et conventus

Endorsement: contemporary including lviii.
Size: 24.8 × 16.5 cm.
Slit for seal tag.
Date: Walter de Suffield was elected before July 1244 (*Fasti*, ii. 57); date of *inspeximus*. This seems to be M. William de Horham's earliest known occurrence as archdeacon; 'R. de Insula' in (a) could be Robert or Ralph (*Fasti* iii. 19–20).
Note: Worlingham church today is dedicated to All Saints. There were two churches there in Domesday (ii. fo 283), and clearly also in the 13th century. Butley claimed both (Evelyn-White, 46) but there seems no other evidence that they possessed All Saints.

INDEX OF NAMES AND PLACES

Places are in Suffolk unless otherwise stated. Numbers in italics are those of charters.

A, clerk of Weybread, *131*.
Ada, *see* Biskele.
Adam, *de monasterio, 90*.
  see Bedingfeld, Mercator, Welbeck, Wereden.
Adric, William son of, *15*.
Agnes, *see* Crek.
Alan, Robert son of, *52*.
  William son of, *17–19, 28, 42, 52, 58, 65, 70, 72–3, 75, 78–81, 84, 86, 88, 94, 98, 102–4, 135*.
  see Carlton, Oki, Valeines, Witherdale.
  see Godfrey, Alan son of.
Alard, *see* William, Alard son of.
Alcred, Robert son of, *89*.
Aldeburgh, Roger son of Warin son of Bonde de, *134*.
Alderton, parson of, *see* Pyssale.
Aldringham (Alringeham, Aldringheam, Alrinham), 26, *30*, *114*.
  church, 2, 19, 21, 24, 31, 33, 35–6, 38, *5, 22–4, 27, 29, 31–6*.
Alencun, Herbert de, 10–11, *41, 74, 126*.
Alexander, son of Elena, *42*.'
  Master Richer, son of, *see* Richer.
  see Walter, Alexander son of.
Aleyn, John son of Roger, *144*.
  William son of Roger, *144*.
Aliz, Robert son of, *77*.
Alkoc, John, *143*.
Alpasia, *see* Biskele.
Alured, Jordan son of, *77*.
Alwin, *139*.
Archdeacons, *see* Geoffrey, Herbert, Insula, Lucy, Ralph, Robert, Thomas, Walkelin, William.
Arden (Ardene, Arderne), Ralph de, 35, *27, 29, 75*.
  Thomas de, *27, 73*.
Arnald, Hubert son of, *14*.
  see Peter, Arnald son of.
Arroasian order, 6.
Arundel, *23*.
  William earl of, *23*.
Ashfield, church, 22.
Aspall, church, 22.
Athies, Girard de, 76 n.
Attebregge, Henry, *114*.
Attleborough (Attleburgh), John de, *136*.
Auberville, Matilda de, 5, 9.
  William de, 5, 9, *27, 146*.
  William son of William de, *27*.
Aubrey, earl, 25, *121*.
  Thomas son of, *131*.
Austyn, Andrew, *112* n 1.
  Richard, *114*.

Auviliers, Richard de, *18*.
Avilers, Richard de, *129*.

Bacheler, Robert, *89*.
Bacoun, John, *115*.
Baldry, *see* Winston.
Baldwin, *see* Canterbury, Archbishops of, Guines, Poteford, Ufford.
Barat, Roger, *132–3*.
Barbere, William, *137*.
Bardolf, Hugh, 23, 28.
Barkere, *see* Winston.
Barlings Abbey (Lincs.), 31.
Bartholomew, *see* Dearneford, Glanville, Norwich.
Basilia, *see* Claude.
Basingeham, William de, 27.
Batalie, John de la, *56*.
Batesford, Henry de, *79–80*.
Bath, Reginald, Bishop of, 24–5, *121*.
Bavent, Beavent, Michael de, *87*.
Bawdsey (Baudreseie, Baudresheia), 27.
  church, 21, *120*.
  Hervey de, *132–3, 153*.
  Osbert, clerk of, *120*.
  Osbert de, *139, 149–50*.
  Rannulf de, *120, 146*.
Baxter, Agnes le, *144*.
Bayham (Sussex) Abbey, 32.
Bealings (Beliges), Robert son of Guy de, *77*.
Beauchief Abbey (Yorks), 2.
Beaufo (Bellafago), Aumary de, *147*.
  Egidia de, 10–11, *84–5*.
  Martin de, 10–11, *84–5*.
Beccles, Robert de, *clericus, 151*.
Bedale, William, *112* n 1.
Bedingfeld, Adam, de, *30, 67* n, *70, 95, 97, 99–100, 108, 126*.
  Hubert de, *126*.
  Philip de, *76*.
Bek, Gilbert de, *145*.
Beleth, Michael, *23*.
  Robert, 11.
Bellehus, Bellus, Mirine, *89*.
  Roger, *89*.
Benhall, 5, *115*.
  church, 21, *120*.
Bernard, Roger son of, *54*.
  see Helle, Stodhage.
Bernesheg, Fulk, *77, 95, 100*.
  Gilbert *capellanus* de, *95, 100*.
  Matilda de, *100*.
  Robert de, 10, 28, *77, 95, 100–1*.
  William son of Hervey de, 10, 28, 43, *95, 99–101*.
Bernier, Hugh le, *18*.

159

Bert, Ric', *89.*
Bertha, *see* Glanville.
Berwick (Berewic), John de, *115.*
Beverley (Beverlac'), Master Thomas de, *130–1.*
Bigod, Hugh, earl of Norfolk, *40.*
    Ida, *40.*
    Juliana, *40.*
    Roger, earl of Norfolk, 16, 18–19, *40–2, 13* n, *40–1, 134.*
Biker (Lincs), church, 22.
Bishops, *see* Bath, Ely, Norwich, Rochester, Winchester.
Biskele, Bischele, Ada de, 11, *53, 55, 92.*
    Alpasia de, 11, *54.*
    Osbert de, 11.
    Saer de, 10–11, 18, 24, 28–9, 42, 47, *13, 53–5, 57, 65–7, 71, 74, 81, 84–5, 92, 98, 103.*
Bixley (Norfolk), 11.
Blame, Blome, John, *114.*
Blanchevill, Robert de, *146.*
    William de, *137, 141.*
Ble(n)cio, Roger, *147.*
Blom, William, *148.*
Blund, Agnes, 13.
    Gilbert, 13, 16.
    Rose, 13.
    William, 13, 16.
Blundeston, Robert de, *17.*
Blundeville, *see* Norwich, bishops of,.
Blythburgh, 12.
Blythburgh Priory, 1, 12–13, 17–18, 40, *17.*
    Prior of, 32.
Bocking, John de, *116.*
    Roger de, *113.*
Bokel, Joan, *114.*
    John, *114.*
    Margery, *114.*
    Richard, *114.*
Bolle, Thomas, *137.*
Boniface IX, 32.
Bordemal, Gilbert, *124–5, 127, 132–3.*
Bosco, Henry de, of Spexhall, 13–14, 28, *17–18.*
Boulogne, Honour of, 13.
Boyton, 77.
    Henry de, *134.*
Bradeker, William de, *126.*
Braham, John de, *13* n, *88, 114.*
    Roger de, *13–14,* 30, *53–5, 57, 61–2, 78.*
Brahuse, Richard de, *142.*
Bramford, Nicholas de, *139.*
Bredfield, church, 9, 22.
Briencuith, Richard de, *19.*
Bringuuam, Gilbert son of, 77.
Brit, William, *29.*
Briwerre, William, *28.*
Brodheye, Thomas, *113.*
Brom, John de, *142.*

Bromholm (Norfolk) Priory, 18, 34, *19* n.
Bruerio, Hugh de, *89.*
Bruisyard (Burgeswerd), 9, 26, *45.*
Brumford, Hubert de, *30.*
Brun, Haldan, 29, *89.*
    Robert le, *59.*
Buch, William de, *29.*
Bule, William, *126.*
Bullok, Robert, *112* n 1.
Bungay Priory, 33.
Bungeye, Roger de, rector of Groton, 49, *145.*
Burdun, Burchard, 11, *70.*
    Reginald, and Alexandria his wife, 11.
Burend', *see* Woodcroft.
Bures, John de, *15.*
Burg, John son of Ralph de, *17.*
Burgstede, Burstede, Richard, parson of Framlingham, *114.*
Burneyle, Robert de, *112.*
Burt, William, *142.*
Bury St Edmunds abbey, 27, 32.
Butley (Butele, Buteleia, Buttele, Butthele), 27.
    church of, 21, *120.*
    land in, *120, 129.*
    Alexander, chaplain of, *131, 153.*
    Nicholas of, *31.*
    Priory, 6–7, *23–4,* 27, 34, *115, 120–54;* church, 1; foundation of, 1–2; library, 8; site of, 5.
    Priors of, 51, *61–2,* 90; Gilbert, 1–2, 37–8, *6, 31–3,* 36, *68;* Robert, 38–9, *33, 68;* Rivers, Augustine, 8; William, 21, 38, *7, 32–3,* 68, *89–90;* W., *133, 153.*
Buurt, Hugh, *140.*
Buxlow, 25, *110, 114.*
Bylaugh (Norfolk), church, 9, 22.

Caen (Caan, Cadomo), Aelina de, *148.*
    Richard de, 11, 48, *140, 148.*
    Richard, son of Richard de, 12.
    Sara de, *148.*
    Walter, 11, *148. See* Richard, clerk of.
Caldecotes, Henry de, *17.*
Caldham, *see* Theberton.
Calne, Master Walter de, 27.
Campo, Gerard son of Wulric de, 12, *149–50.*
    Henry de, 12, *149–50.*
Canterbury, Archbishops of, *11;* Baldwin, 33, 35–6, *8, 10–11, 24–5, 122;* elect of, 121; Hubert, *see* Walter; Richard, 35.
    Archdeacon of, *see* Herbert.
    Christ Church priory, 32, 34.
    St Augustine's abbey, 32.
Capel (Capella, Capele), 27.
    church, 21, *120.*
    John de, *129, 136, 145.*
    Roger, son of Reginald de, *153.*
Caretarius, Roger, *55, 92.*

161

Robert de, 13–14, *15–18*.
Roger de, 14, *15–16*.
Debenham, 16, 21, *123*.
church, 22.
(*places in*) Bromiesedge, Bromiestone-shegg, Debenhambrok, Godleshay-medwe, Goldmereshay, Gooldeshay, Hayesmedwe, Hungerdonne, Hungrisdonne, Katenhowe, Keedyng, Kolersweye, Kurlepetacre, Manshort, Shepwaysh, Wynstonefeeld, Yuluere-dingg, *123*.
Warin Chapman, Mabille Child, Adam le Dextere, John de Hoxne, Adam Ingre, William Ingre, Thomas Spytelman, Walter Towgh, Thomas le Whyte, *123*.
Decanus, Robert, *30*.
Dedham (Essex), church, 22.
Dene, William, *6, 140*.
Dennington (Dinhevetune, Dinieveton, Dinniveton), 15, 26, 28, *18* n, *49, 124–8*.
(*places in*) Holyoak (Holyoc, Halihoc), 15, *49, 125–7*; Luuerunesbusc, *125–7*; Northwall, *125–7*.
Geoffrey, parson of, *49*.
Gerard, son of Benedict of, 15, 29, 48, *124–7*.
Ida, wife of Gerard, 15, *124–5*.
Henry *parcarius,* son of Benedict of, 15, *124–5, 127* (see also *Parcarius*).
Jordan son of Osbert of, *124*.
Margery, wife of Gerard, 15, *124–5*.
Richard son of Henry son of Benedict of, 15, *126*.
Dextere, Adam, *123*.
Dickleburgh (Norfolk), church, 9.
Digkemue, Eustace de, *12*.
Dionis, Thomas, *112* n 1.
Dionysius, *cementarius, 65, 76*.
merchant, *120* D.
Dodnash priory, 3.
Drinkstone, Agnes de, 28.
William de, 28.
Driu, *see* Chediston.
Dune, John de la, *138*.
Dunwich, 6, 14, 16, 24, *11, 61–2, 72, 76, 111–13*.
bailiffs of, *112–13*.
Dean of, *131*.
William, 48, *61–2*.
Hospital, 13, *17*.
William of, *see* Peter, William son of,.
Durford Abbey (Sussex), 2.
Durham, Hugh Bishop of, *23–5, 121*.

Edgefield, Lecia de, 16.
Edrich, John, *144*.
William, *129*.
Edward III, 69.
Ernald son of, *60*.

Eldirhegg, Roger de, *114*.
Elena, wife of Roger Wuluard, 28, *42*.
Thomas son of, 28, *42*.
Elias, *see* Robert, Elias son of,.
Eligham, Richard de, *121*. (*See also* Ellingham.)
Robert de, *121*.
Elinton, John *clericus* de, *12*.
Ellingham, Ric' de, *113*.
Robert de, *113*.
Elmham, South, 38, *22*.
Elmswell, Seman de, *113, 121* A.
Ely, Bishops of, Geoffrey, *23–5, 121*; John of Fountains, *81*; William, elect of, *23*.
prior and convent of, 21, *123, 152*.
Elyot, Roger, *89*.
Engaine, Henry, *15*.
Enges, Henges, Richard de, *clericus, 141–2*.
Enulf, son of Baldwin of Guines, *12*.
Ernald, *see* Edward, Ernald son of,.
the priest, *120*.
Esfeld, Osbert de, *131*.
Eshom, Hesham (in Weybread), Roger, son of Walter de, *138*.
Walter de, 48, *138–9*.
William, son of Walter de, *138*.
Essex, earls of, *see* Peter, Geoffrey son of, Mandeville.
Eston, Estune, John de, *81*.
Robert de, *87*.
Esturmi, Roger, *129*.
William de, *16*.
Eustace, *capellanus, 37*.
Walter son of, *61–2*.
see Digkemue.
see Walter, Eustace son of.
Euston, 13.
Eye, honour of, 1, 23, 32, 34, *112, 114*.
priory, 16, 20, 23, 32, *31–3, 36, 68*.
Roger, prior of, 38, *68*.
William son of Robert of, *148*.
seneschal of, see Gernegan.
Eyken, church, 22.

Faber, Henry, *89*.
Fakenham, Master Henry de, *154*.
Falesham, Aliz, wife of William de, *62*.
William de, 16, 41, *61–2, 78*.
William, son of William de, 16, *72*.
Farnham (Fareham), church, 21, 26, *120*.
Langwade mill, 15, *63–4*.
Ferre, Gydo, junior, 5, *115*.
Fileolus, Roger, *120*.
Finborough, 27.
church, 21.
Fitz Alan family, 13.
Flanders, Philip d'Alsace count of, 48.
Flandrensis, Walter, *30*.
Flegg, Roger de, *124–5, 127*.
Fletheshehe, Hubert, *137*.

163

Harlepin, Rannulf, *89*.
William, *89*.
Harleston, 27.
church, 9, 22.
Harvey, Hervey, *see* Glanville, Koket, Walter.
William son of, *26*; *see* Bernesheg.
see Hunteman, Hervey son of.
Hautboys, Adam de, parson of Cockfield, 7, *152*.
Hawkedon, Gilbert de, 14, *47–8*, *147*.
Hecam, Master Reiner de, *27*, *39*.
Helle, Bernard, 28, *67*.
Helmingham, *116*.
Hemmingesfen, *59*.
Henle, William de, *30*.
➤ Henry, canon of Leiston, 4.
II, 5, *32–5*, *37–8*, *12 n*, *23*, *27–9*, *34*.
Charters of, *24–6*, *121–2*.
III, 5, 15.
son of Gerold, Warin son of, *122*.
see Batesford, Bosco, Caldecotes, Engaine, Grimilies.
see Haldan, Julian, Henry son of.
Herbert, archdeacon of Canterbury, 35, *8*, *25*, *121*.
Roger son of, *89*.
see Alencun.
Hereford, William de, *120*.
Hernald, priest, *147*.
Herol, Geoffrey, *136–7*.
Robert, *135*.
Wulfric, *135*.
Herolf, Al', *135*.
Herst, *see* Mendham.
Hert, *see* Winston.
Hervey, *see* Harvey.
Hesham, *see* Eshom.
Hetfeld, Walter de, *79–80*.
Heveningham, *114*.
Heythe, Henry del, *145*.
Hickling (Hykeling, Ykeling) (Norfolk), priory, *19 n*.
Brian de, *19*.
Geoffrey de, *146*.
Hispania, Jocelin de, *9–10*, 26, 29, *41–2*, *56*, *93–4*.
Holcham, William de, *96*.
Hollesley (Holeslee), Roger de, *73*, *124–5*, *127*, *149–50*.
Holming, Stephen, *54*.
Honorius III, 19, 29, *31–2*, *5*, *20–2*, *91*.
Hopton (Hopetun), (*places in*) Benecroft, *71*; Wrabesheg, *71*.
Alice de, *71*.
John de, 14, *71*.
Roger de, 14, *71*.
Horham, *36* (*Hoxham*).
Master William de, Archdeacon of Suffolk, *154*.
Horkesley (*Horkel'*), John de, *139*.

Horshag, Roger de, *30*.
Horsham St Faith (Horsford) (Norfolk), prior of, *90*.
Horswold, 16.
Hosa, Henry de, *74*.
Houdyn, *see* Oudyn.
Hovel, Alienor, 14, *144*.
Hugh, *144*.
Robert, 14, *137*, *141*.
Howard, John, *114*.
Hoxne, John de, *145*.
Robert de, *114*.
Simon, dean of, *130–1*, *153*.
see Debenham.
Hubert, Geoffrey son of, *124–5*, *127*.
Hubert son of, *124–5*, *127*.
Peter son of, *124–5*, *127*.
see Brumford, Cordebof, Marshal, Walter.
see Arnald, Hubert son of.
Hugh, William son of, *16*.
see Bardolf, Bigod, Cressi, Durham, Gosebech, Lanpernes, Lega, Malaln, Neville, Rickinghall, Ruffus, Rus.
Huleman, Ric', *139*.
Hunipot, Ernald son of John, *151*.
John, 17, *148*.
Hunteman, 60.
Hervey son of, 28, *17–18*.
Huntingfield, Master John de, *130*.
Roger de, *110*.
Hurt, Robert, *89*.
Hykeling, *see* Hickling.

Ingre, Adam, *123*.
William, *123*.
Ingreth, Walter, *152*.
Innocent II, 20, 30.
Innocent III, 29, *31–2*, *2*, *22*.
Innocent IV, 32.
Instead, 11, 14, *146–8*.
(*places in*) Anhand bridge, 11, *148*.
Insula, Master R. de, archdeacon of Colchester, *154*.
Ipswich, Holy Trinity Priory, 3, 32.
Isabel, *see* Wachesham.
Iver (*Evera*) (Bucks.), 35, *29*.
Ixworth Priory, 3.

Joce, Alexander, *112 n* 1.
John, *112 n* 3.
Robert, *112 n* 1.
John, *capellanus*, 44.
Count of Mortain, 16, 32, *34–5*, *29*.
King, 10, 13, 24, 32, 35, *13 n*, *28*, 76.
prince, *27*.
Michael son of, of Dunwich, *111–12*.
Peter son of, *112 n* 1.
see Batalie, Braham, Bures, Burg, Cordebof, Darsham, Dearneford,

164

Lucius III, 2, 22, 29–30, 37, *1, 3, 22.*
Lunetild, Ric', *89.*
Lutewine, *see* Lotewine.
Lynn (Len), Master William de, 37, *35, 38.*

Malaln, Hugh de, *29.*
Malebisse, Richard, 27.
Malet, Robert, 20, 23–4, 87.
    Walter, 10, *46, 130.*
Maleville, William de, *30.*
Maloisel, Alexander, 15, *135, 142.*
    Robert, 14–15, 47, *132–5, 142.*
Mandeville, William de, earl of Essex, 48.
Mannyng, William, *145.*
March, Le Marocis, Alexander, *135, 139–40.*
    Alice, *137.*
Margaret, *see* Culpho, Margaret de.
Margrete, William, *114.*
Marlingford (Norfolk), 9.
Marseilles, 34, 36, *122.*
Marshal, Hubert, *132–4, 153.*
Marthoys, Alan, *137.*
Martin, *see* Beaufo.
Matthew, *capellanus, 139.*
    see Keleshale, Stokes, Valeines.
Meer, Robert, *129.*
Mellis, 18.
    Baldwin, son of Ralph de, 87.
    Peter de, *115.*
    Ralph de, 87.
Mendham, Adam de, *140.*
    Godfrey de, *124–5, 127.*
    John de, *124–5, 127.*
    R., *capellanus* de, *130.*
    Ric' de, *clericus, 130.*
    Richard de, *134.*
    Thomas de, *148.*
    Priory (Herst), 36, 47–9, *130, 139.*
Mengi, Ralph, *54.*
Mercator, Adam, *54.*
    Robert, *47, 89.*
Meriel, Richard de, *114.*
Merum, William, *139.*
Metfield (Medefeld), William de, *137, 142.*
Metinham, John, *112, 115.*
Meus, William, 97.
Michael, canon of Leiston, 76.
    see Beleth, Orford.
    see John, Michael son of.
Middleton (Middelton, Midelton), 13–14, 47, 60, 70.
    church, 8–9, 12, 19–21, 23, 31, 37, *5, 13, 22, 37–41.*
    (*places in*) Brunsiesheg, 70; Sortelond, 70.
Minsmere, 4, 6, *112–13.*
Montalt (Monte Alto), Robert de, 48, *116.*
Moulton (Multun), Gregory de, *151.*
Mouney, Alan de, *140.*
Mountagu, Edward de, *114.*
Murdac, Ralph, 27.
Muriols, Geoffrey de, *120.*

Nereford, Ralph de, 16.
Neve, Walter le, 76.
Nevill, Hugh de, 28.
Newalesclade, *52.*
Newton (Neutun), Ric' de, *151.*
    Sewal de, *126.*
Nicholas, Master, 76, *120.*
    see Butley, Leiston, Somerleyton.
    see Robert, Nicholas son of.
Nigel, Rannulf son of, *120.*
    Thedild daughter of, *51.*
Noloth (Noloht, Nolod, Noloz), Adam, *134, 151.*
    Gerard, *135, 139–40.*
    Richard, *136.*
Norfolk, earl of, 19. *See* Bigod.
    Margaret, countess of, 7, 19.
Norman, *see* Peasenhall.
Normannus, Dionysius, *18.*
Northhaghe, *see* Winston.
Norwich (Norfolk), 22.
    Bishops of, Blundeville, Thomas, *90;* Despenser, Henry, 35, 38, charter of, *118;* Grey, John de, 35, 37, *9, 22;* charters of, *35, 38;* Oxford, John of, 2–3, 19, 30, 35–7, *9, 22, 24–5, 27–8, 35, 38, 121;* charters of, *34, 36–7;* Pandulf, 76; Percy, Thomas, *117;* Raleigh, William, 19. 35, 37–8, *22, 139, 154;* Suffield, Walter, 35, 38; charter of, *154;* William, *120.*
    Dean of, *90.*
    Priors of, 17; Nicholas, *118;* Simon, 35, 37–8, *22, 154.*
    Bartholomew de, *15.*
    William de, *136.*
Novill, Robert de, *30.*

Ode, John, 29, *89.*
    Richard, *89.*
    Walter, *89.*
    William, *89.*
Oki, Alan son of, 86.
Oky, Robert, 29.
Oliver, *see* Vaux.
    see Osbert, Richard son of.
Onehouse (Onhus, Anhus), Petronilla de, 15, *63.*
    Rannulf de, 15–16, 41, *44, 63–4.*
    Robert, parson of, *139.*
    William de, 15–16.
Ording, Robert son of, *134.*
Ordmar, Roger son of, *54.*
Orford, 26.
    Catfoth, 77.
    castle, 17.
    Michael son of Reginald of, 41, 77.
    Robert *capellanus* de, 77.
    Robert son of Ric' de, *132–3, 153. See also* Richard, Robert son of.
Orgar, John, *89.*

Osbert, *see* Glanville, Tuddenham, Uni, Wachesham.
    Ermeg' son of, *120.*
    Richard son of, and Oliver his son, *87.*
    Richard son of, *149–50.*
    Roger son of, *17.*
    Walter son of, *17, 149–50.*
Oselac, William son of, *132.*
Oseberen, John, *151.*
Ostechirche, Adam, *111.*
Otley, Thomas de, *101.*
Oudin, *146.*
Oudyn, Houdyn, Alice, wife of William, *129, 136, 140, 145.*
    Thomas, *137, 141–2.*
    William, of Weybread, *129, 136, 140, 145.*
Oxford, *see* Aubrey, earl.
    see Norwich, bishops of.

Palmar, Haldan, *47.*
    Odo, *89.*
    Robert, *89.*
Pandulf, *see* Norwich (bishops of).
Parcarius, Parker, *see* Dennington, Starston.
    Gerard, *49.*
    Godfrey le, *15.*
    Henry, brother of Robert, *126.*
    Robert, *126; see* Woodcroft.
    Roger, *see* Woodcroft.
    Walter, *15.*
Parchemin, cook, *131.*
Parham, Peter de, *151.*
Parmentarius, John, *67.*
Parmynhood, Peter, *145.*
Parvus, Matthew, *124–5, 127.*
Paumer, Adam le, *89.*
Peasenhall (Pesehale), Norman de, 15–16, *63–4.*
    Ralph de, *15–16, 64, 149–50.*
Pecche, Gilbert, *14.*
    Hamo, *14.*
Penne, Simon, *139.*
Perceval, Jocelin, *112* n 1.
Perres, William, *89.*
Peter, Arnald son of, 11, *48.*
    Geoffrey son of, *23, 27–8.*
    John son of, *115.*
    William son of, 14, *14, 61–2.*
    see Hubert, John, Peter son of.
Petereste, Hugh, son of Roger de, *77.*
    Roger de, *77.*
Petronilla, *see* Onehouse.
Pettaugh (Pethaye), *116.*
Petton, Peter de, *153.*
Peyton, William de, *149–50.*
Philip, *see* Bedingfeld, Leiston, abbots of.
Picot, Roger, *153.*
Picoth, Robert, *29.*
Pipard, Gilbert, *122.*
Pirho, Reginald de, *19, 71.*

Planes, Roger de, 34, *29.*
Playford, 16, 26, *79–80, 108.*
Poer, John le, *116.*
    Thomas le, *114.*
Poier, Walter le, *77.*
Pole, Michael de la, *119.*
Porchester (Hants), *28.*
Poteford, Baldwin de, *81.*
Prémontré, 1, 2, 5.
Pyssale, John de, parson of Alderton, *152.*

Raimes barony, 16.
Rakebald, Geoffrey, *90.*
    Walter, *90.*
Raleigh, *see* Norwich, bishops of.
Ralph, archdeacon of Colchester, 12, *75.*
    Seman son of, *70.*
    see Burg.
Ramsholt, church, 22.
Rannulf *clericus*, 12.
    Richard son of, *77.*
    Testranum (?), 36, *10.*
    see Arden, Cookley, Gedinge, Glanville, Mellis, Mengi, Murdac, Onehouse, St Edmund, Wine.
    see Nigel, Richard, Rannulf son of.
Raveningham, Walter de, *134.*
Ray, Henry le, *112* n 1.
Redenhall (Redehal), William, Dean of, *131.*
Redisham, church, 22.
Redyng, Seman de, *112.*
Reginald, Thomas son of, *149–50.*
    see Bath, Pirho.
Reileia, land of, *120.*
Reiner, *see* Hecam, Waxham.
Rendham (Rindham), 13, 26, *15–18.*
    Elias son of Robert de, *18.*
    Robert de, *89.*
Rendlesham, Richard de, *154.*
Ribo, Walter de, *94.*
Richard I, 32–6, 8, *10–11, 23, 29, 122.*
    II, 5, *119.*
    cancellarius, 36, *10.*
    clerk of Walter de Caen, *148.*
    parson of Theberton, *83.*
    Rannulf son of, *124–5.*
    Robert son of, *61–2, 134.*
    William son of, *122, 124–5, 127.*
    see Auviliers, Briencuith, Coterel, Cransford, Kalestun, London, Lucy.
    see Osbert, Rannulf, Robert, Richard son of.
Richer, Master, son of Alexander, 14–15, *61–2, 72.*
Richmond, Archdeacon of, *see* Lucy.
    honour of, 12.
Rickinghall, Hugh de, son of Robert, 11, 16, *79–80, 108.*
Riebos, Richard de, *120.*
Ringsfield, church, 22.
Ringulf, Ryngulf, Henry, *111, 112* n 1, *119* A.

167

170

Wine, Ralph, *50, 88.*
Winfarthing (Norfolk), church, 22.
Wingfield, 11–12, 27–8, *146–51.*
Winston (Wineston, Wynestune), 21, *116, 123, 152.*
    (*places in*) Bluedonne, *123*; Estmedwe, *123.*
    Roger Baldry, Sayer Barkere, Adam Dexter, William Hert, William Ingre, John Lemman, Stephen de Northhaghe, Henry Towgh of, *123.*
    Geoffrey de, *130.*
    Robert de, *116.*
    William de, *116.*
Wissett, manor of, 76 n.
Witherdale (Wiresdal), *131.*
    Alan de, 16, *108, 126, 135, 138, 140, 151.*
    William son of Alan de, *138.*
Witnesham, 16.
Wivilingham, William de, *18, 65.*

Wix Priory (Essex), 32.
Wilmer, Walter, *89.*
    William, *89.*
Woodbridge, mill, 17, *153.*
    prior and convent of, 3, 17, *153.*
Woodcroft (Wdecrofft), Robert de, son of Roger de Burend' *parcarius, 30.*
    Emma, wife of Roger, *30.*
Worcester, bishops of, Baldwin, *24, 121.*
    Roger, 36.
Worlingham, Little, church, 22, *154.*
Wrthested, Adam de, *154.*
Wuluard, Roger, 28, *42.*
Wyte, John le, *112.*
Wyverstone, 14.

Yarmouth, bailiffs of, 18.
    fair, 17.
Yorkshire, 1, 27.
Yoxford, *114.*